Marriage Records
of
Cumberland County
Virginia
- 1749-1840 -

Compiled By:
Katherine B. Elliott

Southern Historical Press, Inc.
Greenville, South Carolina

Copyright 1969
By: Katherine B. Elliott

Copyright Transferred 1983
To: Southern Historical Press, Inc.

All rights reserved. No part of this publication may be reproduced, stored in a retrieval system or transmitted in any form or by any means without the prior permission of the publisher.

SOUTHERN HISTORICAL PRESS, INC.
PO BOX 1267
Greenville, SC   29601

ISBN #0-89308-382-X

Printed in the United States of America

INTRODUCTION

Many of the marriage bonds of Cumberland County have been lost, and many of the surviving bonds are now fragmented. All of the bonds for the years 1766, 1777, 1778 and 1781 have been lost, apparently, as none for these years were found among the bonds now extant. Only one bond for the year 1782 is now extant. There are no extant bonds for the years 1783, 1796, 1799, 1800, 1801 and 1802.

The compiler copied all of the marriage records for the years 1749 through 1840 which are recorded in the Marriage Register in the Clerk's Office of Cumberland County. She copied, also, the list of Cumberland County marriages compiled by Dr. Joseph D. Eggleston. This list was communicated by Dr. Eggleston to the National Society, Daughters of the American Revolution, and was subsequently published in volume 65 of the magazine of the society. These lists were then checked with the marriage bonds, consents and minister's returns now preserved.

In comparing these lists with the extant original records, many differences or variations in names and dates were found. The names and dates given in the following pages are those found on the bonds or consents. If there was a variation between the copied lists and the bonds or consents, the names and dates given on the bond or consent was used.

During the years 1784 to 1816 quite a few of the bonds bear no date. The printed form of bond in use during this period has the name of the Governor of Virginia in whose administration the bond was issued. While many of the bonds have no date on the face of the bond, some of the bonds bear a date on the back. These dates are assumed to be the dates on which the bonds were issued.

Because there seemed to be so many missing records, the compiler checked marriages in the William and Mary Quarterlies and the Douglas Register. She checked also the extant fee books of Cumberland County. Written in the back of one these was a list of those who had paid the fees for bonds, and the list included the names of the prospective brides.

The compiler listed, also, the names of the married daughters given in a book of abstracts of Cumberland County wills at the Virginia State Library. This list was compared with the bonds, consents and minister's returns. If no marriage record was found, the names were then checked in will, deed and court order books for names of the husband and the approximate date of marriage.

It was not feasible, however, to make an exhaustive search of such records. Because of the migration of people, proof of some marriages can undoubtedly be found in other counties. Search of such records, however, was beyond the scope of this work. There are probably some sources which were overlooked or not found by the compiler.

    A few of the marriage records included in this volume probably should have been omitted since they are to be found in other published works. But because so many of the early records have been lost, they were included to show their Cumberland County connection and to make available in one source book such records.

    I am indebted to the Hon. George F. Abbitt, Jr., Judge of the Fifth Judicial Circuit, Appomattox, and to Mr. William J. Van Schreeven, Archivist, Virginia State Library, for their kind permission to examine and copy the preserved records now under court custody.

    And I am indebted, also, to Mrs. Jewell T. Clark, Archival Assistant, Virginia State Library, for her patience and the time spent in checking names and dates transcribed from the original records.

    My appreciation is extended to Mrs. Imogene W. Tunstall, Clerk of the Circuit Court of Cumberland County, and to Mrs. Betty Walton, Deputy Clerk, for the assistance given me in searching records at Cumberland.

    And I feel that any credit given should include the name of my husband, Herbert A. Elliott, for without his assistance in preparing and indexing the manuscript this volume would never have been completed.

                                          Katherine B. Elliott

C O N T E N T S

Title	1
Introduction	3
Contents	5
Other Books by Katherine B. Elliott	6
Marriage Records - Cumberland County	7
Index to Brides	149
Ministers	169
Index to Other Names	171

Books by Katherine B. Elliott

Early Settlers, Mecklenburg County - Volume I
Postpaid

Early Settlers, Mecklenburg County - Volume II
Postpaid

Early Wills, 1765-1800, Mecklenburg County
Postpaid

Marriage Records, 1811-1853, Mecklenburg County
Postpaid

Revolutionary War Records, Mecklenburg County
Postpaid

Early Wills, 1746-1766, Lunenburg County
Postpaid

Emigration to Other States from Southside Virginia
                                                            Volume I
Postpaid

Emigration to Other States from Southside Virginia
                                                           Volume II
Postpaid

CUMBERLAND COUNTY MARRIAGE RECORDS

ABRAHAM, Mordecai   Sarah J. ANDERSON
M.B. 10 Dec. 1824   M. 11 Dec. 1824
Consent: Richd J. Anderson *   Surety: Bradley S. Glover
* No relation stated   Witness: William Price

ADAMS, John W.   Ann LANCASTER
License: 16 Nov. 1779 *   Fee 20/
* Cumberland County Fee Book - 1754-58 and 1779-1781

ADDAMS, James   Polly MELTON
M.B. 26 Oct. 1789   Surety: Thomas Addams

AGEE, Anthony   Christian WORLEY
Ante 1 May 1751 *
* Cum. Co. D.B. 1, p. 327   Removed Albemarle County
Will of John Worley - Cum. Co. W.B. 1, p. 149
       3-22-1757-3-27-1758

AGEE, James   Martha JOHNSON
M.B. 4 April 1810   Surety: Edwd Walton

AGEE, Samuel   Mary M. ANDERSON
M.B. 26 April 1824   Surety: Bennett Bagby

AGEE, William   Susan WALTON
Consent: 28 Oct. 1803   Teste: Thos M. Walton
Edwd Walton, Sr., for his daughter   Teste: Edwd Walton, Jr.

AIKEN, James   Martha WILSON
M.B. 12 Feb. 1816 *   Surety: Ja^s Wilson
* Date on back of bond - Bond not dated

ALDERSON, Richard   Judith BALLOW
M.B. 4 Dec. 1810   * Consent: 4 Dec. 1810
* Judith writes own consent   Teste: Thomas Hudson
               Teste: Charles Ballowe

ALDERSON, Thomas   Martha OAKLEY
M.B. 29 Nov. 1820   Surety: Erasmus Oakley

ALDERSON, Wilkins   Elizabeth THACKER
M.B. 12 Dec. 1822   Surety: Sam'l Hudson
Note: Sam Hudson appears before William Powell and swears
   that Elizabeth Thacker is above age 21 and a resident
   of this county.

ALLEN, Charles   Sally WILSON
M.B. 26 Aug. 1787   Surety: Yancey Holman

ALLEN, Daniel   * Joanna HILL
M.B. 21 Feb. 1775   Surety: Geo. Carrington, Jr.
* Joanna Hill, Widow

ALLEN, Charles B.   Susan SANDERS
M.B. 26 May 1831   Surety: Peter B. Foster
Married 12 May 1831 (?) by Rev. John T. Watkins *
* Date given in minister's return of John T. Watkins

ALLEN, Drury M.   Sally A. WRIGHT
M.B. 17 June 1806   Surety: Henry Woodson
Consent: William Wright for his daughter   Teste: John A. Allen
Consent dated 17 June 1806   Teste: Henry Ransone

ALLEN, James   Polly ALLEN
M.B. 12 Jan. 1807   Surety: Benj. Allen

ALLEN, John   Mariah C. SCRUGGS
M.B. 19 Sept. 1819   Surety: Ed. Scruggs

ALLEN, John A.   Mary D. COLEMAN
M.B. 14 Jan. 1817   Surety: Wm F. Randolph
Consent: Elliott G. Coleman for his daughter
Consent date 13 Jan. 1817   Teste: Elizabeth Coleman
                                                Teste: Elliott R. Coleman

ALLEN, Joseph   Anne HARRISON
Ante 14 Jan. 1761   Cum. Co. D.B. 6, p. 69, - -1780
Will of Benjamin Harrison, Cum. Co. W.B. 1, p. 215
              1-14-1761-5-25-1761

ALLEN, Josiah   Caroline GORDON
__ Aug. 1813 *   Surety: Wm. A. Allen
* Date on back of bond - Bond not dated

ALLEN, Philip   Elizabeth COLEMAN
M.B. 19 Nov. 1763   Surety: W Coleman
Consent: Daniel Coleman for his daughter
Consent dated 19 Nov. 1763   Teste: Sarah Coleman

ALLEN, Richard   Mary BOYD
No date on bond   Surety: Thomas Atkinson
Consent: Dated 31 Aug. 1791 *
* Mary Boyd writes own consent to marry Richard Allen, <u>Junior</u>

ALLEN, Richard   Sally SMITH
M.B. 13 Dec. 1834   Surety: Pleasant Smith
Pleasant Smith makes affidavit that Sally is of age.
Married 17 Dec. 1834 by Rev. Joseph A. Brown

ALLEN, Richmond   Polly FRANCISCO
Prior to 31 Dec. 1799   Surety: Jno. Michaux
Administration of Gov. James Monroe - 12/19/1799-12/29/1802

ALLEN, Richmond   Fanny ANDERSON
M.B. 18 April 1808   Surety: James Anderson
Married 21 April 1808 by Rev. Drury Lacy

ALLEN, Richmond   Elizabeth JOHNS
Bond not dated   Surety: Francis Anderson
26 December 1816 entered on back of bond
Consent: Thos. Johns for his daughter   Teste: James D. Johns

ALLEN, Robert A.   Martha J. PHILLIPS
M.B. 11 Oct. 1838   Surety: Thomas Phillips
Consent: Randolph Phillips for his daughter
Consent dated 11 Oct. 1838 - Thomas Phillips makes affidavit
that Martha Phillips is of age.

ALLEN, Samuel   Rhoda CAYCE
After 12 Nov. 1788   Surety: A. Guthrie
Administration of Gov. Beverly Randolph   11/12/1788-12/1/1791

ALLEN, Saymer   Anna COOPER
M.B. 29 July 1805   Surety: William North
Consent: Jas. Cooper for his daughter Anna
Consent dated 28 July 1805   Teste: Thomas Cooper

ALLEN, Valentine   Ann ARNOLD
M.B. 26 Feb. 1758   Surety: Nicholas Davies
Note: Daughter of William Arnold

ALLEN, William   Mary BURTON
License: 22 May 1780   Fee 20/
Cumberland County Fee Book - 1779-1781

ALLEN, William   Sarah SLAUGHTER
M.B. 25 Dec. 1785   Surety: Larkin Smith
See: W & M (1) V. 20, p. 3

ALLEN, William   Nanny CHILDRESS
M.B. 28 Nov 1798   Surety: John Holman

ALVIS, David   Nancy ROBINSON
M.B. 24 July 1809   Surety: Walter Jones

AMOS, James   Nancy SIMPSON
M.B. 24 Dec. 1830   Surety: Miller Woodson
Consent: Richd Simpson for his daughter
Teste: Leonard Simpson   Teste: Sam'l R. Simpson
Married 28 December 1830 by Rev. John T. Watkins

AMOS, Littleberry   Elizabeth M. DOWDY
M.B. 20 Dec. 1830   Surety: John Matthews
Consent: Thos Dowdy for his daughter   Teste: Alonza Robinson
Married 22 Dec. 1830 by Rev. Poindexter P. Smith

AMOS, Thomas   Susan MATTHEWS
M.B. 26 Nov. 1821   Surety: Saml G. Pulliam
Consent: Susan Matthews writes own consent
Married 13 December 1821 by Rev. Joseph Jenkins

ANDERSON, Caleb   Rebecca ANDERSON
M.B. 2 Nov. 1838   Surety: Joseph Jenkins
Consent: Rebecca writes her own consent - dated 30 Oct. 1838

ANDERSON, Charles   Anna ALLEN
M.B. 20 Oct. 1789   Surety: Creed Taylor
Consent: Daniel Allen for his daughter Anna Allen
Consent dated 12 Oct. 1789   Teste: Cha^S Allen
Note: Charles Anderson of Lunenburg County

ANDERSON, Chesley   Nancy DOWDY
M.B. 25 Oct. 1820   Surety: Shirley Anderson
Consent: Thomas Dowdy - no relation stated
Consent dated 23 October 1820   Teste: John A. Allen

ANDERSON, Chesley   Jane W. JENKINS
M.B. 27 March 1826   Surety: Elijah Winfree

ANDERSON, Francis   Martha W. MEREDITH
M.B. 3 Dec. 1823   Surety: John C. Allen
Consent: Martha writes own consent   Teste: William Wilson

ANDERSON, Jacob A.   Betsy DAVIS
Bond not dated   Surety: Christopher Woodson
31 May 1813 entered on back of bond

ANDERSON, James   Anny HUBBARD
M.B. 23 Jan. 1786   Surety: John Anderson

ANDERSON, James   Sarah G. PEARCE
Prior to 12 May 1792
Will of Jeremiah Pearce, Cum. Co. W.B. 3, p. 74
                    5-12-1792-1-25-1796

ANDERSON, James   Charlotte Lotey HAZLEGROVE
M.B. 15 Dec. 1817   Surety: Sam Hobson
Consent: P. Hazlegrove for his daughter   Teste: Ed. Booker

ANDERSON, James   Frances S. TALLY
M.B. 23 Feb. 1831   Surety: Wm A. Talley
Consent: Jackey Talley no relation stated
Consent dated 23 Feb. 1831   Teste: Lawrence Anderson

ANDERSON, Jesse   Mary HOLLAND
Prior to 1 August 1812
Note: Jesse Anderson and Mary his wife, both of Cumberland
      County sell to John Anderson for $300.00 all right and
      claim of Jesse Anderson and Mary Anderson as legatees
      to the estate of James Holland, deceased, late of Cum-
      berland County, after the death of Mary Holland, widow
      of James Holland, who lives on the land and has a life
      right in the said land. Cum. Co. D.B. 12, p. 181.
      Deed dated 1 August 1812

ANDERSON, John
M.B. 28 Jan. 1793
         Nancy BRYANT
         Surety: Wm. Austin
         Surety: Reuben Austin

ANDERSON, John
M.B. 2 Nov. 1814
Consent: Nancy writes own consent
Consent dated 2 Nov. 1814
         Nancy CHARLTON
         Surety: Daniel Jones
         Teste: Betsey Anderson

ANDERSON, Jno.
M.B. 14 Jan. 1817
         Mary S. WEBSTER
         Surety: Archer Bevill

ANDERSON, John
M.B. 30 Jan. 1821
Consent: Agnes writes her own consent
Consent dated 29 January 1821
Married 31 Jan. 1821 by Rev. Joseph Jenkins
         Agnes MINTER
         Surety: Isham Bradley
         Teste: Caleb Anderson
         Teste: Elizabeth Ballow

ANDERSON, John
M.B. 7 Dec. 1830
Note: Daughter of John Sanderson
         Elizabeth Jane SANDERSON
         Surety: John Sanderson

ANDERSON, John C.
M.B. 3 May 1816
         Nancy HUTCHARDSON
         Surety: John Hutchardson

ANDERSON, Jonas M.
M.B. 7 Feb. 1825
Consent: Sally writes her own consent Teste: Wm. W. Meredith
William B. Langhorne makes affidavit Sally is of age.
         Sally C. GUTHREY
         Surety: David Molloy

ANDERSON, Joseph J.
M.B. 7 July 1830
Note: Daughter of Benjamin Bradley
         Elizabeth R. BRADLEY
         Surety: Benja. Bradley

ANDERSON, Lawrence
M.B. 24 Sept. 1806
         Ann JENKINS
         Surety: William Jenkins

ANDERSON, Parsons
M.B. 15 Feb. 1758
Consent: Charles Anderson gives consent for his son
Consent dated 13 February 1758
         Mary COCKE
         Surety: Thomas Cocke
         Teste: James Brown

ANDERSON, Richard
M.B. 23 Aug. 1813
         Judith OSBORNE
         Surety: William Osborne

ANDERSON, Richard
M.B. 29 April 1816
Consent: Mary Ann Davis writes own consent Test: Parke Bailey
Consent dated 29 April 1816   Test: Robert Armistead
         Mary Ann DAVIS
         Surety: Matthew Wilson

ANDERSON, Samuel Q.
M.B. 25 Aug. 1825
Married 1 September 1825 by Rev. John Ayres
         Martha G. SCRUGGS
         Surety: T(scharner) Woodson

ANDERSON, Shirley   Elizabeth ANDERSON
M.B. 29 Nov. 1820   Surety: Chesley Anderson
Consent: Jenny Anderson gives consent - no relation stated
Consent dated 29 November 1820   Teste: James Meddoss

ANDERSON, Shirley   * Mary ORSLIN
M.B. 21 Feb. 1823   Surety: Zachariah Talley
* Mary Oslin ?

ANDERSON, William   Sarah KEELING
M.B. 24 Nov. 1794   Surety: Geo. Keeling
Note: Bond signed William Anderson, Junr.

ANDERSON, William B.   Susan BRYANT
M.B. 16 Dec. 1830   Surety: Thos Boatwright
Consent: Charles Bryant gives consent for his daughter
Consent dated 15 December 1830   Teste: Charles LeSeur
Married 22 December 1830 by Rev. Poindexter P. Smith

ANDREWS, William   Catey GAINS
M.B. 5 July 1794   Surety: Larkin Smith
Catey Gains of lawful age writes own consent Teste: B. Gaines
Consent dated 4 July 1794   Teste: James Fretwell

ANGLEA, Andrew   Frances CHARLTON
Bond not dated   Surety: Archibal Brown
25 Dec. 1815 on back of bond   Teste: Archibal Brown
Consent: Samuel Charlton consents for his daughter

ANGLEA, John   Sally DURHAM
M.B. 22 Oct. 1794   Surety: Arch^d E. Anglea
Consent: Sally Durham writes own consent 22 Oct. 1794

ANGLEA, John   Polly PALMORE
M.B. 8 June 1803   Surety: T^s Woodson
Consent: William Palmore gives consent for his daughter

ANGLEA, William   Mary BROWN
M.B. 9 Sept. 1789   Surety: James Durham
Consent: George Brown gives consent for daughter Mary

ANGLEA, William   Nancy CARRINGTON
M.B. 26 Sept. 1805   Surety: Nicholas Durham
Consent: Nancy writes own consent dated 26 September 1805

APPERSON, James *   Sally GUTHREY
M.B. 29 Aug. 1805   Surety: John Guthrey
Consent: William Guthrey gives consent for his daughter to
        marry James Epperson   * Apparently James Epperson

APPERSON, William N.   Elizabeth JONES
M.B. 2 Oct. 1830   Surety: Edmund L. England
Consent: Lewis Jones gave consent 1 Oct. 1830 for daughter
Married 14 October 1830 by Rev. Poindexter P. Smith

ACHEN, James V. *   Mildred D. LEE
M.B. 11 Oct. 1815   Surety: Edm^d P. Lee
Consent: To the Clerk of Cumberland
   11 Oct. 1815
      "My daughter Mildred D. Lee wishes to change her
   situation, she is of lawful age, and has my consent
   to marry Jas. V. Achen."
   Teste: Sarah G. Lee   /s/ Charles Lee
* Signature on bond "James V. Aiken"

ARMISTEAD, Francis   Hannah PRICE
M.B. 8 May 1776   Surety: Joseph Palmore
Consent: Joseph Price gives consent for daughter
Consent dated 8 May 1776   Teste: Edmund Price and Anne Price

ARMISTEAD, Francis   Martha G. FAULKNER
M.B. 14 May 1821   Surety: Smith Criddle
Consent: Martha of lawful age writes own consent
Consent dated 13 May 1821   Teste: William Armistead
Married 15 May 1821 by Rev. Joseph Jenkins

ARMISTEAD, James A.   Sally W. TRENT
M.B. 26 Dec. 1831   Surety: Alexander Trent

ARMISTEAD, John, Junr.   Polly WOOD
M.B. 19 Dec. 1805   Surety: Joseph Price
Consent: Polly Wood writes own consent 17 December 1805

ARMISTEAD, Robert   Joana ALLEN
M.B. 14 Feb. 1804   Surety: Thomas H. Hill
Consent: Elizabeth Allen consents for her daughter
Consent dated 14 Feb. 1804   Teste: Frederick Galloway

ARMISTEAD, William   Judith BLANTON
M.B. 12 May 1817   Surety: James Blanton, Jr.
Consent: David Blanton gives consent for daughter 12 May 1817

ARMISTEAD, William   Rebecca GODSEY
M.B. 30 April 1834   Surety: M. H. Bagby
Consent: Drucilla Godsey gives consent for her daughter
Consent dated 29 April 1834   Teste: Edward Blanton

ARNOLD, John   Patty LEE
M.B. 19 Dec. 1788   Surety: John Lee

ATKINSON, John   Eliza P. HARRIS
M.B. 13 Dec. 1823   Surety: G. H. Matthews

ATKINSON, John   Martha JOHNSON
M.B. 4 Jan. 1827   Surety: Josiah Hix
Consent: Sarah Johnson gives consent as guardian of daughter
           Martha Johnson 1 Jan. 1827   Teste: Wm Armistead

ATKINSON, Robert   Polly GAINES
M.B. 21 Feb. 1793   Surety: Jacob Gauldin

ATKINSON, Thómas   Elizabeth DUPUY
M.B. 25 Sept. 1775   Surety: James Dupuy

AUSTIN, James H.   Jane MERRYMAN
M.B. 26 Nov. 1832   Surety: William Austin
Consent: Signed by both 26 Nov. 1832   Teste: Martha Hudgins

AUSTIN, James M.   Mary SCRUGGS
M.B. 14 Jan. 1812   Surety: John Minter

AUSTIN, James M.   Melissa M. FRAYSER
M.B. 4 Oct. 1832   Surety: William J. Frayser
Note: William J. Frayser makes affidavit that Melissa is of
      lawful age.

AUSTIN, John A.   Frances Ann MEADOR
M.B. 27 Oct. 1834   Surety: William D. Austin
Consent: Drusilla Meador consents for daughter 25 Oct. 1834

AUSTIN, John T.   Jane MONTAGUE
M.B. 23 Nov. 1807   Surety: George Holman
Consent: Peter Montague gives consent for daughter
Married 19 December 1807 by Rev. Lewis Chaudoin

AUSTIN, William   Judith ATKINSON
After 1 Dec. 1791   Surety: A. Austin
Administration of Gov. Henry Lee - 12/1/1791-12/1/1794
Daughter of Samuel and Mary Anne Atkinson

AUSTIN, William A.   Missouri TAYLOR
M.B. 31 August 1837   Surety: Henry Wheeler
Consent: Missouri wrote her own consent 30 August 1837

AUSTIN, William D.   Mildred A. WALTON
M.B. 22 Dec. 1834   Surety: Anthony A. Walton
Consent: Mildred signed own consent   Teste: Sarah Walton

AYRES, John L.   Jane DOWDY
M.B. 19 Dec. 1838   Surety: Robert Starkey
Consent: Thomas Dowdy gives consent for daughter

AYRES, Nathan W.   Martha H. BRADLEY
M.B. 1 Oct. 1821   Surety: William Bradley
Consent: Martha writes own consent   Teste: Carter H. Bradley

AYRES, Peter   Frances A. TANNER
M.B. 24 Nov. 1834   Surety: John F. Tanner
Consent: Frances signed own consent   Teste: Emaline E. Tanner

AYRES, Samuel   Jane GUTHREY
Bond not dated   Surety: Robert Caldwell
Consent dated 26 Jan. 1814   Daughter of Henry Guthrey

BABER, Edward   Rhoda BROWN
M.B. 11 Nov. 1815   Surety: William Turner
Consent: Rhoda signs own consent   Teste: Mary J. Turner

BAGBY, James   Sally BATES
M.B. 26 Aug. 1805   Surety: Samuel Putney
Consent: Signed by Jesse Woodson "as agent for her" 24 Aug.
Relation not stated   Teste: John Walton

BAGBY, John   Mariah FOWLER
M.B. 9 Dec. 1817   Surety: Robert S. Robinson
Consent: Elizabeth Fowler signs consent for her daughter

BAGBY, Madison H.   Martha J. HUDGINS
M.B. 21 Dec. 1833   Surety: Fleming Bagby
Consent: John Hudgins signs consent for daughter
Consent dated 20 Dec. 1833   Teste: Robert W. Hudgins

BAGBY, William   Elizabeth MURRAY
M.B. 25 Sept. 1786   Surety: C. Taylor

BAGBY, William T.   Frances R. SNODDY
M.B. 19 Jan. 1836   Surety: William S. Hudgins
Consent: David Snoddy consents for daughter
Consent dated 17 January 1836   Teste: James Snoddy

BAILY, A. M. *   Martha M. COLEMAN
M.B. 24 March 1836   Surety: E. N. Allen
* Name written Arminadab Monroe Bailey

BAILEY, Henry   Eliza JOHNS
M.B. 26 Dec. 1828   Surety: William Southall

BAILEY, James   Nancy MURPHY
After 30 Nov. 1786   Surety: John Bell
Administration of Gov. Edm'd Randolph - 11/30/1786-11/12/1788

BAILEY, Peter   Frances WINFREE
M.B. 25 Sept. 1770   Surety: John Winfree
Note: Daughter of John Winfree of this county

BAILEY, Thomas   Sarah SPALDING
Married 13 February 1757   Both in Manakin Town
Ref: Douglas Register, p. 10

BAKER, Abraham   * Hannah MOSBY
M.B. 6 October 1750   Surety: Micajah Mosby
* Hannah Mosby, widow

BALLARD, Moorman   Minerva BULLOCH
M.B. 6 Nov. 1769   Surety: Job Johnson

BALLOW, John S.   Sally Clough SELF
M.B. 10 Nov. 1827   Surety: Jo^s Fuqua
Consent: Sally signed own consent 9 Nov. 1827 "being of law-
    ful age".   Teste: John E. Self

15

BALLOW, Thomas Cloe BATTERSBY
Married 17 March 1757 by Rev. William Douglas
Note: Thomas Ballow of Albemarle County
Note: Cloe Battersby of Maniken Town

BALLOW, Thomas Permaly J. NUNNALLY
M.B. 22 Jan. 1824 Surety: Bartlett Cox
Note: Bartlett Cox states <u>Pamelia</u> is age 21 and resident of
 this county.

BALLOW, William, Sr. Elizabeth Smith DAVENPORT
Prior to 1 July 1784
Note: Elizabeth Smith Ballow, wife of William Ballow, Sr.,
 released her dower right - 3 July 1784 - Cum. Co. D.B.
 6, p. 211.
 Will of William Davenport, Cum. Co. W.B. 3, p. 9
 7-10-1792-3-25-1793

BALLOW, William T. Myrie FARIS
M.B. 13 Jan. 1819 Surety: Jacob Faris

BALLOW, William T., Jr. Susanna H. BRANSFORD
M.B. 22 Nov. 1824 Surety: John S. Ballow

BARBEE, John Martha C. ALLEN
M.B. 17 Dec. 1836 Surety: Jerome (?) Bondurant
Consent: Martha signed own consent   Teste: Frances Anderson

BARKER, William W. Jane RANSONE
M.B. 11 May 1805 Surety: Wm. Bond

BARNES, James Janet STEVENSON
M.B. 14 Jan. 1759 Surety: John Stevenson
Note: Will of John Stevenson, Cum. Co. W.B. 1, p. 269
 13 April 1763-26 Sept. 1763

BARNES, John Mary PORTER
Married 30 October 1755 in Maniken Town
Ref: Douglas Register, p. 11.

BASHAM, Nathan Mildridge DICKERSON
M.B. 17 April 1789 Surety: John McCann
Consent: David Dickerson gives consent for daughter
 Teste: William Dickerson

BASKERVILLE, Richard Martha GOODE
M.B. 9 Oct. 1770 Surety: Thompson Swann
Consent: 8 Oct. 1770 by Bennett Goode, Senr., for daughter
Teste: Bennett Goode, Junr.   Teste: John Baskerville, Junr.

BASKERVILLE, William Mary A. M. FERGUSON
M.B. 7 March 1812 Surety: James Brown
Consent dated 24 Feb. 1812 by William Ferguson for marriage
of his daughter Teste: John Brown

BASKETT, William T.   Mary W. HOWARD
M.B. 25 Jan. 1826   Surety: Robert Moseley
Consent: Signed by Mary Howard stating that she is of lawful
        age. Robert Moseley certifies Mary is age 21.
Teste: Wm G. Price   Teste: Wm M. Sheperd

BASS, Frederick W.   Lucy MAYO
M.B. 24 Nov. 1832   Surety: John M. Mayo
Consent dated 22 Nov. by Daniel Mayo for daughter.

BASS, William   Rebekah HASKINS
M.B. 8 Dec. 1762   Surety: Ch. Haskins
Consent: Creed Haskins for daughter   Teste: Thomas Haskins

BASS, William   Martha T. MAYO
M.B. 5 July 1823   Surety: Richd W. Bass
Daughter of D. Mayo - Richd W. Bass makes affidavit that Martha Mayo is of age.

BATES, William   Rosanna MEADER
M.B. 14 March 1785   Surety: Joseph Weatherford

BAUGH, Burwell   Ann NETHERLAND
M.B.. 7 March 1775   Surety: None given

BAUGH, Edward F.   Martha LAMBERT
M.B. 9 June 1825   Surety: Wm. F. Randolph
Consent: Martha states she is of lawful age
Teste: R. H. Montague   Teste: A. Cheatwood

BAUGHAN, James   Jane FLIPPEN
M.B. 10 June 1809   Surety: William Baughan

BAUGHAN, Randolph   Patsy FLIPPEN
M.B. 30 Dec. 1822   Surety: John M. Flippen
Consent: Thos Flippen - no relation stated
Jno. M. Flippen made oath that Patsy Flippen is above age 21

BAUGHAN, Silas   Elizabeth CARTER
M.B. 15 Dec. 1831   Surety: Jonas Meador
Consent: Jane Carter gives consent for her daughter
Consent dated 4 December 1831   Teste: William A. Carter

BAUGHAN, William W.   Sarah JACKSON
M.B. 31 Jan. 1830 (Date on bond)   Surety: Peyton Baughan
Consent: Sarah signed own consent 31 Jan. 1831
Married 1 February 1831 by the Rev. John T. Watkins

BEATY, James F.   Elizabeth JOHNSON
M.B. 22 Oct. 1832   Surety: Berry Smith
Note: William Phaup makes affidavit thet Elizabeth Johnson
      was of age.

BEDFORD, Benjamin   Susannah DANIEL
Before 30 October 1760   Daughter of James Daniel
Will of James Daniel, Albemarle County, W.B. 2, p. 94
                10-30-1760-2-12-1761

BEDFORD, Thomas   Mary Ligon COLEMAN
M.B. 24 Sept. 1750   Surety: Micajah Mosby

BELL, Henry   Rebecca HARRISON
M.B. 10 June 1773   Surety: Cary Harrison

BELLAMY, Richard   Patsy DOSS
M.B. 4 Oct. 1803   Surety: Caleb Green

BELLAMY, William   * Nancy PALMORE
M.B. 20 Dec. 1807   Surety: Josiah Gauldin
* Widow of William Palmore
Married 1 January 1808 by Rev. Rane Chastain
    31 Dec. 1807 - "This is to certify that I, Nancy
    Palmore, widow of William Palmore, deceased, being
    my own guardian do agree to join in bonds of matri-
    mony with Mr. William Bellamy".

BELSHERS, Benjamin   Mary ROGERS
M.B. 6 Sept. 1785   Surety: Arthur Edwards

BELT, Addison   Elizabeth A. CARRINGTON
M.B. 24 March 1817   Surety: Henry B. Montague

BENNETT, John H.   Judith E. MICHAUX
M.B. 19 Sept. 1835   Surety: Coleman D. Bennett
Consent: Judith signs own consent   Teste: Richard K. Raine
Married 29 September 1835 by Rev. John T. Watkins

BENTLEY, Efford   Elizabeth GAY
Prior to 30 Nov. 1796   Surety: Chastain Cocke
Administration of Gov. Robert Brooke - 12/1/1794-11/30/1796

BERNARD, John   Henningham CARRINGTON
M.B. 30 July 1767   Surety: Geo. Carrington, Junr.
Note: Daughter of George Carrington, Gent., of Cumberland Co.

BERNARD, William   Mary FLEMING
M.B. 21 March 1748   Bond in Goochland County
Included because of following references:
    Cum. Co. D.B. 2, pp. 186-230-232 - 28 July 1755
Will of John Fleming, Cum. Co. W.B. 1, p. 122
                11-20-1756-12-27-1756

BILBO, John   Ann WALKER
M.B. 16 June 1760 - Married 16 June 1760 in Manakin Town
Ref: Douglas Register, p. 12

BINFORD, William A.   Hardenia A. SPEARS
M.B. 24 July 1837   Surety: Overton B. Pettus

18

Note: Hardenia A. Spears daughter of Leonard L. Spears

BINGLEY, Joseph   Judith FORSEE
Prior to 28 Aug. 1766
Will of John Forsee, Cum. Co. W.B. 1, p. 317
         8-28-1766-10-27-1766

BLACKWELL, Putnam A.   Perlina BROWN
M.B. 28 April 1840   Surety: John R. Wright
Daughter of Archer Brown   Teste: John Chrisp

BLAIN, Samuel   Susan J. HARRISON
M.B. 13 Dec. 1837   Surety: Geo. W. Dame
Consent: Randolph Harrison gives consent 5 December 1837 for
     marriage of his daughter.   Teste: Ed. Sims

BLANKENSHIP, Joseph   Polly ANDERSON
M.B. 29 Dec. 1806   Surety: Samuel Williams
Married 30 December 1806 by Rev. Abner Watkins

BLANKENSHIP, William   Lucy WOOD
M.B. 7 Feb. 1829   Surety: Henry Blankenship

BLANTON, Alexander   Martha AMOS
M.B. 12 Nov. 1837   Surety: James Amos
Consent: Henry Amos gives consent for daughter
James Amos makes affidavit 13 Nov. 1837 that Martha is of
lawful age.   Teste: Robert Amos

BLANTON, Edward A.   Mary A. MILLER
M.B. 28 Nov. 1836   Surety: Allen Wilson
Consent: William Walker consents for his ward and grand-
     daughter Mary Miller.   Teste: John L. Gauldin

BLANTON, Elisha B.   Elizabeth F. SANDERS
M.B. 27 May 1822   Surety: John L. Gauldin
Consent: John Sanders gives consent for daughter
Married 12 June 1822 by Rev. Abner Watkins

BLANTON, James, Jr.   Nancy WALKER
M.B. 23 Nov. 1818   Surety: Alexander Rice

BLANTON, John   Sarah ANGELEA
M.B. 23 March 1786   Surety: James Blanton

BLANTON, John, Jr.   Nancy DUNCOMBE
Prior to 11 Dec. 1805   Surety: Wade N. Woodson
Administration of Gov. John Page - 12/29/1802-12/11/1805

BLANTON, John   Martha BLANTON
M.B. 25 Dec. 1809   Surety: James Blanton

BLANTON, Joseph   Susanna S. WALKER
M.B. 28 April 1828   Surety: Chas. B. Allen

Consent: William Walker, guardian for Susanna S. Walker,
         gives consent 23 April 1828   Teste: Wm. B. Walker

BLANTON, Laurence   Gilly CORLEY
M.B. 29 May 1809   Surety: William Corley

BLANTON, Lindsey   Rebecca B. WALKER
M.B. 27 March 1820   Surety: William Walker

BLANTON, Meredith   Nancy CHRISP
No date on bond   Surety: William Chrisp
Consent: John Chrisp, Senr., gave consent for his daughter
         <u>3 April 1814</u>   Teste: William Chrisp

BLANTON, Nelson   Elizabeth CRISP
M.B. 23 Nov. 1806   Surety: John Crisp, Jr.
Married 27 November 1806 by Rev. Abner Watkins

BOATRIGHT, Daniel   Jane MARTIN
Prior to 21 May 1758
Will of Valentine Martin, Cum. Co. W.B. 1, p. 203
          5-21-1758-7-28-1760

BOATRIGHT, Daniel   Lucy A. HARRIS
M.B. 14 Jan. 1818   Surety: Joel M. Boatright
Consent: Rebecca Harris for daughter   Teste: Jo^S Harris

BOATRIGHT, Daniel   Elizabeth A. MONTGOMERY
M.B. 13 Oct. 1831   Surety: Nelson Talley
12 Oct. 1831 - Elizabeth age 21 writes own consemt

BOATRIGHT, James   Sally THOMAS
M.B. 28 Sept. 1789   Surety: Valentine Boatright
Consent: James Thomas consents - no relation stated

BOATRIGHT, Joel M.   Ellenor BELLAMY
M.B. 30 May 1820   Surety: Ja^S B. Anderson
Consent: William Bellamy gives consent for his daughter

BOATRIGHT, John   Elizabeth DOSS
M.B. 12 March 1812   Surety: Thomas Hudson
Consent: Elizabeth writes own consent   Teste: Jesse Davenport

BOATRIGHT, Jones A.   Polly MONTGOMERY
M.B. 24 May 1824   Surety: William Montgomery

BOATRIGHT, Leonard   Susanna RODGERS
M.B. 20 Dec. 1815   Surety: Daniel Smith
Consent: Martha Rodgers gives consent for her daughter

BOATRIGHT, Marlow   Elizabeth AYRES
M.B. 17 Oct. 1814   Surety: Henry Skipwith, Jr.
Consent: Wm. Brown states "Elizabeth Ayres is upwards of 21
         years of age and lives in my house. I consent for
         her marriage".

BOATRIGHT, Marlow P.   Catharine CRISON
M.B. 31 May 1816   Surety: John McCormack, Jr.
Consent: Catherine Crison writes own consent.

BOATRIGHT, Langhorne   Sally BOATWRIGHT
M.B. 15 July 1809   Surety: John Palmore

BOATWRIGHT, Reuben, Jr.   Mary A. BRYANT
M.B. 24 Sept. 1827   Surety: Anderson Guerrant
Consent: Charles Bryant for daughter   Teste: Thos Boatwright

BOATWRIGHT, Thomas   Nancy Oslin
M.B. 4 Dec. 1821   Surety: John A. Oslin
Married 5 December 1821 by Rev. Joseph Jenkins

BOHANNON, Henry   Susannah FRETWELL
Prior to 29 Dec. 1786
Will of William Fretwell, Cum. Co. W.B. 2, p. 428
              12/29/1786-2/25/1788

BOLLING, Jesse   Sarah ROBERTSON
M.B. 26 Sept. 1785   Surety: William Robinson
Consent: Samuel Robertson for daughter   Teste: Jesse Flippen

BOLLING, Robert   Sarah HOBSON
M.B. 5 Sept. 1821   Surety: Thomas Hobson

BONDURANT, Charles P.   Caroline E. SMITH
M.B. 8 April 1833   Surety: William P. Daniel
Consent: John R. Palmore gives consent for his ward, Caroline
        Smith, 7 April 1833   Teste: Tho. J. Goodman

BONDURANT, George   Arrina FLIPPEN
M.B. 28 Aug. 1815   Surety: William Flippen
Married 31 August 1815 by Rev. Samuel Woodfin

BONDURANT, James A.   Amelia M. PRICE
M.B. 5 July 1834   Surety: Fred Galloway

BONDURANT, Joseph   Agnes RADFORD
Prior to 10 Nov. 1745
Residents of King William Parish, Cumberland County, until
1772. Goochland County D.B. 5, p. 248

BONDURANT, William   Martha WALTON
M.B. 14 Jan. 1793   Surety: John T. Merryman
Consent: George Walton for Martha Walton Teste: Thomas Walton

BOOKER, Edward   Patsy TAYLOR
M.B. 8 Oct. 1804   Surety: Miller Woodson
Consent: B. B. Woodson consented for Mary P. Taylor - no re-
         lation stated.

BOOKER, George   Louisa Ann CARRINGTON
M.B. 3 Dec. 1818   Surety: Thomas Hobson
Note: Daughter of Benjamin Carrington

BOOKER, German　　　　　　　　　　　　　　Martha W. BALLOW
M.B. 28 Dec. 1818　　　　　　　　　　　Surety: Chas. A. Ballow

BOOKER, German　　　　　　　　　　　　　　Anne F. WOODSON
M.B. 27 March 1822　　　　　　　　　　Surety: Fr^s J. Clarke

BOOKER, German　　　　　　　　　　　　　Adelina LYNCH
M.B. 25 May 1840　　　　　　　Surety: Jesse R. Wilkinson
Consent: Robert Lynch consents for his daughter to marry
　　　　German Booker F.N. (?)　　Teste: John S. Holland

BOOKER, John James　　　　　　　　　　Judith ALDERSON
Prior to 22 Dec. 1828
Ref: Division of estate of John Alderson, Cum. Co. W.B. 8,
　　p. 580
　　　"Thomas Alderson late guardian of his sister Judith
　　Alderson who has intermarried with John James Booker"
　　Will of John Alderson, Cum. Co. W.B. 4, p. 264, rec-
　　orded at Sept. Court 1813 - Division made 12-22-1828
　　recorded 7-27-1829.

BOOKER, Richard　　　　　　　　　　　　　Lucy HOBSON
License 15 June 1780　　　　　　　　　　　　　Fee 10/
Ref: Cumberland County Fee Book -1779-1781

BOOKER, Richard A.　　　　　　　　　　　　Eliza DAVIS
M.B. 21 April 1808　　　　　　　　　Surety: Parke Bailey

BOOKER, Thomas B. W.　　　　　　　　　Sally M. TALLEY
Bond not dated　　　　　　　　Surety: Frederick Hatcher
Consent: 12 Sept. 1810 - William Talley consents for his
　　　　daughter Sally Manning (Talley) to marry.
Teste: John Baughan　　　　　　　　Teste: Robert Scruggs

BOOTH, John　　　　　　　　　　　　　　Ann A. WILSON
M.B. 23 July 1815　　　　　　　　　　Surety: Sam'l Davis
Consent: Richard Wilson consents for his daughter 7-23-1815
Teste: A. Mason　　　　　　　　　　　Teste: Tho. Johnson

BOSHER, Leonard　　　　　　　　　　　　Nancy P. SMITH
M.B. 7 Nov. 1828　　　　　　　　Surety: Peter T. Phillips

BOSTICK, John　　　　　　　　　　　　Tabitha ROBINSON
M.B. 6 July 1785　　　　　　　　Surety: Joseph Robinson

BOWLES, Anderson　　　　　　　　　　　　　Jane THOMAS
M.B. 30 Aug. 1785　　　　　　　　Surety: Richd Taylor
Consent: James Thomas for daughter　Teste: Saml Taylor

BOWLES, Elijah P.　　　　　　　　　　　Sally GUTHREY
M.B. 9 Aug. 1834　　　　　　　　　Surety: John Caldwell

BOWLES, James　　　　　　　　　　　　　Sarah WALDEN
M.B. 18 Jan. 1771　　　　　　　　　　　Surety: T. Swann

BOYDEN, Lucius   Ann N. LEE
M.B. 14 Jan. 1839   Surety: Alfred R. Watkins
Daughter of Joseph D. Lee who consents
Married 23 January 1839 by Rev. John T. Watkins

BRACKETT, Joseph   Jane THOMPSON
M.B. 13 Jan. 1810   Surety: Tho^S Gordon
Consent: Sally Thompson for her daughter
Teste: Francis Bransford & Benj. Bransford Teste: Benj. Hobson

BRACKETT, Thomas H.   Sarah M. BRANSFORD
M.B. 29 Aug. 1834   Surety: Thomas A. Goodman
Note: Philip Old makes affidavit that Sarah is of age.

BRADLEY, Benj.   Lockey MERRYMAN
M.B. 28 May 1804   Surety: John F. Merryman
Consent: Jesse Merryman consents - relationship not stated

BRADLEY, Benj.   Nancy WALKER
M.B. 28 May 1814   Surety: Rice Alexander

BRADLEY, Clement   Polly McGINNIS
M.B. 17 Dec. 1807   Surety: James Minter
Consent: Polly signs own consent   Teste: Beverly Lyall
Married 23 December 1807 by Rev. Rane Chastain

BRADLEY, Clement   Mary BOATRIGHT
M.B. 25 Oct. 1815   Surety: Valentine Boatwright

BRADLEY, Daniel   Jenny HUDGINS
M.B. 20 Jan. 1808   Surety: Walter Keeble
Consent: Holloway Hudgins consents for his daughter
Married 25 January 1808 by Rev. William Walker

BRADLEY, Daniel R.   Mary WINFREE
M.B. 4 Nov. 1822   Surety: John Winfree

BRADLEY, David   Nancy MEADOR
M.B. 23 Nov. 178_   Surety: John Bradley
Consent: Nancy signs own consent 22 Nov. 1789
                                     Teste: Hezekiah Bradley

BRADLEY, David   Mary L. FRAYSER
M.B. 13 Dec. 1815   Surety: William Frayser

BRADLEY, Isham   Catherine HUDGINS
M.B. 6 Oct. 1832   Surety: William Austin
Consent: Both consent for themselves   Teste: John Hudgins

BRADLEY, Joseph S.   Mary HUDGINS
M.B. 8 Jan. 1815   Surety: Holloway Hudgins

BRADLEY, Phineas   Ann B. BOATWRIGHT
M.B. 22 Oct. 1806   Surety: James Osborne
Consent: John Boatwright consents for daughter

BRADLEY, Samuel B.   Polly RYE
M.B. 19 Dec. 1808   Surety: John W. Rye
Note: John Rye appears before the Clerk and states that Polly
      is above age 21 years, and a resident of this County.
Married 19 January 1809 by Rev. Rane Chastain

BRADLEY, Thomas   Frances MINTER
M.B. 9 Dec. 1812   Surety: Turner Brown
Frances signs consent   Teste: Jesse Minter - William Minter

BRADLEY, William   Mary Price ROWTON
M.B. 22 Oct. 1770   Surety: William Routon
See: Charlotte County Deed Book 5, page 362

BRADLEY, William   Betty HARRISON
Prior to 8 Oct. 1793
Will of Carter Henry Harrison, Cum. Co. W.B. 3, p. 20
                10-8-1793-1-27-1794

BRADLEY, William E.   Ann E. LEWIS
M.B. 14 March 1840   Surety: William P. Seay
4 March 1840 - Thomas Lewis guardian for Ann E. Lewis gives
            consent   Teste: Wm C. Talley
17 Feb. 1840 - Goochland County Court
        "Thomas Lewis qualified as guardian for Ann
        Lewis, orphan of John Lewis, deceased."
                        /s/ Wm Miller Clk

BRADLEY, William R.   Ellen S. CARRINGTON
M.B. 15 Dec. 1829   Surety: Joseph N. Carrington
Consent: William E. Carrington gives consent as guardian
        for Ellen S. Carrington, daughter of late Wm.
        Carrington, deceased.   Teste: Maria L. Watkins

BRADSHAW, Charles   Jemima HENDRICK
Prior to 25 Jan. 1758
Ref: Cum. Co. O.B. 4, p. 44 - Deed of Gift - April Court 1759
Will of Adolphus Hendrick, Cum. Co. W.B. 1, p. 273
                1-25-1758-10-24-1763

BRADSHAW, Ch.   Nancy ROBINSON
License 6 April 1780   Fee 20/
Cumberland County Fee Book - 1779-1781

BRADSHAW, Feild   Judith ROBERTSON
Prior to 11 December 1767
Will of John Robertson, Cum. Co. W.B. 1, p. 343
                12-11-1767 - 4-25-1768

BRADSHAW, Josiah   Elizabeth ARMISTEAD
M.B. 20 Dec. 1763   Surety: John Armistead
Note: Daughter of John Armistead of Cumberland County

BRAIG, Benj: (Bragg ?)   Lucy McCORMACK
M.B. 26 Aug. 1822   Surety: Joseph Davidson

Note: Lucy McCormack daughter of Pleasant McCormack.

BRANCH, Daniel   Elizabeth PORTER
Prior to 1 Nov. 1761
Will of Thomas Porter, Cum. Co. W.B. 1, p. 321
                 4-15-1765 - 4-27-1767

BRANSFORD, Benjamin   Lucy HATCHER
After 15 June 1782
Daughter of Frederick and Sarah (Woodson) Hatcher
Will of Frederick Hatcher, Cum. Co. W.B. 2, p. 317
Will of Sarah Hatcher, Cum. Co. W.B. 4, p. 214
                        See: Bransford Family Records

BRANSFORD, Francis   Sarah HATCHER
After 15 June 1782   - See references above

BRANSFORD, John   Lucy Jane ALLEN
M.B. 8 Dec. 1836   Surety: Benja. Allen

BRIERS, Edward   Lucy HAWKINS
Married 18 October 1761 in Maniken Town
Ref: Douglas Register, p. 13

BRIGHTWELL, John   Frances H. GLENN
M.B. 9 Dec. 1811   Surety: William Glenn, Jr.
Note: Daughter of William Glenn

BRIGHTWELL, John James   Sarah Ann Thomas APPERSON
M.B. 30 Dec. 1839   Surety: James Jenkins
Prince Edward County - 23 December 1839
    Col. W. Wilson, I wish you to order the Clerk of Prince
    Edward County to issue licens (sic) to marry my daugh-
    ter Sarah Ann Thomas Apperson and John James Brightwell.
                             /s/ Elizabeth Ann Apperson
Consent: 30 Dec. 1839 - Wm. Wilson, administrator of Thomas
          Apperson, deceased, has since acted as guardian of
          the children by request of their mother. consents
          for Sarah Ann.   Teste: Robert F. Gibson

BRITT, Obadiah   Elizabeth HOLEMAN
M.B. 16 Sept. 1806   Surety: Tandy Holman
Note: Daughter of John Holeman who states she is of lawful
     age.
Married 18 September 1806 by Rev. Abner Watkins

BROWN, Archibald   Polly ANGLEA
M.B. 15 Aug. 1789   Surety: James Durham

BROWN, Archer   Sally ANGELEA
No date on bond   Surety: Jacob Durham
Consent: Sally writes own consent **15 Dec. 1813**
Witness: Jacob Durham   Teste: John Durham

BROWN, Archer   Nancy GODSEY
M.B. 27 May 1835   Surety: William H. Armistead
Consent: Nancy signs own consent   Teste: Rebecah Armistead
Married 28 May 1835 by Rev. John T. Watkins

BROWN, Archer, Jr.   Magary BROWN
M.B. 22 Dec. 1817   Surety: Pleasant Colley
Note: Daughter of Archibald Brown, Senr.   Teste: Josiah Ward

BROWN, Chesley   Mary BRADLEY
M.B. 7 Nov. 1817   Surety: John M. Flippen

BROWN, Daniel   Nancy L. H. WALTON
M.B. 7 Nov. 1808   Surety: Robert Walton

BROWN, George   Sarah CORLEY
M.B. 10 Jan. 1789   Surety: William Dickenson
Note: Daughter of Valentine Corley   Teste: George Brown

BROWN, George   Sally JONES
M.B. 6 March 1793   Surety: William Anglea
Note: Daughter of Hanner (sic) Jones   Teste: James Durrum
Teste: William Anglea, Junr.   Teste: Archibald Brown

BROWN, German   Eliza CARR
M.B. 23 Dec. 1829   Surety: Ludwell Brown
Note: Ludwell Brown swears that Eliza is above age 21 years.
Married 24 December 1829 by Rev. John T. Watkins

BROWN, James   Polly PALMORE
M.B. (no date) - on back of bond 17 Dec. 1807
                            Surety: John Caldwell

BROWN, Jesse   * Mary DUSKINS
M.B. 7 Feb 1806   Surety: William Bond
* Mary Dunkins ?   Teste: Sally Clements
Consent: Mary signed own consent 23 Jan. 1806

BROWN, Jesse   Judith MOSS
M.B. 8 Aug. 1815   Surety: John Steward
Consent: Judith signed own consent and states that she is of
        age 21 years.   Teste: Savery Dunkum

BROWN, John   Polly HATCHER
M.B. 19 Dec. 1826   Surety: Thos. Cooper
Note: Thos. Cooper states Polly is over 21 years of age.

BROWN, Robert   Mary TABB
M.B. 5 Sept. 1758   Surety: Thomas Tabb

BROWN, Robert   Sally I. SANDERSON
M.B. 15 April 1820   Surety: William Turner
Consent: John Sanderson for daughter
Consent dated 11 April 1820   Teste: Elizabeth P. Sanderson

26

BROWN, Spencer					Amanda FLIPPEN
M.B. 23 Sept. 1822			Surety: Robert W. Flippen

BROWN, Thomas					Susanna G. PARKER
M.B. 21 Dec. 1825				Surety: Isham Parker
Note: Daughter of Jesse Parker
　　　John Parker makes affidavit that Susanna is of age.

BROWN, Thomas C.				Martha J. GOODMAN
M.B. 18 Dec. 1837				Surety: Thos. D. Flippen
Consent: James H. Hobson gives consent for his ward Martha.

BROWN, Turner					Sally MINTER
Prior to 12 Dec. 1808			Surety: John Minter, Jr.
Administration of Gov. William H. Cabell　Teste: James Hobson
　　　　　　　12/11/1805-12/12/1808
Will of John Minter, Cum. Co. W.B. 4, p. 242 - Division of
estate recorded at June Court 1813

BROWN, William					Jane ADAMS
M.B. (no date) on back of bond Oct. 1809
						Surety: John M. Hambleton
Consent: Jane Adams gives consent for daughter 15 Oct. 1809

BROWN, William, Jr.				Jane C. PALMORE
M.B. 7 Feb. 1814				Surety: James Brown
Consent: Jane Palmore gives consent for her daughter.

BROWN, William J.				Mary J. MATTOX
M.B. 9 Sept. 1837				Surety: James W. Reynolds
Consent: Willis S. Brown gives consent for his son
Consent: William G. Mattox gives consent for his daughter
Teste: Valentine Meador		Teste: Elizabeth Richardson

BROWN, Willis S.				Nancy B. BROWN
M.B. (no date on bond)			Surety: Thomas Brown
Note: William Turner listed as surety but did not sign bond.
Consent: Thos Brown gave consent 26 Sept. 1818 for daughter
Teste: William Turner			Teste: John Brown

BROWN, Wilson					Cynthia MONTAGUE
M.B. 1 April 1805				Surety: William Amonett

BRYANT, Charles				* Delphia B. HUDGINS
* Philadelphia B. Hudgins
M.B. 10 June 1834				Surety: Phineas B. G. Wright
Note: Phineas B. G. Wright makes affidavit that Delphia is of
　　　age.					Teste: Elijah Glover

BRYANT, John					Sarah BROWN
M.B. 15 Feb. 1788				Surety: Ben Brown
Witness: Miller Woodson		Witness: Laban Hawkins

BRYANT, Silas S.				Elizabeth D. ANDERSON
M.B. 25 Nov. 1830				Surety: Richard J. Anderson
Note: Daughter of Richard J. Anderson

BUGG, Samuel S.   Delilah JOHNSON
M.B. 5 Nov. 1831   Surety: Reuben F. Davidson
Consent: Mary Johnson for her daughter Teste: James A. Thomas
Married (6 ?) November 1831 by Rev. Poindexter P. Smith

BURCH, John   * Charity WOODSON
* Charity Woodson, widow
M.B. 28 August 1756   Surety: Benja. Childrey

BURTON, Allen   Mary BURTON
M.B. 27 Feb. 1775   Surety: Tapley Merritt
Note: Daughter of late William Allen Burton, deceased, of
      this county.

BURTON, Benjamin   Elizabeth SMITH
M.B. 16 Feb. 1789   Surety: Harry Smith
Note: 16 February 1789
      Elizabeth Smith and Martha Smith write a joint
      consent to allow Benjamin Burton and George
      Slaughter to get license to marry them.
      Teste: Harry Smith   /s/   Elizabeth Smith
      Teste: John Burton   /s/   Martha Smith

BURTON, John   Agnes MERRYMAN
M.B. 24 August 1752   Surety: Ben Harris
Consent: John Merryman gives consent for daughter Agnes
Consent signed by - John Merryman and Agnes Merryman
Teste: Thomas Merryman   Teste: Allen Burton

BURTON, Seth   Martha WALTON
M.B. 8 Nov. ___ (no year date given) Surety: Thos. G. Walton
Prior to 11 Dec. 1805
Administration of Gov. John Page - 12/29/1802-12/11/1805

BURTON, William   Judith DOSS
M.B. 24 April 1780   License 20/
Cumberland County Fee Book - 1779-1781

BURTON, William A.   Polly GAULDING
M.B. 26 Dec. 1808   Surety: Jn⁰ Nunnally
Consent: Susannah Gaulding, mother of Polly, gives consent
Teste: Jesse M. Armistead, William Nunnally, Gregory Matthews

BURWELL, William M.   Susanna M. CARRINGTON
M.B. 30 June 1823   Surety: Ro. H. Carrington
Note: Daughter of Paul I. Carrington

BUTLER, Isaac   Maria W. OVERTON
M.B. 16 Dec. 1805   Surety: Ro. Butler
Consent: State of Tenn., Soldiers Rest, Tho. Overton, con-
        sents for his daughter - 12 October 1805

BYERS, Elijah M.   Jane FRITTER
M.B. 10 Nov. 1831   Surety: William Hatch
Consent: Jane Fritter signs own consent

BYRAM, William   Mary FRETWELL
Prior to 29 Dec. 1786
Will of William Fretwell, Cum. Co. W.B. 2, p. 428
                 12/29/1786-2/25/1788

BYRD, Job   Judith SCOTT
M.B. 15 Aug. 1786   Surety: William Walker
Consent: Saymer Scott consents for his daughter

BRYANT, James   Jane GUERRANT
Married 11 June 1758 - in Maniken Town
Ref: Douglas Register, p. 13

CABELL, Nicholas, Jr.   Hannah CARRINGTON
M.B. 16 April 1772   Surety: Jos. Carrington

CADWELL, Harlow W.   Rebecca B. BLANTON
M.B. 14 Aug. 1833   Surety: James B. Sanders

CALDWELL, Anthony   Elizabeth AIKEN
M.B. 24 Jan. 1785   Surety: James Aiken
Note: Daughter of James Aiken   Witness: Creed Taylor

CALDWELL, John   Mary FARIS
M.B. 17 Dec. 1821   Surety: Jacob Faris
Married 19 December 1821 by Rev. Joseph Jenkins

CALDWELL, Robert   Ann MASON
M.B. 10 Aug. 1835   Surety: P. H. Nunnally

CANTRELL, Anselm M.   Ann N. STRATTON
M.B. 25 Aug. 1834   Surety: D. C. Smith
Consent: Peter Stratton gives consent for his ward Ann, exact
        relationship not stated   Teste: Martha Stratton

CARDOZA, David N.   Mary Ann ATKINSON
M.B. 3 Sept. 1819   Surety: Richd S. Eggleston
Consent: Ro. Scruggs, guardian for Mary Ann Atkinson, gives
        Consent. Teste: G. P. Scruggs Teste: William Frayser

CARR, Thomas *   Ann HAMBLETON
* Bond signed "Thomas Kerr"
M.B. 2 March 1793   Surety: Jas. Hambleton

CARRINGTON, Codrington   Mary Ann CARRINGTON
M.B. 23 Feb. 1789   Surety: Miller Woodson

CARRINGTON, Codrington   Martha A. CARRINGTON
M.B. 20 Aug. 1832   Surety: Geo. C. Walton
Note: George C. Walton makes affidavit that Martha is of age.

CARRINGTON, Edward J.   Sarah A. THORNTON
M.B. 1 June 1821   Surety: William M. Burwell

Note: Sarah Ann Thornton daughter of William M. Thornton who
     gives consent.   Teste: Ro. H. Carrington

CARRINGTON, Paul I.   Patsy GILLIAM
Prior to 30 November 1796   Surety: Blake B. Woodson
Administration of Gov. Robert Brooke - 12/1/1794-11/30/1796

CARRINGTON, William E.   May Gay HATCHER
M.B. 10 Nov. 1831   Surety: John Hatcher, Jr.
Consent: Daughter of Samuel Hatcher   Teste: Benja. Hatcher
Married 15 November by Rev. Joshua Leigh

CARTER, Charles   Judith CARTER
Married 24 June 1756 by Rev. William Douglas
Note: Charles Carter of Cumberland County
Note: Judith Carter of Goochland County
Ref: Douglas Register, p. 14

CARTER, Charles   Susanna WRIGHT
M.B. 27 March 1789   Surety: Isaac Stephens
Note: Daughter of Thomas Wright   Teste: Martin Stephens

CARTER, Edward A.   Ann R. JOHNSON
M.B. 10 August 1840   Surety: William W. Price
Note: Daughter of Polly Johnson   Teste: W. H. Johnson

CARTER, Edward H.   Louisa JONES
M.B. 16 June 1812   Surety: Leonard Daniel
Consent: Fred^k Jones gives consent - No relation stated

CARTER, Edward M.   Sarah C. TOLER
M.B. 9 Jan. 1833   Surety: David Snoddy
Consent: Sarah signs own consent   Teste: James A. Thomas

CARTER, James   Jenny WINGER
M.B. 18 Jan. 1808   Surety: John Colquitt
Consent: Jenny Winger signs own consent Teste: Miller Woodson

CARTER, James   Susan MAYO
M.B. 18 Nov. 1831   Surety: Levi Davis
Consent: Susan Mayo signs own consent   Teste: John M. Mayo

CARTER, Pleasant   Sally HENDRICK
M.B. (no date on bond)   Surety: Bern^d Sims
Prior to 31 Dec. 1799 (Bond mutilated but   17 shown)
Administration of Gov. James Monroe - 12/19/1799-12/29/1802

CARTER, Wilson   Sarah DAVIS
M.B. (no date) 2 Dec. 1815 on back of bond   Sur: Jesse Davis

CARLYLE, John   Frances NETHERLAND
M.B. 19 February 1752   Surety: Benj^a. Netherland
Note: George Carrington writes consent to Rev. Robert Mc-
     Laurine, or any other orthodox minister of the Church
     of England, to join together John Carlyle and Frances,
     spinster daughter of Wade Netherland.

CAYCE, Fleming							Prudence FOWLER
M.B. (none) consent only dated 27 November 1788
Note: Daughter of Alexander Fowler

CHAFFIN, Nathan							Elizabeth WATKINS
M.B. 28 Nov. 1768						Surety: T. Swann

CHAPMAN, James							Phebe PEARCE
Prior to 12 May 1792
Will of Jeremiah Pearce, Cum. Co. W.B. 3, p. 74
            5-12-1792 - 1-25-1796

CHARLTON, Abraham						Judith BLANTON
M.B. 24 Dec. 1813					Surety: Meredith Blanton
Consent: Judith signs own consent		Teste: Elisha Blanton

CHARLTON, Elijah						Jane FOWLER
M.B. (no date) 25 Nov. 1816 on back of bond
Note: Daughter of Sherwood Fowler		Surety: Andrew Anglea

CHARLTON, James							Agnes DICKERSON
M.B. 16 August 1804					Surety: James Anglea
Note: "Whereas a marriage contract has taken place between
      Mr. James Charlton and myself, I have no objection to
      his getting a license to marry me".
      16 Aug. 1804   /s/ Agnes (X) Dickerson
Teste: Seth Webber			 Teste: Samuel Webber
Note: See Cumberland County Deed Book 14, page 253

CHARLTON, Samuel						Nancy ANGLEA
M.B. 7 August 1789					Surety: James Anglea

CHARLTON, Samuel						Fanny DICKERSON
M.B. 20 Feb. 1807					Surety: Josiah Cayce

CHAUDOIN, Francis						Sarah WEAVER
Prior to 16 November 1761
Will of Samuel Weaver, Cum. Co. W.B. 1, p. 461
            12/16/1763-8/28/1769

CHEATHAM, Alfred C.						Nancy MERRYMAN
M.B. 27 Feb. 1832					Surety: John T. McAshan
Note: Daughter of Edward Merryman who gives consent
Married by Rev. Poindexter P. Smith (date mutilated)

CHEATWOOD, Alexander					Elizabeth MONTAGUE
M.B. 25 Jan. 1814					Surety: Anderson Johnson
Note: Daughter of Peter Montague who gives consent, 1-21-1814

CHEATWOOD, Alex'r						Jane STRATTON
M.B. 25 Sept. 1820					Surety: Sam Hatcher

CHENAULT, Benj. C.						Mary ANDERSON
M.B. 20 Jan. 1837				Surety: Benj. P. Hambleton
Note: Benj. P. Tyree makes affidavit that Mary is of age.

CHENAULT, James   Sally BARKER
M.B. 9 May 1811   Surety: William D. Coleman
Note: Daughter of Anney Barker who consents

CHENAULT, James   Polly WHITE
M.B. 17 June 1819   Surety: Miller Woodson, Jr.

CHENAULT, Patrick   Rebecca BARKER
M.B. 23 Dec. 1807   Surety: Samuel Wheeler
Married 24 December 1807 by Rev. Rane Chastain

CHENAULT, Patrick   Miss _____ BOATWRIGHT
M.B. (not dated)   25 Dec. 1817 on back of bond
                                             Surety: Pryor Boatwright

CHENAULT, William   Eliza Ann HUTCHINSON
M.B. 16 Oct. 1816   Surety: John Hope
Note: Daughter of James Hutchinson who gives consent.

CHESLEY, George C.   Martha H. BRACKETT
M.B. 18 Jan. 1823   Surety: Thomas H. Brackett
Note: Thos. H. Brackett makes oath that Martha is above age
     21 and a resident of this county.
Note: Daughter of L. Brackett, deceased.

CHILDERS, Jacob   Mary RAILEY
Married 23 April 1767 by Rev. William Douglas
Ref: Douglas Register, p. 15

CHILDRESS, John M.   Sally HAMBLETON
M.B. 23 Sept. 1833   Surety: Henry Hambleton
Note: Henry Hambleton makes affidavit that Sally is of age.

CHILDRESS, Joseph   Maria OLIVER
M.B. 9 Aug. 1824   Surety: John Hord
Consent: Maria signs own consent and says she is over age 21.

CHILDRESS, Nelson   Polly COOPER
M.B. 23 Oct. 1817   Surety: Jnº W. Nash
Note: Daughter of James Cooper who gives consent.
Teste: Robert J. Yancey   Teste: John Minor

CHILDRESS, William   Nancy JOLLEY
M.B. 30 May 1822   Surety: Richard A. Booker

CHRISP, James   Sarah BUCKSTON
M.B. 10 Nov. 1817   Surety: Rawleigh Stott
Consent: Jacob Buckston, guardian for Sarah

CHRISP, James   Julia Anne BLACKWELL
M.B. 27 Dec. 1831   Surety: John Chrisp
Consent: Julia Anne signs own consent   Teste: D. M. Wallis

CHUMLEY, Richard   Grace MILAM
Married 9 May 1756 by Rev. William Douglas

CLARKE, Francis J., Jr.   Nancy HOBSON
M.B. 15 August 1809   Surety: Miller Woodson, Jr.
Consent: Daughter of William Hobson who gives consent
                                          Teste: Epa Hobson

CLARKE, John   Ann HOBSON
M.B. 26 Feb. 1780   License 20/
Cumberland County Fee Book - 1779-1781

CLARKE, Joseph   Elizabeth HENDRICK
M.B. 27 Nov. 1816   Surety: Alexander Hendrick

CLARKE, Richard   Mary TONEY
Married 6 December 1768 by Rev. William Douglas
Note: Both residents of Cumberland County

CLARKE, Richard   Catharine MORELAND
M.B. 23 Nov. 1818   Surety: William Clarke

CLARKE, Robert   Anne POWERS
M.B. 14 Dec. 1825   Surety: John White
Note: John White makes affidavit that Anne is of age.

CLARKE, Thomas B.   Elizabeth A. PALMORE
M.B. 10 Oct. 1835   Surety: Charles S. Palmore
Consent: Daughter of William A. Palmore who gives consent
                                          Teste: John A. Caldwell

CLARKE, William   Martha MEREDITH
M.B. 27 July 1754   Surety: William Luck
Note: Martha Meredith, widow and relict of James Meredith
See: Cumberland County Order Book 4, page 156 Feb. Court 1760

CLARKE, William   Martha JAMES
Prior to 17 December 1759
Will of Mary James, Cum. Co. W.B. 1, p. 205
                12/17/1759-8/25/1760

CLARKSON, John   Judith WOMACK
Married 28 March 1765 by Rev. William Douglas
Note: John Clarkson of Goochland County
Note: Judith Womack of Cumberland County

CLAY, Henry   Rachel POVALL
M.B. 9 April 1753   Surety: Richard Povall
Note: Son of Henry Clay   Witness: John Netherland

CLAY, Thomas   Susanna WATKINS
M.B. 23 April 1770   Surety: Samuel Hobson

CLEMENTS, James   Mary OLIVER
Married 15 December 1757 by Rev. William Douglas
Note: Both of King William Parish, Cumberland County
Ref: Douglas Register, p. 16

CLIBOURN, John   Lucy Ann MONTGOMERY
M.B. 14 Nov. 1827   Surety: Patrick H. Barker
Consent: Lucy Ann signs own consent   Teste: Mary A. Boatright
Married 14 November 1827 by Rev. Joseph Jenkins

CLOPTON, Benjamin   Agnes MORGAN
M.B. 23 June 1755   Surety: Alex. Moss

CLOPTON, Reuben F.   Maria A. TAYLOR
M.B. 15 Feb. 1815   Surety: William Wallace
Note: Daughter of William Taylor who gives consent

COBBS, Augustus   Frances A. ABRAHAM
M.B. 8 August 1816   Surety: William Smith
Note: Daughter of Jacob L. Abraham, Senr., who gives consent
Teste: William Spencer   Teste: Jacob L. Abraham, Jr.

COCKE, Anderson   Elizabeth MICHAUX
M.B. 12 Sept. 1782   Surety: Unknown *
* Listed in Marriage Register of Prince Edward County
Note: Daughter of Joseph and Judith (Woodson) Michaux
Will of Joseph Michaux, Cum. Co. W.B. 3, p. 347

COCKE, John   Judith HATCHER
M.B. 13 May 1817   Surety: Benj. Hatcher
Note: Daughter of Drury Hatcher who gives consent
                                    Teste: John Hatcher

COCKE, Walter T.   Susanna COUPLAND
M.B. 7 Oct. 1816   Surety: David O. Coupland
Note: Daughter of David Coupland, Senr., who gives consent
Teste: William A. Trent   Teste: Stephen W. Trent

COLEMAN, Augustus   Lucy C. EDWARDS
M.B. 25 Oct. 1831   Surety: Flemstead Edwards

COLEMAN, Benja.   Sally APPERSON
M.B. (not dated) 24 Dec. 1813 on back of bond
                             Surety: Gulielmus Coleman
Consent: Daughter of Jacob Apperson, Senr., who gives consent
Teste: B. D. Lee   Teste: William Guthrey

COLEMAN, Daniel   Sally COLEMAN
M.B. 29 Oct. 1817   Surety: Samuel A. Coleman
Consent: Daughter of Henry Coleman, Senr., who gives consent
Teste: Zachariah Talley, James W. Coleman, William D. Coleman

COLEMAN, Edward T.   Sarah H. BALLOW
M.B. 17 March 1809   Surety: William Taylor

COLEMAN, (Elias) Henderson   Lavinia DOWDY
M.B. 4 Feb. 1840   Surety: Thos. J. Smith
Consent: Daughter of Jesse Dowdy who consents
                                    Teste: Shelton Davis

COLEMAN, Elisha M.   Fanny WHEELER
Prior to 15 January 1811   Surety: Samuel Wheeller
Administration of Gov. John Tyler, Sr.
                12/12/1808-1/15/1811

COLEMAN, Elliott   Elizabeth DANIEL
M.B. 23 Nov. 1789   Surety: William Daniel

COLEMAN, Ferdinand G.   Eliza PHILLIPS
M.B. 31 December 1821   Surety: Peter T. Phillips

COLEMAN, Gulielmus   Sarah WHITE
M.B. (not dated) *   Surety: William Guthrey
* Date __ July 1812 listed on back of bond

COLEMAN, Gulielmus   Nancy GUTHREY
M.B. 20 March 1826   Surety: David Molloy
Consent: Josiah Gauldin consents to marriage and states that
         Nancy is of age - No relation stated
Francis Cox states Nancy is of age   Teste: Frances Hendrick

COLEMAN, Henry   Charity HUDGINS
M.B. 29 April 1825   Surety: William Coleman
Consent: Charity signed own consent 28 April 1825
Teste: John W. Flippen who makes oath that she is age 21.

COLEMAN, Henry, Jr.   Oraha COLEMAN
M.B. 11 Nov. 1811   Surety: Elliott Coleman

COLEMAN, Henry W.   Eliza G. COX
M.B. 8 Oct. 1834   Surety: William Wilson
Note: Eliza Cox a ward of William Wilson

COLEMAN, James   * Ann COOCKE
M.B. 19 Dec. 1764   Surety: Daniel Coleman, Jr.
Consent: Daughter of John Coocke who gives consent.
Teste: James Coock   Teste: Stephen Coock
* Ann Cooke ?

COLEMAN, James C.   Nancy WRIGHT
M.B. 6 Oct. 1818   Surety: Robert Wright

COLEMAN, John S.   Sarah WHITE
M.B. 29 Oct. 1822   Surety: William Guthrey

COLEMAN, Joseph S.   Martha RANSONE
M.B. 24 Sept. 1827   Surety: John W. Wilson
Married 4 October 1827 by Rev. Joseph Jenkins

COLEMAN, Julius   Elizabeth COLEMAN
M.B. 23 Sept. 1789   Surety: James Coleman

COLEMAN, Thomas   Nancy EDWARDS
M.B. 28 Dec. 1826   Surety: Benjamin Hubbard
Note: Benjamin Hubbard makes affidavit that Nancy is of age.

COLEMAN, Thomas Jefferson   Delilah HUDGINS
M.B. 5 May 1830   Surety: John M. Hudgins
Note: Delilah daughter of John M. Hudgins

COLEMAN, William D.   Mary BARKER
Prior to 15 January 1811   Surety: Patrick Shenault
Administration of Gov. John Tyler, Sr.
            12/12/1808-1/15/1811

COLES, John   * Jane HUGHES
M.B. 4 Dec. 1758   Surety: Paul Michaux
* Jane Hughes, widow of Joseph Hughes, deceased
See: Cumberland County Order Book 4, p. 28 - Feb. Court 1759

COLLEY, Thomas   Sarah MARKHAM
Prior to 6 December 1799   Surety: Tscharner Woodson
Administration of Gov. James Wood   - 11/30/1796 - 12/6/1799

COLLEY, William   Julia E. BLANTON
M.B. 10 July 1837   Surety: Lawrence Blanton

COLQUITT, Henry   Louisa Anne DAVENPORT
M.B. 3 Dec. 1821   Surety: Zach. Goodman
Married 4 December 1821 by Rev. Joseph Jenkins

COLQUITT, John   Elizabeth HENDRICK
M.B. 29 May 1753   Surety: Robert Hudgins
Note: Elizabeth Hendrick, orphan of William Hendrick, dec'd.

COLQUITT, John   Judith HOBSON
M.B. 25 May 1795   Surety: Caleb Hobson

COLQUITT, John   Rebecca DAVENPORT
M.B. 30 Oct. 1820   Surety: Dudley S. Montague
Consent: Rebecca signs own consent   Teste: John S. Ballow

COLQUITT, Robert   Susanna HUBBARD
M.B. 28 Oct. 1785   Surety: John Colquitt
Consent: Susanna daughter of Joseph Hubbard who consents
Teste: Thomas Moody   Teste: Bennett Hubbard

COLQUITT, Samuel   Molly WOODRUFF
M.B. 26 Dec. 1788   Surety: Robert Colquitt
Molly, daughter of Clifford Woodruff   Teste: Jesse Holland

COLVARD, John Butterworth   Judith MERRYMAN
M.B. 25 Dec. 1762   Surety: Simon Gentry
Consent: John Merryman consents for Judith, no relation
            stated in consent
Teste: John Hoggard   Teste: William Bernard

CONNER, Benjamin   Elizabeth ANDERSON
M.B. 1 January 1790   Surety: Charles Watkins
See consent on next page

Consent: 1 January 1790
    "We give our free consent to a marriage license being granted to Benjamin Conner to marry Elizabeth Anderson as witness our hands and seals this date".
    Teste: Mary Chamberlin   /s/   Samuel Phelps
           Peggy Watkins   /s/   Mary Ann Peak

Note: No relationship stated in consent, but Mary Hughes and Elizabeth Hughes, daughters of Anthony Hughes, married respectively William Chamberlin and Samuel Phelps.

COOKE, Abraham   Elizabeth MORROW
M.B. 20 Oct. 1812   Surety: Ewing Morrow

COOKE, John R.   Judith VAUGHAN
M.B. 28 Oct. 1820   Surety: Samuel W. Venable
Consent: Jos. Vaughan for daughter   Teste: Abraham Cook

COOKE, Stephen   Ellener T. COLEMAN
M.B. 28 May 1832   Surety: Guielmus Coleman

COOKE, Stephen, Jr.   Polly BOOKER
M.B. 9 Feb. 1805   Surety: William Wallace
Note: Daughter of Edward Booker
Consent: Francis Anderson, guardian, consents for his niece
         Polly Booker   Teste: William Emanuel

COOKE, William B.   Elizabeth LANCASTER
M.B. 23 Nov. 1820   Surety: Josiah Lancaster
Consent: Daughter of John Lancaster who gives consent.

CORLEY, George   Polly BROWN
M.B. 26 Sept. 1809   Surety: Nicholas Durham
Consent: Daughter of James Brown who gives consent.
Teste: Ludwell Brown   Teste: Archibald Brown

CORLEY, James   Temperance BROWN
M.B. 22 Feb. 1779   Surety: Miller Woodson
Consent: Daughter of George Brown who gives consent.
                        Teste: Benjamin Walker

CORSON, William   Mary Ann BLAKE
M.B. 19 Jan. 1836   Surety: James Blake

COUPLAND, David O.   Catharine JELLIS
M.B. 24 Nov. 1823   Surety: William A. Trent

COUSINS, David   Evaline BARNETT
M.B. 23 May 1817   Surety: Randolph Mayo
Consent: Daughter of Tarlton Barnett who gives consent.
                        Teste: Isham Cousins

COX, Benjamin A.   Mary R. ALLEN
M.B. 28 Feb. 1835   Surety: James Lockland
Consent: Daughter of Benja. Allen who gives consent.
                        Teste: Chs. S. Palmore

COX, Henry   Ann HARRIS
M.B. 7 Jan. 1765   Surety: John Woodson
Note: The infant daughter of Benjamin Harris, deceased, of
    this county.

COX, John   Phebe WILLIAMSON
M.B. 7 Nov. 1757   Surety: Tho. Ballow

COX, John   Elizabeth FORE
Married 22 June 1766 by Rev. William Douglas
Ref. Douglas Register, p. 17

COX, John H.   Nanny HARRIS
M.B. (no complete date) __ __ 1760   Surety: John Harris
Note: Daughter of Mary Harris - Consent: Brother Jos. Harris
Witness: John Skip Harris   Witness: Mary Harris

COX, Jonathon   Sally WALLER
M.B. 14 July 1807   Surety: W. Keeble, Jr.
Married 16 July 1807 by Rev. John Pollard

COX, William   Francinia CANNON
M.B. 21 Dec. 1768   Surety: Benj. B. Cannon
Note: Daughter of Benjamin Cannon of this county.

COX, William   * Chuziah LEE
* Keziah Lee
M.B. 8 Feb. 1785   Surety: Samuel Williams
Consent: Daughter of Joseph Lee who gives consent.
Teste: William Russell   Teste: Anne Russell

CRAIG, William   Sarah BLAKE
M.B. 29 March 1831   Surety: Joseph Clarke

CRAWFORD, Cleon A.   Pamelia HOLT
M.B. 16 Dec. 1820   Surety: Robert Scruggs
Consent: Philip Holt consents for daughter Wit: Richard Holt

CREASY, John   Martha EDWARDS
M.B. 8 Oct. 1827   Surety: Fleming Palmore
Note: Fleming Palmore makes affidavit that Martha is of age.
Consent: Polly Edwards gives consent for daughter.
Teste: John Hix   Teste: William Creasy
Married 17 October 1827 by Rev. Joseph Jenkins

CREASY, William   Nancy CARTER
M.B. 26 Sept. 1785   Surety: Peter Montague

CREASY, William   Elizabeth HIX
M.B. 23 Jan. 1827   Surety: Josiah Hix

CRENSHAW, Anthony W.   Nancy COLQUITT
M.B. 31 Oct. 1820   Surety: Henry Colquitt
Consent: Nancy signs own consent   Teste: Colquitt, Jr.

CRENSHAW, Anthony W.   Martha C. BRANSFORD
M.B. 14 April 1829   Surety: Epa Hobson
Note: Epa Hobson swears that Martha is above age 21 years.

CRENSHAW, Crawford   Frances D. BAGBY
M.B. 29 Nov. 1825   Surety: Lewis M. Isbell
Note: Lewis M. Isbell uncle of Frances D. Bagby
Consent: Daughter of R. (Reuben) Bagby   Teste: Martha Isbell

CRENSHAW, Nathaniel A.   Catharine COLQUITT
M.B. 16 March 1813   Surety: Miller Woodson, Jr.
Consent: Jn⁰ Colquitt gives consent - no relation stated.

CRENSHAW, Thomas B.   Grace BOOKER
M.B. 13 March 1824   Surety: Abner Nash
Consent: Merret N. Booker gives consent - no relation stated.

CRIDDLE, Jesse *   Sally BRADLEY
M.B. 17 May 1809   Surety: Robert Richardson
* Jesse Creedle ?
Married 18 May 1809 by Rev. Rane Chastain

CRIDDLE, John   Mary JONES
M.B. 26 Jan. 1835   Surety: Robert Jones

CRIDDLE, John B.   Catherine ROBERTSON
M.B. 22 August 1831   Surety: Robert Robertson
Note: Catherine, ward of Robert Robertson

CRIDDLE, William S.   Elvira Ann ROBINSON
M.B. 12 Oct. 1833   Surety: William D. Austin
Note: Daughter of Robert Robinson   Wit: William A. Robinson

CROWDER, John M.   Nancy A. FLIPPEN
M.B. 11 Dec. 1840   Surety: Daniel B. Flippen
Note: Daniel B. Flippen makes affidavit that Nancy is of age.
Married 16 December 1840 by Rev. M. A. Dunn

CRUMP, George William   Ann P. MACON
M.B. (no date) __ April 1813 on back of bond
                                              Surety: Thomas T. Swann

CRUMP, Jos. P.   Martha P. MATTHEWS
M.B. 6 May 1816   Surety: Francis Childress
Note: Daughter of Mary Matthews   Teste: Sarah Mathis ?

CRUMP, Thomas   Phaney TAYLOR
M.B. (no date) __ 1785 on back of bond   Surety: Sam Taylor
Consent: 12 Feb. 1785 by Sam¹ Taylor for Phaney Taylor to
         marry Mr. Thomas Crump - no relation stated.
Teste: Richard Taylor   Teste: Thos Wilkinson

CRUMPTON, Joseph   * Mary BARNES
* Mary Barnes, widow of James Barnes
M.B. 27 Sept. 1756   Surety: James Aiken

CULLIN, Benjamin   Sarah WRIGHT
M.B. 27 Jan. 1794   Surety: Samuel Wright

CULLIN, James M.   Mary LIPFORD
M.B. 30 March 1811   Surety: Jesse Wilbourne
Consent: Daughter of Henry Lipford who consents.
Teste: Robert Walton, Daniel Brown   and   William Bondurant

CUNNINGHAM, Albert   Mary J. Woodson
M.B. 26 June 1837   Surety: Tarlton H. Woodson
Note: Daughter of Tarlton Woodson   Teste: T. T. Womack

CUNNINGHAM, Edward   Catharine J. MILLER
M.B. 11 Nov. 1840   Surety: Richard J. Gilliam
Consent: Daughter of John Miller who gives consent.

CURD, Edward W.   Ann Jane WATKINS
M.B. 20 Oct. 1830   Surety: Miller Woodson
Note: Daughter of John T. Watkins who gives consent and says
     his daughter is not 21 years of age.
Teste: A. W. Yancey   Teste: A. R. Watkins
Married 21 October 1830 by Rev. John T. Watkins

CUSHING, J. P. *   Lucy Jane PAGE
M.B. 30 July 1827   Surety: Nelson Page
* Signature Jon^a P. Cushing - Jonathon P. Cushing ?

DABNEY, Robert K.   Jemima G. WOODSON
M.B. 31 Oct. 1815   Surety: Maurice L. Hobson
Consent: Chr. Woodson for his daughter   Wit: Miller Woodson

DAGNEL, Richard   Sarah CAYCE
M.B. 7 April 1792   Surety: Chas. McNeal
Consent: Shadrack Cayce for his daughter   Teste: A. Guthrey

DAINGERFIELD, William   Mildred ROBERTSON
M.B. 28 Oct. 1836   Surety: John G. Thurston
Note: John G. Thurston makes affidavit Mildred is of age.

DAME, George W.   Mary M. PAGE
M.B. 18 July 1835   Surety: Henry P. Irving
Note: Nelson Page certifies that Mary is over age 21 years.

DAMRON, Samuel   Elizabeth THOMAS
M.B. 1 August 1823   Surety: James A. Thomas
Note: James A. Thomas makes affidavit that Elizabeth is of
     age.

DANIEL, George W.   Judith E. SPENCER
M.B. 22 Nov. 1833   Surety: John Daniel
Note: Daughter of John Spencer who consents

DANIEL, Leonard   Polly SPEARS
M.B. 27 Jan. 1794   Surety: Jesse Thomas

DANIEL, Nimrod   Susanna BURTON
M.B. (no date) - 30 Dec. 1812 on back of bond
Note: Susanna of lawful age.   Surety: Wiltshire Burton

DANIEL, Robert   Mary STRATTON
M.B. 28 Sept. 1827   Surety: James C. Mayo
Note: Daughter of Robert Stratton who consents 23 Sept. 1827
                                      Teste: Isham D. Goolsby

DANIEL, William   Patty Field ALLEN
M.B. 28 March 1768   Surety: John Cox
Consent: Samuel Allen gives consent for his daughter.
Teste: Robt Anderson   Teste: Richd Crump

DAVENPORT, Absalom   Elizabeth STEGAR
Before 24 March 1767   Daughter of Francis George Stegar
Cumberland County Order Book, 1764-1767, page 453
Chancery Suit - Court 24 March 1767

DAVENPORT, Jesse   Elizabeth HOBSON
M.B. 24 Nov. 1794   Surety: John Baughan
Consent: Thomas Hobson consents, but no relation stated.
Teste: Sally Hobson   Teste: Catherine Hobson

DAVENPORT, Satterwhite   Sarah MARTIN
M.B. 26 May 1828   Surety: William Hamilton
Note: Hezekiah Martin appeared before the clerk and swore
      that both parties are above age 21 years.

DAVENPORT, Satterwhite   Nancy FLIPPEN
M.B. 1 Dec. 1836   Surety: Azariah Orange
Consent: Thomas Flippen gives consent for his daughter.
                                      Teste: Peter Winfree

DAVENPORT, Thomas, Jr.   Lucy RANSONE
M.B. 28 April 1750   Surety: (not given)
Consent: Ambrose Ransone for daughter Teste: Gideon Glenn

DAVENPORT, Thomas   Betsey GUERRANT
M.B. ___ Aug. 1781   License 10/
Cumberland County Fee Book - 1779-1781

DAVENPORT, William B.   Sarah J. GOODMAN
M.B. 22 April 1823   Surety: James Hobson
Note: Daughter of Noton Goodman   Teste: Samuel Hobson

DAVIS, Alexander K.   Frances H. HENDRICK
M.B. 7 Dec. 1835   Surety: Josiah Gauldin
Note: Josiah Gauldin makes affidavit that Frances is of age.

DAVIS, Benjamin P.   Mary Ann L. FULCHER
M.B. 21 Dec. 1833   Surety: Peyton P. Davis
Note: Zachariah Davis consents for son "who is in the 20th
      year of his age."   Teste: Stephen W. Davis

41

Note: Mary Ann L. Fulcher, daughter of Sarah Quarles
Teste: James Quarles

DAVIS, Edmund   Martha Ann DAVIS
M.B. 25 Dec. 1839   Surety: A. Smith
Consent: Beverly Davis consents for son   Wit: W. H. Dunnavant
Note: A. Smith makes affidavit that Martha Ann is of age.

DAVIS, George   Mary MAXEY
Prior to 27 May 1768
George Davis, son of James Davis - Cum. Co. W.B. 2, p. 3
Will of William Maxey, Cum. Co. W.B. 1, p. 356

DAVIS, Hardin   Mary E. THOMPSON
M.B. 10 Dec. 1840   Surety: William C. England
Note: Daughter of John Thompson   Teste: Eliza J. Thompson
Married 10 December 1840 by Rev. M. A. Dunn, Methodist Minister of Buckingham County.

DAVIS, Jeduthan H.   Eliza W. FRAYSER
M.B. 28 Dec. 1832   Surety: John R. Frayser
Note: Eliza Frayser of full age.   Teste: James M. Austin

DAVIS, John B.   Mary A. PENICK
M.B. 27 Nov. 1837   Surety: J. W. Brightwell

DAVIS, Peyton P.   Rebecca QUARLES
M.B. 21 August 1828   Surety: William Jones
Note: Peyton, son of Zachariah Davis Teste: Stephen W. Davis
Consent: Rebecca, daughter of Nancy Quarles who consents

DAVIS, Shelton   Mary H. MEADOR
M.B. 4 Nov. 1833   Surety: Thomas L. Meador
Consent: Mary daughter of Jonas Meador   Wit: Isham A. Meador

DAVIS, Zachariah   Matilda QUARLES
M.B. 30 March 1820   Surety: John Falwell

DAVIDSON, Andrew J.   Selender Frances GARRETT
M.B. 11 Dec. 1838   Surety: James A. Thomas
Note: Daughter of John D. Garrett who gives consent.

DAVIDSON, Joseph   Arnah SMITH
M.B. 23 Dec. 1816   Surety: John E. Lennly ?
Consent: Daughter of Janie Smith who gives consent.

DAVIDSON, Reuben   Lucy PEASLEY
M.B. 6 Feb. 1816   Surety: John E. Sandidge
Note: Lucy daughter of Gabriel Peasley

DeJARNETTE, James   Polly PRICE
M.B. 21 March 1816   Surety: Warren W. Meredith
Consent: Polly daughter of John L. Price who consents
Note: James DeJarnette of Pittsylvania County

DESHAZAWAY, Henry   Keziah WILLIAMS
M.B. 25 Dec. 1788   Surety: John Woodson

DILLON, Edward   Elizabeth GILLIAM
M.B. (no date)   on back of bond __ Feb. 1794
                                                Surety: Miller Woodson
DILLON, Thomas
Prior to 12 Nov. 1788   Elizabeth KEELING
Administration of Gov. Edmund Randolph   Surety: C. Taylor
           11/30/1786-11/12/1788

DODSON, John   Nancy CAYCE
M.B. 22 Sept. 1894   Surety: Samuel Allen
Consent: Daughter of Shadrack Cayce who gives consent

DOLLINS, James H.   Polly HOLT
M.B. 24 Sept. 1817   Surety: Robert R. Scruggs
Note: Daughter of Joseph Holt

DONAHOE, Edward   Nancy DOSS
M.B. 25 Oct. 1788   Surety: Richd Webber
Consent: James Doss consents for daughter Nancy Doss
Teste: Parker Doss   Teste: Susannah Doss

DONAHOE, Thomas   Drusilla DAVENPORT
M.B. 12 Oct. 1785   Surety: Richard Walden

DOSS, James   Susannah LEE
M.B. 18 June 1811   Surety: Arthur Horner
Consent: Susannah Lee signs own consent   Teste: James Allen

DOWDY, Albert J.   Mary FLIPPEN
M.B. 23 Nov. 1829   Surety: Collin Shuffield
Consent: Daughter of Thomas Flippen   Teste: William F. Ligon

DOWDY, Albert T.   Eliza COOPER
M.B. 26 Sept. 1831   Surety: Alex'r H. Glenn
Consent: Daughter of James Cooper   Teste: A. H. Glenn
Married ( ) Sept. 1831 by Rev. Poindexter P. Smith

DOWDY, George W.   Jane HUDGINS
M.B. 4 Oct. 1832   Surety: Bennett Bagby
Consent: Daughter of Mary Hudgins   Teste: Chas. W. Lewis

DOWDY, Horace   Artimisia BOSHER
M.B. 19 Oct. 1840   Surety: Thomas J. Smith
Note: Horace son of Thomas Dowdy   Teste: Thomas J. Smith
Consent: Daughter of John Bosher who gives consent
Teste: Leonard Bosher   Teste: Gideon Bosher
Married 21 October 1840 by Rev. William H. Kinckle

DOWDY, James   Martha SMITH
M.B. 10 April 1822   Surety: Bird Smith
Note: Martha daughter of Bird Smith

DOWDY, Jesse   Dorothea DAVENPORT
M.B. 4 July 1804   Surety: Martin S. Davenport

DOWDY, John   Nancy MARTIN
M.B. 21 Feb. 1806   Surety: Thos Mosby
Note on back of bond:
    "Lady is present and declaring herself of age
    says she is willing that Dowdy shall marry her".

DOWDY, John   Lucy Ann JOHNS
M.B. 22 Jan. 1838   Surety: Albert Dowdy
Note: Albert Dowdy makes affidavit that Lucy Ann is of age.

DOWDY, Obediah   Mary DAVENPORT
M.B. 7 Nov. 1789   Surety: Henry Davenport
Consent: Mary Davenport writes own consent - Marshall Booker

DOWDY, Poindexter   Martha MARTIN
M.B. 22 Oct. 1832   Surety: Albert J. Dowdy

DOWDY, Poindexter   Emily DUNNAVANT
M.B. 14 June 1836   Surety: Thos. H. Brackett
Note: John Dunnavant makes affidavit that Emily is of age.

DOWDY, Richard S.   Elizabeth SHELTON
M.B. 21 Dec. 1830   Surety: Robert Hudgins
Note: Daughter of Richard Shelton   Teste: David W. Monroe

DOWDY, Thomas   Martha C. HASKINS
M.B. 4 May 1831   Surety: Thos. H. Brackett
Married 12 May 1831 by Rev. Poindexter P. Smith

DOWDY, William H.   Ava SMITH
M.B. 20 Dec. 1831   Surety: Benj. A. England
Consent: James Dowdy Guardian for Ava Smith "a legatee of
    Bird Smith, deceased".   Teste: John Thompson

DRUEN, William   Nancy JENKINS
M.B. 28 Feb. 1831   Surety: Thos. F. Womack

DROUIN, James   Mary WEAVER
M.B (Prior to 5 June 1757)
Will of Samuel Weaver, Cum. Co. W.B. 1, p. 461

DUFFER: Isaac   Nancy SCOTT
M.B. 10 Nov. 1790   Surety: Stephen Hughes

DUFFIELD, John   Amanda Ann ROSS
M.B. 29 May 1806   Surety: Charles W. Baird
Consent: 27 May 1806 - Witnesses: W. Mewburn - John F. Price
    "John Duffield, Esq., late of Philadelphia and
    my daughter Amanda Ann Ross of Cumberland have agreed
    to be married by holy rites of the Church, I give my
    consent as she is under age".
           /s/ David Ross, City of Richmond

DUNFORD, Philip T.   Anne ENGLAND
M.B. 5 Dec. 1816   Surety: Robert Caldwell

DUNFORD, William   Polly CHESHIRE
Prior to 1 Dec. 1794   Surety: Thomas Hobson
Administration of Gov. Henry Lee   -   12/1/1791 - 12/1/1794

DUNFORD, William   Ann BARKER
M.B. (not dated) 21 Dec. 1818 on back of bond
                                        Surety: Robert Caldwell
Consent: Ann signs own consent as she is of full age.

DUNGAN, George   Rebecca JOHNSON
M.B. 22 August 1814   Surety: Thom^s Johnson
Note: George Dungan of Kentucky

DUNGAN, Johnson M.   Harriet E. ALLEN
M.B. 5 Sept. 1834   Surety: Samuel C. Allen
Consent: Daughter of John C. Allen   Teste: George Dungan

DUNGEY, George   Mary Ann BROWN
M.B. 15 Jan. 1823   Surety: Wm Ransone
Consent: Daughter of Betsey (Elizabeth) Jenkins, wife of
        David Jenkins, and late relict of John Brown.
        Betsey Jenkins is guardian for Mary Ann, she
        being under age.

DUNKUM, John   Elizabeth BROWN
M.B. 15 Dec. 1806   Surety: Joseph Jenkins

DUNKUM, Mathias   Sally DUNKUM
M.B. 8 Nov. 1830   Surety: Chisley Anderson
Note: The signature on the bond reads "Mathias Duncan"
Consent for Sally signed by Phebe Robertson - no relationship
stated.

DUNKUM, John *   Rachel BRADLEY
M.B. 27 Sept. 1813   Surety: Miller Woodson, Jr.
* Name on bond given as "Duncombe" but signature "Dunkum".

DUNKUM, Jonas   Sabra FLIPPEN
M.B. 20 July 1811   Surety: Thomas Flippen

DUNCUM, Moses *   Nancy MEGINNES
M.B (not dated)   Surety: Clement Bradley
Consent: Nancy Meginnes signed own consent 28 October 1813
* Bond in name of Moses Duncum but signature Moses Dunkum

DUNKUM, William   Phebe ANDERSON
M.B. 16 Oct. 1805   Surety: Geo. Anderson

DUNKUM, William L.   Elizabeth S. BRADLEY
M.B. 18 Nov. 1833   Surety: Chesley Brown
Note: Elizabeth Bradley listed as ward of Chesley Brown.

DUNNAVANT, William   Rebecca JOHNSON
M.B. 18 Sept. 1820   Surety: Peter Johnson
Consent: Daughter of Mary Johnson   Teste: Jesse Street

DUNLOP, John   Hannah M. BLAIN
M.B. 10 May 1836   Surety: Samuel W. Blain
Note: Samuel W. Blain makes affidavit that Hannah is of age.

DURHAM, Allen W.   Lucinda BERRY
M.B. (not dated) 29 Jan. 1831 on back of bond
                                 Surety: Robert P. Jordan
Note: Robert P. Jordan swears that Lucinda is upwards of 21
    years old.

DURHAM, Jacob   Patsy BROWN
M.B. 5 Feb. 1810   Surety: Nicholas Durham
Consent: Patsy daughter of Archibald Brown who gives consent.

DURHAM, Jacob A.   Elizabeth ALLEN
M.B. 28 Sept. 1829   Surety: James Blake
Consent: Daughter of Simeon Allen   Teste: Jacob Anderson

DURHAM, James *   Pasey SAMMONS
M.B. 27 Dec. 1792   Surety: William Anglea
* Signature James Durrum
Consent: Pats(y) Dey Sammons signs own consent.
                                         Teste: James Anglea

DURHAM, James *   (* Signature Durrum)   Betsy CORLEY
M.B. 1 Jan. 1806   Surety: Clemons Dickerson
Consent: Betsy "a woman of 21 years age" writes own consent.
Teste: Daniel Jones   Teste: Bartlett Dickerson

DURHAM, William   Ann SWILLEY
M.B. 13 Feb. 1757 - Married by Rev. William Douglas
Ref: Douglas Register, p. 19

DURHAM, William W. C. *   Finetta R. BROWN
M.B. 6 Feb. 1837   Surety: John Baughan
* Signature "Durrum"
Consent: Daughter of Archer J. Brown who consents
Married 22 February 1837 by Rev. J. T. Watkins

EANES, James M.   Sally P. WOMACK
M.B. 9 August 1833   Surety: Arch'd M. Webster
Consent: Daughter of Charles Womack   Teste: Dabney P. Miller

EASLEY, Daniel   Ann DAVID
Prior to 18 Oct. 1750
Will of Ann David, Cum. Co. W.B. 1, p. 28

EATON, Minor   Elizabeth WOOD
M.B. 9 March 1840   Surety: John F. Wood
Note: Elizabeth daughter of John F. Wood.

EDWARDS, Charles   Hannah MOSEBY
Married 27 Jan. 1754 by the Rev. William Douglas
Note: Charles Edwards of Goochland County
      Hannah Moseby of Cumberland County

EDWARDS, Daniel C.   Elizabeth EGGLESTON
M.B. 17 Dec. 1812   Surety: William Edwards
Consent: Elizabeth signs own consent.   Teste: John E. Edwards

EDWARDS: F.   Elizabeth ELLYSON
M.B. 7 Jan. 1780   License 20/
Cumberland County Fee Book - 1779-1781

EDWARDS: George   Judith EDWARDS
M.B. 26 Dec. 1810   Surety: Daniel C. Edwards

EDWARDS, John   Sarah SHUFFIELD
M.B. 5 Sept. 1828   Surety: Collin Shuffield

EDWARDS, William   Grisel COLEMAN
M.B. 27 March 1750   Surety: James Adams
Note: Daughter of Burril and Grisel Coleman
Burwell Coleman ?   Teste : Patience Coleman

EDWARDS, William   ? Gazelle GHEE
M.B. __ 24, 1779   License 20/
Cumberland County Fee Book - 1779-1781

EDWARDS, William W.   Martha Ann Jane Taylor CHRISP
M.B. 9 Nov. 1839   Surety: Sam'l C. Chrisp
Married 4 Dec. 1839 by Rev. J. M. Cofer

EGGLESTON, Edmund   Sarah H. COLLEY
M.B. 20 Jan. 1827   Surety: Richd B. Eggleston
Note: Richard B. Eggleston makes affidavit Sarah is of age.

ELAM, William   Frances COX
M.B. 12 Dec. 1758   Surety: John Cox

ELLINGTON, Boswell F.   Judith W. ADAMS
M.B. 22 April 1833   Surety: William L. McAshan
Note: Daughter of Judith F. Adams   Teste: Sam C. Hooton
Note: William L. McAshan makes affidavit Judith is of age.

ELLINGTON, Branch H.   Mary S. WALTON
M.B. 27 Jan. 1823   Surety: Peter F. Anderson
Note: Daughter of William S. Walton Teste: Nathan W. Walton

ELLINGTON, Luke   Mary ROBERTSON
Minister's return - no bond found
Married 14 Nov. 1822 by Rev. Abner Watkins

ELLINGTON, Thos. S. H.   Elvira LANGHORNE
M.B. 18 Dec. 1833   Surety: William Powell
Consent: Elvira signs own sonsent   Teste: Wm. B. Langhorne

ELLINGTON, William   Elizabeth WEBBER
M.B. (not dated)   Surety: Richd Webber
Prior to 30 November 1796
Administration of Gov. Robert Brooke - 12/1/1794-11/30/1796

ELLIOTT, John   Mary Watson ALLEN
M.B. 26 Oct. 1807   Surety: John E. Ritchie
Note: Daughter of Charles Allen   Teste: John C. Allen
Married 5 November 1807 by Rev. Drury Lacy

ELLIOTT, Richard   Philadelphia GUTHRIE
M.B. 29 April 1768
Richard Elliott of Cumberland County Douglas Register, p. 19
Will of Sarah Guthrey, Cum. Co. W.B. 2, p. 59

ELLIOTT, William   Sarah W. ALLEN
M.B. __ ___ 1814 (date incomplete)   Surety: John E. Ritchie

ELLIS, Armistead E.   Polly Y. PANKEY
M.B. 24 April 1815   Surety: Thomas Pankey

ELSON, John   Lucy WOOD
M.B. 3 May 1817   Surety: John P. Palmore
Consent: Lucy signs own consent   Teste: Robert Scott

ENGLAND, Edmund   Rebecca J. APPERSON
M.B. 20 Dec. 1831   Surety: John Lunsford
Note: Daughter of James Apperson   Wit: Sterling G. Apperson
Married 21 December 1831 by Rev. Joshua Leigh

ENGLAND, Edward   Mary PHILLIPS
M.B. 22 Dec. 1789   Surety: Larkin Smith
Note: Daughter of James Phillips   Teste: William England

ENGLAND, Thomas   Elizabeth NOELL
M.B. (not dated) 10 Nov. 1795 on back of bond
                                                Surety: Charles Noell

ENGLAND, William   Arenatta ALLEN
M.B. (not dated) 5 Sept. 1810 on back of bond
                                                Surety: Peter T. Phillips

ENGLAND, William C.   Martha A. HIX
M.B. 28 Dec. 1835   Surety: Fleming Cayce
Note: Son of W. England   Teste: Fleming Cayce
Note: Daughter of Samuel Hix   Teste: Mary Ann E. Hix

ENGLAND, William N.   Salinah HAZLEGROVE
M.B. 2 March 1840   Surety: Pleasant Hazlegrove
Note on back of bond: Pleasant Hazlegrove present and assenting to the licenses

EPPERSON, Jacob, Jr.   Rebecca ARNOLD
M.B. __ Jan. 1810   Surety: James Harris
Consent 15 December 1809 by Moses Arnold for daughter.

EPPERSON, John   Milly Wilson COLEMAN
M.B. 27 Dec. 1817   Surety: John S. Coleman

EPPERSON, Joseph   Martha PEARCE
M.B. 25 August 1752   Surety: Benj. Mosby
Consent: "This is to certify that 'We who are concerned are
         agreed and desire a license to be granted, and given
         under our hand this 25th day August 1752".
         /s/ Martha Pearce   /s/ Elizabeth Chambers

EPPERSON, Richard   Susanna RADFORD
By 1750   Daughter of John Radford
Will of Richard Epperson, Cum. Co. W.B. 1, p. 127
Will of John Radford, Cum. Co. W.B. 2, p. 103

EPPERSON, Richard C.   Keziah MAXEY
Prior to 1772   Daughter of William and Mary Maxey
After 20 May 1771 - Will of Mary Maxey
Will of Richard Epperson, Cum. Co. W.B. 2, p. 180
Will of William Maxey, Cum. Co. W.B. 1, p. 328

EPPERSON, William   Martha STEGAR
Before 24 March 1767   Daughter of Francis George Stegar
Chancery Suit 24 March 1767 - Cum. Co. O.B. - 1764-1767, page
453

ERAMBERT, Edward J.   Melvina ANDERSON
M.B. 31 Oct. 1821   Surety: Philemon H. Anderson
Note: Daughter of Charles Anderson Wit: Presley D. Richardson

ESTES, Christopher T.   Jane C. HOWARD
M.B. 15 April 1822   Surety: Valentine Parrish

ESTES, Francis C.   Caroline M. WILKINSON
M.B. 25 March 1835   Surety: William B. Hobson
Note: William B. Hobson makes affidavit that Caroline is of
      age.

EDMUNDS, Pizarro   Ann E. Howard
M.B. 24 June 1833   Surety: Ro. A. Walton
Note: Thomas H. Walton consents for his ward Ann E. Howard.
                                      Teste: Ludwell Brackett

EUSTACE, Joel   Ann HARRIS
Married 15 Oct. 1770 by Rev. William Douglas
Note: Joel Eustace of Lunenburg County
Note: Ann Harris of King William Parish, Cumberland County
Ref: Douglas Register, p. 20

EVANS, William   Martha HENDRICK
M.B. 6 Jan. 1786   Surety: William Hendrick

FALWELL, John   Elizabeth FORD
M.B. (not dated)   Surety: Jesse Street
Date 27 September 1813 on back of bond
Daughter of Mattie Ford who consents   Teste: Ed. Scruggs

FARGUSON, William   Mary TAYLOR
Prior to 8 October 1758
Will of John Taylor, Cumberland County W.B. 1, page 161

FARIS, Jacob   Susanna SIMS
M.B. 17 Oct. 1818   Surety: Richd S. Eggleston

FARIS, James   Elizabeth Ann JENKINS
M.B. 4 March 1824   Surety: Henry Robertson
Note: Daughter of Joseph Jenkins   Teste: Edmund Pearce

FARIS, John   Elizabeth WINFREE
M.B. 12 December 1780   License 10/
Cumberland County Fee Book - 1779-1781

FARIS, Martin   Rebecca AMOS
M.B. 26 Sept. 1785   Surety: John Carter

FARIS, Samuel   Nancy GRIFFIN
M.B. 7 May 1818   Surety: James M. Daniel
Note: Daughter of Joseph Griffin   Teste: Nelson Griffin

FARRIS, William   Eliza M. DANIEL
M.B. 28 May 1821   Surety: Leonard Daniel
Note: Daughter of Micham Daniel   Teste: James M. Daniel

FARISS, Jackson   Rebecca FARISS
M.B. 9 Feb. 1805   Surety: Walter Keeble, Jr.

FARMER, Burnell   Edith ORANGE
M.B. 8 Dec. 1812   Surety: Joel Orange

FARMER, Byrd   Polly W. MELTON
M.B. 24 May 1806   Surety: Nathan Melton

FARMER, Byrd   Sally C. BALLOW
M.B. 7 Oct. 1840   Surety: Hez(ekiah) Ford

FARMER, Cary   Jane WHEELER
Prior to 11 December 1822   Surety: Samuel Wheeler
Administration of Gov. Thomas Mann Randolph
                     12/11/1819-12/11/1822

FARMER, John   Fanny ALLEN
M.B. 18 April 1808   Surety: William Childress
Note: Daughter of Ann Allen who consents   Teste: John Farmer
Married 22 April 1808 by Rev. William Walker

FARMER, John A.   Nancy DOWDY
M.B. 6 March 1819   Surety: William W. Hanley
Daughter of Lucy Dowdy only surviving parent. Cary A. Farmer

FARRAR, Joseph Royal   Phebe HARRIS
M.B. 26 July 1762   Surety: Joseph Woodson
Married 3 August 1762 by Rev. William Douglas
Note: Daughter of James Harris, Cum. Co. W.B. 1, p. 327

FARRAR, Joseph Royal   Mary GAINES
M.B. 26 Sept. 1774   Surety: Thomas Turpin, Jr.

FEARNE, George   Nancy TAYLOR
M.B. 28 Jan. 1805   Surety: John Richardson

FERGUSON, Edm.   Elizabeth HAWKINS
M.B. 17 Nov. 1779   License 20/
Cumberland County Fee Book - 1779-1781

FISHER, Edward C.   Lavinia A. PAGE
M.B. 21 Feb. 1832   Surety: Thos. Page
Consent of John C. Page for his daughter to marry Dr. Edward
C. Fisher   Teste: Robert B. Page

FITZGERALD, Charles W.   Sarah A. L. HOBSON
M.B. 21 Sept. 1838   Surety: Peter B. Foster

FITZGERALD, Nace   Martha Jane COLLEY
M.B. 27 June 1836   Surety: William W. Colley

FLIPPEN, Abner   Eliza G. HOBSON
M.B. 11 Oct. 1826   Surety: Asa Hubbard
Consent: Daughter of Thomas Hobson   Teste: Thomas Booker

FLIPPEN, Daniel B.   Mary A. GOODMAN
M.B. 3 Dec. 1832   Surety: Thomas A. Goodman
Consent: Daughter of Mary Goodman   Teste: R. J. Goodman

FLIPPEN, Elijah   Prudence BAUGHAN
M.B. 21 Oct. 1822   Surety: John Baughan
Note: Daughter of John Baughan of Cumberland County

FLIPPEN, Henry   Susan DURHAM
M.B. 7 March 1826   Surety: Jacob Anderson
Consent: Daughter of Frances Durham   Teste: Jacob A. Durham

FLIPPEN, J. L.   Martha PENICK
M.B. 8 Jan. 1781   License 10/
Cumberland County Fee Book - 1779-1781

FLIPPEN, James W.   Mary M. HATCHER
M.B. 26 Nov. 1832   Surety: Joseph Hatcher
Consent: Daughter of John H. Hatcher, Sr.   John Hatcher, Jr.

FLIPPEN, John M.   Nancy BROWN
M.B. 11 Dec. 1807   Surety: James Baughan
Consent: Daughter of Clement Brown who gives consent.
Teste: Samuel Brown   Teste: Turner Brown
Married 12 December 1807 by Rev. Rane Chastain

FLIPPEN, Josiah H.
M.B. 15 Sept. 1826
                        Anne S. WOODSON
                  Surety: Tarlton Woodson

FLIPPEN, Robert W.
M.B. 29 Oct. 1824
                 Manervia C. PALMORE
             Surety: Joseph S. Palmore

FLIPPEN, Thomas
M.B. 20 August 1838
                        Martha TRENT
                Surety: Chas S. Palmore

FLIPPEN, William
M.B. 22 Oct. 1804
Consent: Daughter of Rober^t Walton who consents.
Teste: Robert Flippen
                        Agnes WALTON
                  Surety: Thos. Hobson
                  Teste: Robert Wilbourn

FLIPPEN, Wailliam A.
M.B. 24 Sept. 1832
Married 26 September 1832 by Rev. M. M. Dance
                 Rebecca H. HARRIS
             Surety: Benjamin Harris

FLOURNOY, David
M.B. 25 Sept. 1830
Consent: Daughter of Chas. Womack
                       Anne WOMACK
            Surety: Charles H. Womack
              Teste: Geo. L. Aiken

FLOURNOY, Jacques
Married 27 October 1755 by Rev. William Douglas
Ref: Douglas Register, p. 21
                 Elizabeth BURNER

FLOWERS, Valentine
M.B. 28 Nov. 1785
                 Elizabeth FLIPPEN
             Surety: Jesse Flippen

FLOWERS, Valentine
Prior to 30 Nov. 1796
Administration of Gov. Robert Brooke
                       Mary MARTIN
             Surety: John Martin
            12/1/1794 - 11/30/1796

FLOYD, Samuel
M.B. 22 May 1797
                 Rebecca MARTIN
             Surety: Joshua Jones

FORD, Ballard
M.B. 15 Nov. 1823
             Judith M. BRANSFORD
           Surety: William Powell

FORD, Chesley
M.B. 7 Oct. 1805
                   Fanny FALWELL
         Surety: Maurice M. Langhorne

FORD, Edward
M.B. 24 July 1820
Note on bond: "Hugh French, guardian, personally consented!"
                 Harriott BOOKER
            Surety: John W. Wilson

FORD, Hezekiah
M.B. 16 Dec. 1812
Consent: Dated 14 December by Elizabeth S. Ballow - no re-
       lation stated. Teste: John S. Ballow Wm. B. Ballow
                Elizabeth G. BALLOW
             Surety: John Ballow

FORD, James T.
M.B. 24 March 1836
Note: Daughter of Edward Merryman
Note: James T. Ford of Fluvanna County
                 Lucy F. MERRYMAN
         Surety: Alfred C. Cheatham
                Teste: John Ford

FORD, Jesse   Elizabeth FALWELL
M.B. (not dated) __ Nov. 1811 on back of bond
Note: Both signed consent and of age   Surety: John Falwell

FORD, John, Jr.   Frankey PRYOR
M.B. 25 Jan. 1773   Surety: William Davenport
Frankey being of lawful age writes consent.   Thoas Davenport

FORE, Peter   Mary PHILLIP
Note: Daughter of Thomas Phillip - Prior to 27 Nov. 1752
Cumberland County Deed Book 2, page 23

FORE, Peter M.   Sally B. GALLOWAY
M.B. 22 Sept. 1829   Surety: Edwin W. Woodson
Note: Daughter of Rhoda H. Galloway   Teste: A. Shields
Married 23 September 1829 by Rev. Poindexter P. Smith

FOSTER, Alexius Mador   Ann GLENN
M.B. 17 Feb. 1779   Surety: Gideon Glenn
Note: A. M. Foster requests Geo. Carrington to send bond by
      Mr. Glenn

FOSTER, John   Eliza DUNKUM
M.B. 27 Dec. 1828   Surety: W. H. Foster
Consent: Nancy Dunkum consents for Eliza - no relation stated
Test: George Eubank   Teste: Willis W. Dunkum

FOSTER, Peter B.   Martha H. HOBSON
M.B. 5 Feb. 1834   Surety: William B. Hobson

FOSTER, Peter B.   C. C. THORNTON
M.B. 15 March 1837   Surety: Maurice L. Hobson

FOWLER, Albert G.   Harriott S. LYLE
M.B. 21 Aug. 1832   Surety: John B. Fowler
Note: Daughter of Sarah E. Lyle who signed consent 8/13/1832

FOWLER, Holeman R.   Sarah WEBBER
M.B. 6 Dec. 1808   Surety: Dabney Kerr
Consent: Holeman Fowler swore that Sarah was over age 21.

FOWLER, Thomas   Polly SPEARS
M.B. 20 Jan. 1810   Surety: Robert Spears
Note:Cartersville, 19 Jan. 1810, John G. Daniel acting guar-
     dian consents for Polly daughter of William Spears, dec-
     eased.   Teste: Leonard D. Spears

FOWLER, William S.   Ann FOWLER
M.B. 24 Dec. 1806   Surety: B. W. Walker
Note: Daughter of Sherwood Fowler who consents
Married 24 December 1806 by Rev. Abner Watkins

FRANCIS, Thomas   Hellender BASSETT
Married 7 April 1760 by Rev. William Douglas
Ref: Douglas Register, p. 21

FRANCISCO, James A.   Judith MICHAUX
M.B. (not dated)   Surety: Alexander Woodson
Date 11 June 1814 on back of bond.

FRANCISCO, Peter   Susannah ANDERSON
Prior to 1 March 1787 - Chancery suit - Decree of March
Court 1787, Cumberland County, Will Book 2, page 432
Daughter of James Anderson - Will Book 2, page 302

FRANCISCO, Peter   Catherine BROOKE
M.B. (none) - Consent only dated 8 December 1794
    "Catherine Brooke, being of lawful age, signs letter
    of consent for a marriage license to marry Peter
    Francisco. Certificate of Humphrey Brooks, John
    Macon and Laban Micou that Catherine Brooke is up-
    ward of age 21 years".

FRANKLIN, Edmund *   Elizabeth HAMBLETON
M.B. 5 Feb. 1788   Surety: Bartlett Thomson
* Edmund Franklin on bond, but Edward on consent.
Consent: John Sims, guardian, gives consent to Mr. Edward
       Franklin to marry one of William Hambleton's
       orphans that he is guardian for.

FRAYSER, Roderick   Nancy EDWARDS
M.B. 14 Feb. 1825   Surety: James Aiken
Note: Daughter of Flemstead Edwards - Consent 11 Feb. 1825

FRAYSER, Roderick   Maria C. FLIPPEN
M.B. 22 Sept. 1834   Surety: William Frayser
Note: Frances Flippen, mother, gives consent 13 Sept. 1834
                                    Teste: Francis J. Flippen
Will of Frances Flippen, Cum. Co. W.B. 12, page 284
Married 25 September 1834 by Rev. Joseph A. Brown.

FRAYSER, William   Margaret LYNCH
M.B. 22 Nov. 1788   Surety: Feild Robinson

FRAYSER, William   Mary B. FLIPPEN
M.B. 13 Dec. 1832   Surety: Daniel B. Flippen
Note: Daughter of Frances Flippen   Teste: James W. Flippen

FRAYSER, William A.   Judith BRANSFORD
M.B. 19 Dec. 1826   Surety: Henry Bransford
Consent: Daughter of Benjamin Bransford

FREEMAN, Joseph   Sarah HARRIS
M.B. 26 Nov. 1750   Surety: John Netherland
Consent: 24 Nov. 1750 - Wade Netherland guardian for Sarah.
Teste: John Woodson   Teste: William Barley

FRENCH, Hugh   Elizabeth HATCHER
M.B. 23 Oct. 1815   Surety: Tho. Gordon

FRENCH, Hugh　　　　　　　　　　　　　　　　　　Lucy L. NASH
M.B. 23 Nov. 1818　　　　　　　Surety: Miller Woodson, Jr.

FRENCH, John　　　　　　　　　　　　　　　　　　Sarah SMITH
M.B. 24 Dec. 1810　　　　　　　　　Surety: Lewis Isbell

FRENCH, Robert　　　　　　　　　　　　　　　　Nancy HATCHER
M.B. 7 Jan. 1817　　　　　　　　　Surety: Fre^d Hatcher
Note: Daughter of John Hatcher　　　Teste: Frederick Hatcher

FRENCH, William L.　　　　　　　　　　　　　　Jane H. HOBSON
M.B. 25 April 1831　　　　　　　Surety: John Daniel, Jr.

FRITTER, Aden C.　　　　　　　　　　　　　　　Jane FAULKNER
M.B. 2 Jan. 1821　　　　　　　　　Surety: Thos Booker
Married 8 January 1821 by Rev. Joseph Jenkins

FUQUA, Albert D.　　　　　　　　　　　　　　Judith R. SCRUGGS
M.B. 20 Sept. 1827　　　　　　　Surety: Tscharner Woodson
Consent: Edward L. Scruggs, brother, and guardian for Judith.

FUQUA, Albert D.　　　　　　　　　　　　　　Judith H. HOBSON
M.B. 24 April 1832　　　　　　　Surety: Patrick H. Nunnally
Consent: Daughter of Thomas Hobson, Senr. Teste: M. L. Hobson

FUQUA, Benjamin　　　　　　　　　　　　　　Polly W. WOODSON
M.B. 29 Jan. 1823　　　　　　　　Surety: Miller Woodson

FUQUA, John　　　　　　　　　　　　　　　　　Sally BOOKER
M.B. 15 August 1812　　　　　　　Surety: Joseph McLaurine
Consent: Daughter of Edward Booker　　Teste: Jno Baughan

FUQUA, William　　　　　　　　　　　　　　　　　Mary FORD
Prior to 3 Sept. 1753
Will of John Ford, Cum. Co. W.B. 1, page 71

FURGUSON, William J.　　　　　　　　　　　　Rebecca GUTHREY
M.B. 18 Feb. 1824　　　　　　　　　Surety: John Guthrey

GAFFORD, John　　　　　　　　　　　　　　　　Polly NELSON
M.B. 28 May 1817　　　　　　　　　Surety: Andrew Nelson

GALLOWAY, Frederick L.　　　　　　　　　　　Martha WOODSON
M.B. 14 Dec. 1839　　　　　　　　　Surety: B. R. ALLEN
Consent: Booker Woodson consents - no relation stated.

GANNAWAY, Bob　　　　　　　　　　　　　　　　Lucy WALTON
M.B. 8 Oct. 1779　　　　　　　　　　　　　License 20/
Cumberland County Fee Book - 1779-1781

GANNAWAY, John　　　　　　　　　　　　　　Martha WOODSON
M.B. 14 April 1773　　　　　　　　　　Surety (None)
Daughter of John Woodson - Will of John Woodson, W.B. 3, page 10.

GANNAWAY, Money ?   Drucilla WALKER
M.B. 22 Nov. 1788   Surety: William Walker

GANNAWAY, Theoderick C.   Judith B. GILLS
M.B. 27 Dec. 1824   Surety: Nat. Lancaster
Judith signs her own consent 22 December 1824

GANNAWAY, Thomas   Judith WOODSON
Prior to 11 Dec. 1816   Surety: Joseph Williams
Administration of Gov. Wilson Cary Nicholas
                    12/11/1814-12/11/1816

GANNAWAY, Thomas A.   Edith W. ANDERSON
M.B. 21 Dec. 1812   Surety: William C. Binford
Edith "being of lawful age" signs own consent.

GARRETT, John   Polly WOODSON
M.B. __ Jan. 1808   Surety: Benj^a. Woodson

GARRETT, John   Julian (Julia Ann) FLIPPEN
M.B. 28 Nov. 1831   Surety: John Hatcher, Jr.
Married 30 November 1831 by Rev. Joshua Leigh

GARRETT, John D.   Susanna TOLER
M.B. 22 Dec. 1817   Surety: James Daniel
Note: Daughter of Benjamin Toler

GARRETT, John D.   Rebeccah DUNCAN
M.B. (no date given)   Surety: William L. Boatwright
Consent: Dated 4 August 1837   Teste: James A. Boatwright

GARRETT, John W.   Lucy W. LEE
M.B. 22 Nov. 1830   Surety: William Jeter
Note: Daughter of Joseph D. Lee   Teste: Barrett C. Lee
Married 30 November 1830 by Rev. John T. Watkins

GARRETT, Peter   Mary PERRUE
Married 25 November 1756 by Rev. William Douglas
Ref: Douglas Register, p. 22

GARRETT, Samuel   Elizabeth ALLEN
M.B. 21 Dec. 1835   Surety: Joseph S. Palmore
Note: Daughter of Elizabeth A. Allen Teste: James E. Cooke

GARTH, Garland   Sarah McLaurine
M.B. 20 June 1827   Surety: D. C. Garth
Consent: James McLaurine gives consent for his daughter to
         marry Dr. Garland Garth   Teste: M. B. Jarman

GARTHRIGHT, Joel   Mary JENNINGS
M.B. 26 Nov. 1815   Surety: John H. Jones

GAULDING, Alexander   Frances ANDERSON
M.B. (not dated) 22 Jan. 1805 on back   Sur: Jesse Anderson

GAULDING, Alexander   Nancy NOWEL
Prior to 12 Dec. 1808   Surety: Jnº Hill
Administration of Gov. William H. Cabell
              12/11/1805-12/12/1808

GAULDING, Jesse   Polly NOEL
M.B. ___ ___ 17__   Surety: Jesse Anderson
Prior to 19 Nov. 1799   Teste: Miller Woodson

GAULDIN, William   Elizabeth ANGLEA
M.B. 10 Sept. 1789   Surety: William Anglea

GAULDIN, William   Mary F. EDWARDS
M.B. (not dated) Prior to 12/11/1822 Surety: James B. Woodson
Administration of Gov. Thomas Mann Randolph
              12/11/1819-12/11/1822

GAULDIN, Willis W.   Martha Ann HENDRICK
M.B. 8 Sept. 1829   Surety: Benjamin F. Sims
Note: Daughter of William Y. Hendrick   Teste: James Hendrick

GAY, William   Frances TRENT
M.B. 20 Sept. 1769   Surety: Daniel Bates
Note: Daughter of Alexander Trent   Surety: Jnº Scott
Consent: Neill Buchanan, Jr., guardian for William Gay who is
under age.   Teste: Ann Murray   Teste: Thomas Bolling

GENTRY, Simon   Susanna BROWN
M.B. 9 May 1760   Surety: John Brown

GOLSON, John *   * Frances TOURMAN
* John Gholson - Frances Tureman   ?
M.B. 25 November 1770 - Married by the Rev. William Douglas
Both parties residents of Cumberland County.

GHOLSON, William Y.   Mary Anne Jane TAYLOR
M.B. 25 Dec. 1827   Surety: Creed Taylor
Consent: William G. Gholson consents for his ward William
         Yates Gholson of Brunswick County to marry Miss
         Anne Jane Taylor of Cumberland County.

GIBBONS, Peter   Jane BOATWRIGHT
M.B. 16 Feb. 1810   Surety: Joel Elam
Note: Daughter of Jesse Boatwright Wit: Thomas T. Boatwright

GIBSON, Benjamin   Priscilla BRADBERRY
Married 21 January 1769 by Rev. William Douglas
Ref: Douglas Register, p. 22

GIBSON, George H.   Arabella B. MICHAUX
M.B. 15 April 1817   Surety: William Jones
Note: Daughter of John Michaux   Teste: George B. Woodson

GIBSON, John   Elizabeth WORLEY
Prior to 22 March 1757
Will of John Worley, Cum. Co. W.B. 1, p. 149   Rec. 3-27-1758

GILLIAM, Charles   Elizabeth WOODSON
M.B. 22 April 1793   Surety: None listed

GILLIAM, Charles M.   Elizabeth A. CARTER
M.B. 27 Feb. 1826   Surety: Joseph W. Riddle
Note: Daughter of Elizabeth Carter who gives consent for the
      marriage of her daughter Eliza Ann. Wit: Matilda Watson

GILLELAND, William S.   Elizabeth MAYES
M.B. 2 March 1831   Surety: Blake B. Woodson
Note: Elizabeth signs her own consent and states she is over
      age 21 years.   Teste: Jane Mayes   Teste: Polly Mayes

GILLS, George   Judith B. LANCASTER
M.B. 22 Feb. 1814   Surety: Josiah Lancaster
Note: Daughter of John Lancaster   Teste: Henry Ransone
Note: George Gills of Amelia County.

GILLS, James   Polly A. PHILLIPS
M.B. 30 Oct. 1838   Surety: Albert Caldwell
Consent: Charles S. Palmore consents for his ward Polly A.
         Phillips   Teste: Peter T. Phillips

GLENN, Nathan   Lucy COLEMAN
M.B. 24 May 1756   Surety: Stephen Davenport
Note: Daughter of Daniel Coleman

GLENN, Nathan   Nancy MOSEBY
M.B. 29 Oct. 1807   Surety: Thomas Moseby

GLENN, Nathan   Mary D. FOWLER
M.B. (not dated)   Surety: Osborne L. Fowler
Note: Date on back of bond - 13 December 1819

GLENN, Nehemiah   Ann COLEMAN
Prior to 29 August 1763
Will of Daniel Coleman, Cum. Co. W.B. 2, p. 4

GLENN, Thomas, Jr.   Jemima C. SPENCER
M.B. 7 July 1834   Surety: Benj. A. Allen
Note: Jemima makes oath before John Holeman, J.P., that she
      is of age.

GLENN, William   Elizabeth WRIGHT
M.B. 16 July 1788   Surety: Thomas Wright

GLOVER, Elijah   Fanny ARMISTEAD
M.B. (not dated)   Surety: Joshua M. Bernard
Note: Daughter of Frances Armistead   Teste: Hannah Armistead
Married 10 March 1808 by Rev. Rane Chastain

GLOVER, John   Polly JOHNSON
M.B. 29 July 1806   Surety: Drury Woodson

GLOVER, Joshua   Elinor CROW
M.B. 27 Feb. 1793   Surety: Jesse Thomas

GLOVER, Robert   Hannah H. Armistead
M.B. 24 August 1807   Surety: Joshua M. Bernard
Note: Daughter of Frances Armistead
                                    Teste: Francis Armistead, Jr.
Married 24 March 1807 by Rev. Lewis Chaudoin

GODSEY, John   Ann ELAM
Married 14 November 1762 by Rev. William Douglas
Ref: Douglas Register, p. 22

GODSEY, Royal F.   Delilah MEADOR
M.B. 17 Nov. 1828   Surety: William Meador

GOFF, Henry   Caty SMITH
M.B. (not dated)   Surety: Morton Davis
Consent: Caty signs own consent 1 Sept. 1807

GOODE, Francis   Alice HARRIS
M.B. 28 Nov. 1774   Surety: William Harris
Note: Daughter of William Harris of this county.

GOODMAN, Charles J.   T. ALDERSON
M.B. 27 Nov. 1838   Surety: Thomas Alderson

GOODMAN, James H.   Eliza A. GOODMAN
M.B. (not dated)   Surety: R. J. Goodman
Consent: Date 27 September 1837
Note: Daughter of Josiah Goodman   Teste: C. J. Goodman

GOODMAN, Josiah   Sukey (Susanna) HATCHER
M.B. 29 June 1811   Surety: Benjamin Hatcher
Consent: Drury Hatcher consents - no relation stated

GOODMAN, Robert   Sarah BOLES
Consent only - dated 27 October 1797
Consent: Sarah Boles signed consent   Teste: Byrd Smith

GOODMAN, Robert J.   Frances J. DUNKUM
M.B. 26 March 1838   Surety: William N. Booker
Consent: John H. Parker gives consent for his ward Frances
         Dunkum   Teste: Charles W. Parker

GOODMAN, Samuel   Martha GOODMAN
M.B. 12 Dec. 1815   Surety: John S. Walker
Note: Daughter of Elizabeth Goodman who gives consent.
Teste: Merit Booker   Teste: M. Carpenter

GOODMAN, Thomas A.   Jane G. BRANSFORD
M.B. 10 December 1832   Surety: John H. Bransford

GOODMAN, Thomas B.   Elizabeth Ann GOODMAN
M.B. 26 Nov. 1838   Surety: Zachariah Goodman

GOODMAN, Zachariah   Elizabeth M. DAVENPORT
M.B. 27 March 1807   Surety: Jesse Michaux

GORDON, Alexander   Susanna LEAKER
M.B. 20 July 1785   Surety: James Leaker

GORDON, John   * Judith Moracet
Married 25 March 1758 by Rev. William Douglas
Note: John Gordon of Goochland County
Note: Judith Moracet of King William Parish, Cumberland Co.
Ref: Douglas Register, p. 23   * Judith Morisset ?

GORDON, Thomas   Nancy HATCHER
After 15 June 1782 - Prior to 23 May 1804
Will of Frederick Hatcher, Cum. Co. W.B. 2, p. 317
Will of Sarah Hatcher, Cum. Co. W.B. 4, p. 214
Note: Daughter of Frederick and Sarah (Woodson) Hatcher

GORMUS, Gustus   Judith OLIVER
M.B. 27 Feb. 1816   Surety: Hammon Oliver

GOTTIE, Peter (Peter Gorrie ?)   Sally TSCHEFELI
M.B. 28 August 1758   Surety: John Woodson

GOSS, James   Mary Ann DUTOY
Married before 26 November 1750
Note: Sister of Isaac Dutoy - Will of Isaac Dutoy, W.B. 1,
      page 51, Cumberland County.

GOWING: Thomas (Thomas Goins)   Mary P. MAYO
M.B. 13 Jan. 1823   Surety: Tarlton Jenkins
Note: Tarlton Jenkins makes oath that Mary P. Mayo is above
      age 21 years, and is a resident of this county.

GREEN, Caleb   Dianna HUDSON
M.B. 23 Dec. 1839   Surety: Richard T. Green
Note: Daughter of William Hudson

GREEN, Henry W.   Frances ANDERSON
M.B. 16 Feb. 1833   Surety: Burwell D. Deaton
Note: Frances daughter of Nancy Anderson who gives consent.

GRIFFIN, Michael   Polly MARTIN
M.B. 28 July 1828   Surety: Kiah Martin

GUERRANT, Daniel   Mary PORTER
Married 19 July 1770 by Rev. William Douglas
Ref: Douglas Register, P. 22 - Will of Elizabeth Porter, Cum.
     Co. W.B. 2, p. 63

GUTHREY, Beverly   Sarah COLQUITT
M.B. 17 Dec. 1793   Surety: James Colquitt
Note: Daughter of John Colquitt   Teste: William Colquitt

GUTHREY, Bernard   Rebecca BIRD
M.B. (not dated)   Surety: Harman Oliver
Note: On back of bond - 21 July 1817

GUTHREY, John   Betty Ann ALLEN
M.B. 25 May 1785   Surety: William GUTHREY

GUTHREY, John J.   Martha Ann GOODMAN
M.B. 25 March 1839   Surety: Z. Goodman

GUTHREY, Levingston   Hannah DAVIS
M.B. 10 April 1819   Surety: Jesse Davis

GUTHREY, Thomas   Polly BASKERVILLE
M.B. 6 Dec. 1793   Surety: William Guthrey
Note: Daughter of Richard Baskerville Wit: George Baskerville

GUTHREY, William P.   Eliza J. ENGLAND
M.B. 30 Sept. 1833   Surety: John H. Stratton
Note: Daughter of John England   Teste: Fleming Cayce

HACKLEY, Richard   Harriet RANDOLPH
Prior to 11 Dec. 1805   Surety: William Randolph
Administration of Gov. John Page   Teste: Peyton Randolph
                 12/29/1802-12/11/1805

HACKNEY, John J.   * Anne C. MARTIN
M.B. 16 July 1821   (a) Surety: Absalom Applebury
(a) Signature: Absalom Appelbury
* Consent of Francis Thomas for his daughter Anne C. Martin,
   now a widow, formerly Anne C. Thomas.   Teste: James Thomas
Married 19 July 1821 by Rev. Joseph Jenkins

HACKNEY, Richard   Ann NORRIS
M.B. (no date)   Surety: John Duffield
Date on back of bond - 6 Oct. 1819

HALL, Nelson   Sally DAVIS
M.B. 3 Dec. 1833   Surety: Zach A. Sandige
Consent states Sally is above age 21 years.   Phineas Wright

HALL, William C.   Eliza Ann SANDERSON
M.B. 2 June 1838   Surety: S. S. Pettit
Consent: Thos. B. Sanderson for Eliza Ann - no relation
         stated   Teste: C. G. Sanders

HAMBLETON, Benjamin   Elizabeth ANDERSON
M.B. 18 June 1833   Surety: William S. Swann
Note: Daughter of Nancy Anderson   Teste: James Hambleton

HAMBLETON, David   Elizabeth A. MAXEY
M.B. 27 March 1823   Surety: Timothy Tyree
Note: Elizabeth A. Maxey above age 21 and a resident of Co.

HAMBLETON, Henry   Julia HAMBLETON
M.B. 1 Jan. 1833   Surety: John M. Childress

HAMBLETON, James   Sarah COLEMAN
M.B. 25 Nov. 1793   Surety: Wyatt S. Coleman

HAMBLETON, James   Eliza BLANTON
M.B. 24 Dec. 1838   Surety: John Anderson
Consent: Eliza being of age signs own consent   Polly Blanton

HAMBLETON, John   Fanny FLIPPEN
M.B. (not dated)   Surety: Francis Flippen
Note: Back of bond has incomplete date, Viz: ___ ___ 1808

HAMBLETON. John F.   Rebecca F. LYLE
M.B. 23 Nov. 1835   Surety: William Lyle
Note: Daughter of Sarah E. Lyle   Teste: William Holman
Married 25 November 1835 by Rev. John T. Watkins

HAMMONTREE, John M.   Sarah A. E. BLANTON
M.B. 15 Dec. 1840   Surety: S. S. Reynolds
Note: Daughter of Anderson Blanton   Teste: Alexander Blanton

HANKLEY, James   Fanny LOCKETT
Prior to 21 Sept. 1768
Will of Joel Lockett, Cum. Co. W.B. 1, p. 440 Rec. 2-27-1769
Note: James Hankley one of executors.

HANLEY, William   Harriet MONTGOMERY
M.B. 8 March 1819   Surety: William Montgomery

HARDICK, Maurice (?)   Sally C. WHEELER
M.B. 18 March 1829   Surety: John Oliver
Note: Daughter of Nancy Wheeler who gives consent for Sally
Teste: Robert N. Anderson   Teste: Elva H. Anderson

HARLOW, Allen M.   Mary Ann AUSTIN
M.B. 9 May 1840   Surety: James Meador
Note: Daughter of Sarah H. Austin   Teste: D. H. Whitlock

HARPER, Isaac   Mary Ann CARTER
M.B. 22 March 1819   Surety: John Carter

HARRIS, Allen H.   Eliza FORD
M.B. 25 Jan. 1814   Surety: Sterling Ford
Note: Daughter of Newton Ford   Teste: George B. Hughes

HARRIS, Allen H.   Elizabeth E. SCRUGGS
M.B. 15 Oct. 1833   Surety: John Caldwell
Note: John Caldwell makes affidavit that Elizabeth is of age.

HARRIS, Benjamin   Priscilla WAGER
Married between 1750 and 1753
Ref: Douglas Register, p. 24

HARRIS, Francis   Anne DIUGUID
M.B. 7 June 1773   Surety: Thompson Swann

HARRIS, Giles   Martha BRANSFORD
M.B. 16 Dec. 1828   Surety: Henry Bransford
Note: Daughter of Benjamin Bransford   Wit: James P. Patterson

HARRIS, James   Ursely FLOURNOY
Married 26 May 1769 by Rev. William Douglas
Ref: Douglas Register, p. 25

HARRIS, John   Obedience TURPIN
M.B. 27 August 1754   Surety: Alexander Trent
Note: Daughter of Thomas Turpin who gives consent
Teste: Thomas Turpin, Junr.   Teste: James Smith

HARRIS, John   Nancy SIMS
M.B. 16 Oct. 1817   Surety: Alexander Cheatwood
Consent: Reuben T. Sims, brother, and guardian for Nancy.

HARRIS, John Skip   Sarah WALKER
M.B. 23 Nov. 1772   Surety: Henry Cox
Note: Daughter of Warren Walker who gives consent.
Teste: William Smith   Teste: Henry Cox, Junr.

HARRIS, Joseph   Rebekah HOWARD
Married 6 February 1766 by Rev. William Douglas
Note: Joseph Harris of Cumberland County
Note: Rebekah Howard of Goochland County

HARRIS, Joseph   Elizabeth R. FARISS
M.B. 1 December 1806   Surety: Jacob Fariss

HARRIS, Richard   Judith SIMS
M.B. 5 Nov. 1794   Surety: James Roper
Note: Daughter of Benjamin Sims   Teste: Payton Sims

HARRIS, Richard J.   Phebe HARRIS
M.B. 23 December 1819   Surety: John Griffin
Consent: Susannah Carter - no relation stated   Teste: D. Mayo

HARRIS, Samuel   Elizabeth SCRUGGS
M.B. 16 April 1839   Surety: Asa Hudgins
Note: Daughter of Sally Scruggs   Teste: Joseph Fuqua

HARRIS, Thomas   Jane TAYLOR
M.B. (not dated) *   Surety: Saml Harris
Date on back of bond 7 Oct. 1812 - Consent dated 8 Oct. 1812
Note: Daughter of Milly Taylor   Teste: John Harris
Teste: Samuel Harris, Senr.   Teste: Anthony M. Hudgens

HARRIS, William   Elizabeth EVANS
Married 15 June 1770 by Rev. William Douglas
Both parties of Cumberland County - Douglas Register, p. 25

HARRIS, William E.   Martha Ann HARRIS
M.B. 24 July 1837   Surety: Charles H. Blake

HARRIS, Zephaniah   Ann LEE
M.B. 9 August 1794   Surety: John Holman
Consent: Ann Lee signs own consent 4 August 1794
Teste: David Blanton   Teste: William Cox

HARRISON, Carter Henry   Susannah RANDOLPH
Married 9 November 1760 by Rev. William Douglas
Note: Susannah daughter of Isham Randolph, deceased.
Note: M.B. 7 November 1760 - Goochland County
Note: Carter Henry Harrison of Cumberland County
Note: Susannah Randolph of Goochland County

HARRISON, Cary   Sarah LANGHORNE
M.B. 29 January 1789   Surety: Joseph Michaux
Note: Sarah signs own consent   Teste: Cary Harrison

HARRISON, Thomas R.   Eliza M. CUNNINGHAM
M.B. 30 Nov. 1812   Surety: John Trent
Consent: A. Taylor for his ward Eliza Cunningham.

HARRISON, William B.   Mary HARRISON
M.B. 6 Feb. 1827   Surety: William F. Randolph
Note: Daughter of Randolph Harrison of Cumberland County
Note: William B. Harrison of Prince George County
Teste: R(andolph) Harrison, Jr.   Teste: F. H. Drew

HARTSOOK, Daniel J.   Elizabeth H. CARRINGTON
M.B. 3 February 1840   Surety: Joseph N. Carrington
Consent: Lawrence Carrington for his ward Elizabeth
                                                     Teste: Henry Walton
Married 11 March 1840 by Rev. J. M. Cofer

HARVEY, Jesse   Julia BERRY
M.B. 6 May 1834   Surety: Joshua Butler

HARVEY, Thomas   Mary VAWTER
M.B. 4 December 1793   Surety: John Vawter
Note: Daughter of Agnes Vawter who gives consent

HASKINS, Benjamin   Phebe HASKINS
M.B. 9 November 1757   Surety: Ch. Haskins
Note: Phebe Haskins signs own consent   Wit: Capt. Thos Swann

HASKINS, Creed   Harriot DOWDY
M.B. 25 Dec. 1833   Surety: Miller Woodson
Note: Daughter of Thomas Dowdy

HASKINS, John T.   Elvira SMITH
M.B. 17 November 1824   Surety: Thos H. Brackett
Note: Daughter of Martin P. Smith   Teste: Andr. H. Armistead

HASKINS, William G.   Elizabeth S. M. MORROW
M.B. 19 Feb. 1821   Surety: Miller Woodson, Jr.

HATCHER, Benjamin   Lucinda B. FLIPPEN
M.B. 18 December 1830   Surety: Henry Hatcher, Jr.
Note: Daughter of John M. Flippen   Teste: William A. Southall

HATCHER, Frederick   Sarah WOODSON
M.B. 13 January 1756   Surety: John Woodson
Note: Sarah daughter of John and Mary (Miller) Woodson

HATCHER, Frederick   Milly TALLY
M.B. (not dated)   Surety: Joseph McLaurine
Note: Date on back of bond - 25 February 1811

HATCHER, Henry   Susan M. A. SPEARS
M.B. 24 October 1825   Surety: Benj. L. Belt
Consent: A. Wharton as guardian for Susan   Wit: Saml Hatcher

HATCHER, Henry   Polly K. EDWARDS
M.B. 17 August 1838   Surety: William Ransone
Consent: Polly signs own consent   Teste: James M. Austin

HATCHER, John   Nancy GANBY
M.B. ___ Sept. 1780 - Date incomplete   License 10/
Cumberland County Fee Book - 1779-1781

HATCHER, John   Mary M. FLIPPEN
M.B. 24 Sept. 1832   Surety: Josiah Hatcher
Note: Daughter of William Flippen   Teste: Archibald Flippen
Married 27 September 1832 by Rev. M(atthew) M. Dance

HATCHER, Martin R.   Mary SUTPHIN
M.B. 10 January 1825   Surety: William Smith
Consent: Hendrick Sutphin, brother, gives consent.
                                 Teste: Robert McCormack

HATCHER, Samuel   Elizabeth BOOKER
M.B. 14 Dec. 1812   Surety: Samuel Hobson
Note: Daughter of Edward Booker who gives consent.
Teste: Fred^d Hatcher   Teste: Thos. Booker

HATCHER, Samuel   Maria L. WATKINS
M.B. 28 April 1832   Surety: John Hatcher, Jr.
Consent: Maria signs own consent - 27 April 1832
Teste: George W. Pace   Teste: Catharine P. Pace
Married 3 May 1832 by Rev. Hiram R. Howe

HATCHER, Thomas   Sarah PORTER
M.B. 25 May 1762   Surety: William Porter
Note: Daughter of Thomas Porter   Teste: Ann Porter
Will of Thomas Porter, Cum. Co. W.B. 1, p. 321
Married 3 June 1762 by Rev. William Douglas
Ref: Douglas Register, p. 25

HAZLEGROVE, Newton   Lucy Ann PHILLIPS
M.B. 11 Dec. 1826   Surety: Peter T. Phillips

HAZLEGROVE, William R.   Malinda V. ANDERSON
M.B. 10 January 1840   Surety: Jacob Anderson
Note: Daughter of Jacob Anderson who gives consent

HAZLEGROVE, Winston N.   Nancy M. JOHNSON
M.B. 12 Dec. 1831   Surety: William Allen
Note: Daughter of Thomas Johnson, deceased
Note: Daughter of Lucy Johnson who gives consent
Married 15 December 1831 by Rev. Joshua Leigh

HENDERSON, Robert   Louisa BRACKETT
M.B. 28 March 1820   Surety: William A. Howard
Note: Daughter of Ann E. Brackett who gives consent.
Teste: Tho^S H. Brackett   Teste: Benjamin H. Powell

HENDRICK, Alexander   Lydia GODSEY
M.B. 8 January 1827   Surety: Henry Godsey
Note: Lydia Godsey above age 21 writes her own consent.

HENDRICK, David   Sally P. PALMORE
M.B. 21 July 1821   Surety: Henry P. Scruggs

HENDRICK, John   Sabrine GARRETT
Married 4 April 1757 by Rev. William Douglas
Ref: Douglas Register, p. 25

HENDRICK, Joseph C.   Mary T. STOKES
M.B. 26 May 1818   Surety: Sam^1 Hix
Consent: Mary T. Stokes signs own consent 23 May 1818
Note: Both parties of Cumberland County
Teste: Benjn B. Johnson   Teste: Benjamin H. Powell

HENDRICK, Matthew   Frances GAULDIN
Prior to 11 Dec. 1816   Surety: Josiah Gauldin
Administration of Gov. Wilson Cary Nicholas
           12/11/1814-12/11/1816

HENDRICK, William   Judith MICHAUX
M.B. 10 February 1786   Surety: Creed Taylor
Note: Joseph Michaux consents as guardian for Judith Michaux.
     Capt. Miller Woodson Clerk, attached the following
     note to the marriage bond. "Yourself and Family are
     desired to dine with us tomorrow".

HENDRICK, William W.   Polly T. GORDON
M.B. (not dated) - Date 1811 on bond   Surety: William Evans
Prior to 26 December 1811 - Administration of Gov. Smith

HENDRICK, William Y.   Elizabeth COOPER
M.B. 7 April 1807   Surety: Thomas S. Cooper
Consent: Daughter of James Cooper   Teste: Thomas S. Cooper

HENSEN, William   Jane BOATWRIGHT
M.B. 9 December 1822   Surety: Joel M. Boatwright
Married 12 December 1822 by Rev. Abner Watkins

HEWLETT, Thomas H.   Jane W. S. WALTON
M.B. 27 July 1839   Surety: Edward G. Walton
Consent: Edwd G. Walton gives consent for his daughter Jane
        to marry Col. Thos. H. Hewlett.

HIGGASON, John   Ann SCRUGGS
M.B. 28 October 1771   Surety: Drury Scruggs

HILL, Alfred A.   Sarah H. PHILLIPS
M.B. 11 Nov. 1835   Surety: John A. Caldwell
Consent: Charles S. Palmore gives consent for his ward Sarah
        Phillips to marry.   Teste: Joseph R. Hill

HILL, Jesse   Molly SCRUGGS
M.B. 23 Feb. 1789   Surety: Philip Holt
Consent: Tabitha Scruggs give consent for daughter.
                                     Teste: William Frayser

HILL, John   Sarah BONDURANT
M.B. 18 February 1806   Surety: Thos Caldwell
Consent: Sally Fleming Bondurant signs own consent.

HILL, Samuel   Nancy SMITH
M.B. 16 July 1817   Surety: Robert Smith

HILL, William   Sallie HOBSON
M.B. _____ 1779 (Date incomplete)   License 20/
Cumberland County Fee Book - 1779-1781

HINES, Henry, Jr.   Mary Ann WALKER
M.B. 27 July 1807   Surety: William Walker
Married 1 August 1807 by Rev. Abner Watkins

HITTSON, Alexander   Nancy G. DAVENPORT
M.B. 12 Dec. 1817   Surety: Thos Dowdy, Jr.

HIX, Jesse   Betsy P. ORANGE
M.B. 30 January 1809   Surety: Joshua Orange
Married 2 February 1809 by Rev. William Walker

HIX, John   Martha COX
M.B. 25 Nov. 1828   Surety: John F. Cox
Note: Daughter of Bartlett Cox who consents   Teste: Mary Cox

HIX, William   Elizabeth HOLLOWAY
Prior to 13 December 1757   Daughter of John Holloway
Will of John Holloway, Cum. Co. W.B. 1, p. 153

HOBSON, Adcock   Edith FARMER
M.B. 29 Nov. 1819   Surety: James Allen, Jr.

HOBSON, Benjamin
M.B. 18 July 1812
Note: Daughter of John Hatcher who consents

Sally W. HATCHER
Surety: Sam¹ Hatcher
Richd Moseley

HOBSON, Frederick
M.B. 29 January 1828
Note: Daughter of Tho. A. Morton

Betsy MORTON
Surety: Landon C. Read
Teste: Thomas F. Womack

HOBSON, James
M.B. 11 Nov. 1816

Eliza H. GOODMAN
Surety: Miller Woodson, Jr.

HOBSON, John
Married circa 1777
Will of Frederick Hatcher, Cum. Co. W.B. 2, p. 317
Daughter of Frederick and Sarah (Woodson) Hatcher

Susannah HATCHER

HOBSON, John
M.B. 25 February 1789

Polly LANGHORNE
Surety: Miller Woodson

HOBSON, Joseph
M.B. 2 Oct. 1806
Consent: W. Wilson, guardian consents

Mary MUNFORD
Surety: Thomas Brackett
Teste: Alex Trent

HOBSON, Maurice L.
M.B. 22 May 1820
Note: Daughter of T. M. Deane

Ann W. DEANE
Surety: Miller Woodson, Jr.
Teste: M. J. Deane

HOBSON, Samuel
M.B. 24 November 1760

Sarah POVALL
Surety: Richard Povall

HOBSON, Samuel
M.B. 4 March 1813

Elizabeth Maria HOBSON
Surety: Tho^S Hobson

HOBSON, Thomas
Prior to 30 Nov. 1796
Administration of Gov. Robert Brooke
12/1/1794-11/30/1796

Judith LANGHORNE
Surety: Miller Woodson

HOBSON, Thomas
M.B. 23 Jan. 1809
Cert: Uphan Jennings is over 21 years of age.

Uphan JENNINGS
Surety: John H. Jones

HOBSON, Thomas Jr.
M.B. 18 Dec. 1805

Mary W. BAUGHAN
Surety: Tucker Baughan

HOBSON, Thomas, Jr.
M.B. 27 June 1832
Consent: John R. Palmore consents for his ward Mary G. Smith
       to marry.

Mary G. SMITH
Surety: George W. Daniel
Teste: Thomas J. Goodman

HOBSON, Thomas L.
M.B. 27 November 1833
Note: Daughter of John C. Page

Virginia R. PAGE
Surety: Thomas Page
Teste: Edward W. Fisher

HOBSON, William   Elizabeth MERRYMAN
M.B. 28 January 1750   Surety: John Merryman

HOBSON, William B.   Patience Turner GORDON
M.B. 23 April 1824   Surety: Ben Holman
Note: Daughter of Richard Gordon   Teste: B. B. Woodson

HODGES, Jesse   Mary J. CULLINGE
M.B. 11 October 1835   Surety: George W. Pace
Consent: Mary signs own consent   Teste: William Amonett

HOGAN, William   Elizabeth ROBERTSON
Prior to 11 December 1767
Will of John Robertson, Cum. Co. W.B. 1, p. 343 - 4-25-1768

HOLLAND, Jesse   Rhody DAGNELL
M.B. 5 Jan. 1790   Surety: John Holland
Note: Daughter of Richard Dagnell   Teste: Thomas Hill

HOLLAND, John   Jane BOND
Prior to 10 Oct. 1756
Will of William Bond, Cum. Co. W.B. 1, p. 181
Will of John Holland, Cum. Co. W.B. 1, p. 268

HOLLAND, William, Jr.   Mary MOSBY
M.B. 27 February 1759   Surety: (none named)

HOLMAN, Benjamin   E. ALLEN
M.B. 28 May 1827   Surety: William Phaup

HOLMAN, William   Martha W. ALLEN
M.B. 15 August 1836   Surety: Benj. Holman
Married 25 August 1836 by Rev. John T. Watkins

HOLEMAN, William T.   Sarah L. SANDERS
M.B. 14 Jan. 1828   Surety: Chas. B. Allen
Note: Daughter of John Sanders   Teste: Joseph Blanton

HOLT, Philip   * Elcy RICHARDSON
M.B..23 February 1789   Surety: Jesse Hill
Consent: Martin Richardson consents - no relation stated
* Elsie Richardson ?   Teste: William Bond

HOLT, Phillip   Altzera B. SUTPHIN
M.B. 26 Feb. 1838   Surety: James M. Austin
Consent: James M. Austin consents for his ward Altzera.
Teste: A. B. Sutphin   Teste: Roderick Frayser

HOLT, Richard R.   Elizabeth B. MANN
M.B. 17 April 1830   Surety: William F. Mann, Jr.
Note: Daughter of William F. Mann, Jr.

HOOPER, John M.   Catherine A. COX
M.B. 28 August 1837   Surety: James Lackland

69

HOOTON, Samuel C.   Susan J. WINFREE
M.B. 3 July 1816   Surety: Parke Bailey
Consent: 1 July 1816 - Susan J. Winfree signs own consent and
        certifies that she is above 21 years old.

HOOTON, Samuel C.   Elizabeth JOHNSON
M.B. 22 April 1833   Surety: William Powell

HOPKINS, Charles B.   Sally C. SCRUGGS
M.B. 3 July 1827   Surety: Henry P. Scruggs

HOPKINS, Francis   Jane COX
M.B. 24 November 1762   Surety: John Holman

HOWARD, William A.   Rebecca E. T. ANDERSON
M.B. 16 Dec. 1817   Surety: Jn⁰ T. Anderson
Note: Daughter of Jane Anderson   Teste: Robert N. Anderson

HOWELL, Peter M.   Caroline M. A. PANKEY
M.B. 11 June 1829   Surety: Pleasant F. Agee
Note: Daughter of Thomas Pankey who gives consent
Teste: Elizabeth Ann Lyall   Teste: Alexander Langhorne

HOWLE, Jeffrey   Frances DURHAM
M.B. (no complete date) *   Surety: Bartlett Anglea
* Listed as "25 day of 1795"

HOWLETT, Edwin   Nancy McLAURINE
M.B. 19 Dec. 1820   Surety: James McLaurine, Jr.
Note: James McLaurine consents for daughter - Jane McLaurine

HOWLETT, Edwin   Eliza FLIPPEN
M.B. 23 July 1834   Surety: John Flippen
Note: Edwin Howlett and wife Eliza G. of County of Marengo,
       State of Alabama, sold their interest in the estate of
       John Flippen, deceased, of Cumberland County, that was
       assigned to daughter Eliza G. Cum. Co. D.B. 25 P. 556.

HOY, John Booker *   (a) Madeline MOSBY
(a) Madeline Mosby, widow - * Listed also as John Bowker
M.B. 22 Nov. 1773   Surety: James Mosby

HUBBARD, Asa   Betsy BAUGHAN
M.B. 30 August 1809   Surety: William Baughan
Note: Daughter of James Baughan who gives consent
Teste: John Baughan   Teste: Richard Anderson

HUBBARD, James M.   Martha J. BOOKER
M.B. 1 February 1836   Surety: Charles S. Palmore
Note: Daughter of Richard A. Booker   Teste: Thos. Caldwell

HUBBARD, Thomas   Mary B. SWANN
M.B. 12 October 1785   * Surety: Th⁰ T. Swann
* Listed also as Thomas Thompson Swann

HUDLESTONE, Benjamin *   ** Elizabeth PANKIE
* Benjamin Huddleston   ** Elizabeth Pankey
Married 23 September 1762 by Rev. William Douglas
Note: Daughter of John and Dorothy Pankey, Cum. Co. D.B. 5
      p. 107 - Ref: See also Douglas Register, p. 27

HUDDLESTON, James   Mary Mosby JENKINS
M.B. 29 Jan. 1830   Surety: Frederick Hatcher
Note: Daughter of William Jenkins   Teste: John Cock

HUDDLESTON, Robert   Elizabeth WHEELER
M.B. 27 August 1832   Surety: Patrick H. Barker
Note: Daughter of Samuel Wheeler   Teste: Cary Farmer
Married by Rev. Poindexter P. Smith - List illegible no date.

HUDDLESTON, William   Nancy MEADOR
M.B. 19 December 1823   Surety: John H. Jones
Note: Daughter of William Meador   Teste: John Garrett, Jr.

HUDGINS, Albert G.   Delphia B. GLOVER
M.B. 12 October 1825   Surety: Bradley S. Glover
Note: Daughter of Elijah Glover   Teste: James M. Montague

HUDGINS, Anthony M.   Elizabeth HARRIS
M.B. 6 April 1812   Surety: Jacob Seay

HUDGINS, Asa   Delila BRADLEY
M.B. 3 December 1832   Surety: Thos. Hobson

HUDGINS, Benjamin   Mary A. SNODDY
M.B. 26 December 1837   Surety: William T. Bagby
Note: Daughter of David Snoddy   Teste: James C. Snoddy

HUDGINS, John   Martha HOLLOWAY
Prior to 13 December 1757
Daughter of John Holloway - Will of John Holloway, Cum. Co.
                    W.B. 1, p. 153

HUDGINS, John A.   Elizabeth M. CARTER
M.B. 25 Jan. 1830   Surety: George C. Walton
Note: Daughter of Elizabeth Carter   Teste: Lewis T. Miller
Married 28 January 1830 by Rev. Poindexter P. Smith

HUDGINS, Robert   Mary Jane TATUM
M.B. 18 August 1840   Surety: Albert Hudgins
Married 19 August 1840 by Rev. M. A. Dunn
Daughter of Mary Tatum   Teste: Martha L. Tatum

HUDGINS, Smith   Hannah T. SOUTHALL
M.B. 22 January 1838   Surety: Cary Southall

HUDGINS, William   Emily MORRIS
M.B. 13 Nov. 1833   Surety: John Hudgins
Note: Consent of Osborne Morris - no relation stated.

HUDGINS, William D.   Martha MERRYMAN
M.B. 29 July 1832   Surety: Isham Bradley
Note: Elizabeth H. Merryman gave consent, but no relation
      stated in consent.   Teste: Jane Merryman

HUDGINS, William S.   Eliza MURRAY
M.B. 22 October 1822   Surety: Jesse S. Street

HUDSON, Thomas   Patsy DOWDY
M.B. 24 January 1809   Surety: James Dowdy

HUDSON, Thomas   Lucy JENKINS
M.B. 19 Feb. 1840   Surety: Samuel Hudson

HUDSPETH, William   Lucy POVALL
M.B. 26 January 1756   Surety: Richard Povall

HUDSPETH, William   Mary STAMPS
M.B. 17 April 1759   Surety: Frederick Hatcher

HUGHES, Anthony   Nancy PALMORE
M.B. 3 Nov. 1807   Surety: John Hudgins
Note: Daughter of Fleming Palmore
Married 5 November 1807 by Rev. Lewis Chaudoin

HUGHES, David   Mary MURRAY
M.B. 18 December 1788   Surety: Billy Hughes
Note: Daughter of John Murray   Teste: Joseph Hughes

HUGHES, Edward   Nancy WOODFIN
M.B. 2 October 1820   Surety: Allen Smith
Consent: "Elisha Woodfin consents for his daughter to marry
         Doctor Edward Hughes".   Teste: Martha A. Pearce

HUGHES, Joseph   Jane HOPSON
Prior to 1 February 1759
Note: Jane Hughes, widow and relict of Joseph Hughes, dec-
      eased, and Henry Hopson, her brother, administrators.
      Cum. Co. O.B. 4, p. 28 - February Court 1759.

HUGHES, Robert   Molly MOSBY
M.B. 3 April 1775   Surety: Joseph Carrington
Consent: Daughter of Littleberry Mosby who gives consent.
Teste: John Mosby   Teste: Littleberry Mosby, Junr.

HUGHES, Samuel   Frances REYNOLDS
M.B. 28 October 1834   Surety: Rowland W. Foster
Consent: Henry Reynolds for Frances, but relation not stated.
Married ___ October 1834 by Rev. Robert J. Carson

HUNDLEY, Charles   Dorothy NELSON
M.B. 28 January 1771   Surety: Samuel Williams
Note: Daughter of Matthew Nelson   Teste: John Nelson, Junr.

HUNNEBUS, Henry   Anne MINTER
Prior to 3 June 1785
Will of John Minter, Cum. Co. W.B. 2, p. 475

HUNT, Ira R.   Hannah POLLOCK
M.B. 10 Nov. 1818   Surety: Jn° Pollock
Note: Daughter of Susanna Pollock   Teste: Joseph Travis

HUNT, Samuel   Rhoda THOMPSON
M.B. 2 November 1785   Surety: Claiborne Sims
Note: Daughter of Bartlett Thompson who gives consent.
Teste: Joseph Jenkins   Teste: Ann Hambleton

HUNTER, George, Jr.   Martha A. W. MITCHELL
M.B. 27 Sept. 1836   Surety: Vincent C. Ryall

HURT, Cary   Polly SOUTHALL
M.B. 29 December 1814   Surety: Turner Southall

HUTCHERSON, George   Jane JENKINS
M.B. 24 Jan. 1825   Surety: Jos. Jenkins

HUTCHERSON, John   Mary CARTER
M.B. 27 October 1814   Surety: Thomas Hobson

IRVING, Henry P.   Williana M. HARRISON
M.B. 3 October 1836   Surety: Thos. Page
Note: Daughter of Randolph Harrison Wit: Richard S. Eggleston

IRVING, Robert   Elizabeth H. DEANE
M.B. 25 February 1819   Surety: Henry Page
Consent: T. B. Deane consents, but no relation stated.

IRWIN, William   Cynthia CARTER
M.B. 12 April 1819   Surety: Henry Newton
Consent: Cynthia signs own consent   Teste: John Carter

ISBELL, James   Polly D. MONTAGUE
M.B. 2 January 1812   Surety: Thomas Montague

ISBELL, James T.   Elenor B. ISBELL
M.B. 26 August 1812   Surety: Peter T. Phillips

ISBELL, John   Betsy BRANSFORD
M.B. 2 December 1820   Surety: Thos H. BRACKETT
Note: Daughter of Benjamin Bransford   Wit: Francis Bransford

ISBELL, William   Nancy WALTON
M.B. 23 November 1795   Surety: Robert Walton

ISBELL, William P.   Elmina H. STEGAR
M.B. 7 Nov. 1831   Surety: Albert G. Stegar
Note: Daughter of Thomas H. Stegar   Teste: Francis E. Stegar
Married 24 November 1831 by Rev. Joshua Leigh

JACKSON, Daniel * ** Betsy NORRIS
M.B. 15 July 1808 Surety: Benj. P. Baltimore
* A free man of color. ** A woman of color.
Consent: Thomas Norris, who emancipated Betsy about 15 years
    ago, gives permission for both.
Teste: Robert Spear Teste: John Carter

JACKSON, Francis Jane MANN
M.B. 19 August 1808 Surety: Cain Mann

JACKSON, Lewis Frances RICHARDSON
M.B. 4 January 1764 Surety: Thomas Whorthy
Consent: Henry Cox, guardian for Frances gives consent.
Teste: Mary Richardson Teste : Samuel Vawter

JAMES, Francis Mary HARRIS
Prior to 12 April 1753
Will of Sarah Harris, Cum. Co. W.B. 1, p. 72   Rec: 9-24-1753

JAMES, Richard Mary TURPIN
M.B. 10 March 1761 Surety: Thomas Turpin, Junr.
Note: Daughter of Thos Turpin Teste: William Turpin

JAMES, Richard Elizabeth TURPIN
M.B. 6 January 1814 Surety: Thomas Hobson
Consent: William Turpin consents for his daughter to marry
    Dr. Richard James.

JEFFERS, John B. Martha McLAURINE
M.B. 7 Sept. 1825 Surety: Joseph S. Wingfield
Consent: James McLaurine consents for daughter
                    Teste: Garland A. Garth
Married __ September 1825 by Rev. George C. Chesley.

JEFFERSON, Peterfield Elizabeth ALLEN
M.B. 29 May 1762 Surety: John Jefferson
Consent: Sam Allen gives consent for his daughter to marry.
Teste: Daniel Bates Teste: Dick Holland

JELLIS, Thomas Mary J. DEANE
M.B. 24 Jan. 1825 Surety: D. O. Coupland
Consent: Mary J. Deane signs own consent. Wit: Anne H. Deane

JENKINS, Anthony Elizabeth BROWN
M.B. (not dated)   - Consent dated 9 Dec. 1812
Teste: William Ransone Surety: William Smothers

JENKINS, Anthony * ** Elizabeth TURPIN
* A free man of color. ** A free woman of color.
M.B. 9 Nov. 1840 Surety: Tarlton Jenkins
Married 11 November 1840 by Rev. Lewis Chaudoin, Sr.

JENKINS, David Elizabeth BROWN
M.B. 19 July 1817 Surety: William Ransone

JENKINS, Edward * Thurza CHEATAM
M.B. 10 June 1816   Surety: William Clarke
* Thurza Cheatham ?

JENKINS, John   Betsy HAMBLETON
M.B. 23 Nov. 1795   Surety: Obediah Hendrick

JENKINS, John D.   Maria B. SANDERSON
M.B. 23 October 1837   Surety: Jerman L. Stratton

JENKINS, Joseph H.   Julia A. E. COLLEY
M.B. 20 August 1833   Surety: Joseph Jenkins

JENKINS, Obediah   Elizabeth McGINNIS
M.B. (On bond 2   1815)   Surety: Norvell H. Robertson
Consent: Dated 27 May 1815 * Elizabeth signs own consent.
Teste: Sam Hatcher   Teste: Norvell H. Robertson, Jr.

JENKINS, Reuben   Elizabeth OAKLEY
M.B. (not dated)   Surety: Erasmus Oakley
Consent: Dated 28 December 1795 - Elizabeth signs own consent
Teste: John Jenkins   Teste: Stephen Winfree

JENKINS, Tarlton   Betsy MAYO
M.B. 6 Dec. 1820   Surety: Strabber Turpin

JESSE, William   Mary Ann PARKER
M.B. 6 Jan. 1820   Surety: John H. Parker
Note: Daughter of Jesse Parker   Teste: Isham Parker

JETER, Anderson   Laura S. ALLEN
M.B. 5 December 1809   Surety: Peter T. Phillips

JOHNS, Daniel   Judith C. ANDERSON
M.B. (not dated)   Surety: Parke Bailey
On back of bond - __ May 1816   Daughter of Mary Anderson

JOHNS, John   Martha JOHNS
M.B. 25 December 1780   License 10/
Cumberland County Fee Book - 1779-1781

JOHNS, John, Jr.   Martha G. GORDON
M.B. 17 Dec. 1810   Surety: Hez. Cheshier
Note: Daughter of Richard Gordon   Teste: A. T. Gordon

JOHNS, John A. S.   Betsy A. S. MILLER
M.B. (date incomplete) __ June 1815   Surety: John S. Walker

JOHNS, John T.   Mary BOOKER
M.B. 18 Nov. 1815   Surety: Thomas Booker
Note: Daughter of Edward Booker   Teste: Ann Hatcher

JOHNS, Reuben   Fanny GARRETT
M.B. (not dated) On back - 3 Oct. 1807 Surety: John Garrett
Married 8 October 1807 by Rev. Abner Watkins.

JOHNS, Thomas   Patty (Martha) FLIPPEN
Prior to 1 July 1794
Will of John Flippen, Cum. Co. W.B. 3, p. 80   Rec: 5-23-1796

JOHNSON, Benjamin B.   Elizabeth T. JORDAN
M.B. 24 August 1818   Surety: William Anderson
Consent: "The Clerk of Cumberland is hereby authorized to
         grant license of marriage between Elizabeth T.
         Jordan of Cartersville and Benj. B. Johnson of the
         same place". /s/ Elizabeth Jordan Wit: T. B. Deane

JOHNSON, Decker   Demaris TAYLOR
M.B. 27 Dec. 1825   Surety: Bennett Toler
Note: Daughter of Richard Taylor   Teste: Susannah Taylor
Teste: Admine Taylor   Teste: William Dunnavant

JOHNSON, Isaac   Judith WOODSON
M.B. 27 December 1773 - Daughter of Drury Woodson

JOHNSON, Job   Sarah MOSBY
M.B. 2 June 1770   Surety: Thomas Hobson

JOHNSON, John   Nancy (Ann) ATKINSON
Prior to 7 May 1794
Will of Samuel Atkinson, Cum. Co. W.B. 3, p. 34

JOHNSON, John   Mary BOATWRIGHT
M.B. (not dated)   Surety: Jesse Boatwright
Married 27 February 1808 by Rev. Rane Chastain

JOHNSON, Maker   Sally RUSSELL
M.B. 10 Dec. 1805   Surety: Jas. Russell
Note: Daughter of William Russell   Teste: Yancey Russell

JOHNSON, Obediah   Polly MERRYMAN
M.B. 1 August 1786   Surety: Jn° Flippen

JOHNSON, Peter   Selinder TOLER
M.B. 11 March 1822   Surety: James M. Daniel
Note: Daughter of Benjamin Toler   Teste: Bennett Toler

JOHNSON, Robert   Nancy COX
M.B. 20 May 1806   Surety: Charles Womack
Note: Daughter of William Cox   Teste: Thos. and Lucy Johnson

JOHNSON, William   Mary WEAVER
Married 20 August 1770 by Rev. William Douglas
Ref: Douglas Register, p. 29

JOHNSON, William   Eleanor DEPPE
Married 17 September 1776 by Rev. William Douglas
Ref: Douglas Register, p. 29

JOHNSTON, Alexander   Mary B. ANDERSON
M.B. 23 Dec. 1822   Surety: Richd J. Anderson

JONES, Albert   Elizabeth BROWN
M.B. 7 Jan. 1828   Surety: John H. Jones
Note: Albert son of Joel Jones of Hanover County
Note: Elizabeth daughter of Thomas Brown of Cumberland County
Teste: William A. Jones   Teste: Washington Jones
Teste: Thos. H. Isbell   Teste: Obadiah J. Reynolds

JONES, Daniel   Susanna ANDERSON
M.B. 27 March 1809   Surety: John Anderson

JONES, Drury J.   Elizabeth STONE
M.B. 1 December 1828   Surety: Henry P. Scruggs

JONES, Orlando   Judith WOODSON
Prior to 9 April 1793
Will of John Woodson, Cum. Co. W.B. 3, p. 16   Rec: 8-26-1793

JONES, Richard   Ann Jane TAYLOR
M.B. 10 August 1830   Surety: John Daniel, Jr.
Note: Daughter of Zachariah Taylor   Teste: William M. Woodson

JONES, William S.   Ann C. RANDOLPH
M.B. 27 Oct. 1825   Surety: Tho^S Hobson

JONES, William W.   Elizabeth DURHAM
M.B. 17 Dec. 1821   Surety: Jacob Anderson
Note: Daughter of Frances Durham   Teste: Jonas Anderson
Married 19 December 1821 by Rev. Joseph Jenkins.

JORDAN, Edwin H.   Emeline M. LEWIS
M.B. 5 July 1830   Surety: William Browning
Note: Albemarle - 2 July 1830 - Howell Lewis, guardian for
      Emeline M. Lewis, gives consent.   Teste: William Hix

JORDAN, Robert P.   Elizabeth W. ADAMS
M.B. 16 July 1821   Surety: Sam C. Hooton
Consent: Tho^S Adams - no relation stated

JORDAN, William B.   Mary G. PHAUP
M.B. 11 February 1829   Surety: Isaac R. Janney
Note: 10 Feb. 1829 - Lunenburg - Nicholas E. Davis consents
      for his ward Wm B. Jordan   Teste: Edmund C. Winn
Note: William Phaup consents for Mary - no relation stated
Married 19 February 1829 by Rev. John T. Watkins

JURNEY, William   Martha JAMES
M.B. 5 October 1795   Surety: A(braham) Sandifur
Note: Daughter of Richard James   Teste: R^d James

KEEBLE, Walter   Hannah G. DAVENPORT
M.B. 21 April 1794   Surety: Thomas F. Davenport
Note: Ann Davenport gives consent for her daughter Hannah
      Glenn Davenport to marry.   Teste: Elijah Jones

KEITH, Alexander   Nancy JOHNSON
M.B. 16 Dec. 1812   Surety: Matthew Bagby
Consent: Nancy signs own consent   Teste: John Bagby

KENNON, John   Elizabeth WOODSON
M.B. 10 February 1779   Surety: John Woodson
Note: Daughter of John Woodson - Cum. Co. W.B. 3, p. 16

KENT, Obadiah   Susannah DAVENPORT
M.B. 6 Jan. 1789   Surety: Thos Davenport
Note: Daughter of Henry Davenport   Teste: William Davenport

KERR, Dabney   Elizabeth A. DODSON
M.B. 22 Dec. 1794   Surety: Jno. Kerr
Note: Daughter of John and Edith Dodson who give consent
Teste: John Dodson   Teste: Thomas Pankey

KIDD, James B.   Elizabeth BALTIMORE
M.B. 22 April 1793   Surety: Christopher Baltimore

KIDD, Pleasant   Judy ELLISON
M.B. 24 March 1828   Surety: Leonard Bosher
Note: David Ellison swears that Judy is over age 21 years.

KILPATRICK, Joshua W.   Sally HOBSON
M.B. 11 January 1809   Surety: Joseph N. Kilpatrick
Note: Daughter of William Hobson   Teste: Epa Hobson

KING, Isaac   Lavinia HIX
M.B. 19 March 1832   Surety: John Atkinson
Consent: Lavinia signs own consent Teste: Anthony A. Wallace

KING, John P.   Ann C. JONES
M.B. 20 February 1835   Surety: Harrison Jones
Note: Daughter of Mary Ann Jones   Teste: William A. Ford

KING, Phillip *   Elizabeth BOOTH
M.B. 26 Jan. 1782   Surety: Benja. Harrison
Consent: Elizabeth signs own consent   Teste: Cary Harrison
* Phillip King of Charlotte County

KING, Phillip   Nancy WOODSON
M.B. 22 April 1788   Surety: (none named)

KING, William   Polly WOODSON
M.B. 7 January 1789   Surety: Phillip King

KIRKPATRICK, John   Jane Maria JELLIS
M.B. ___ March 1825 (bond torn)   Surety: Thos Jellis
Note: Cartersville - .26 March 1825
Consent: Jane Maria signs own consent   Wit: Francis B. Deane

LACY, Drury * Willian WILKINSON
* Willie Ann Wilkinson ?
M.B. 21 December 1824   Surety: James Lyle
Consent: W. B. Smith, guardian for his ward Willian, gives
        consent for her to marry Mr. Drury Lacy.

LACY, Elkanah   Mary BROWN
Married 18 Jan. 1756 by Rev. William Douglas
Ref: Douglas Register, p. 30

LAMBERT, Patrick   Martha MONTAGUE
M.B. 22 Nov. 1813   Surety: Hugh Watson
Note: Daughter of Peter Montague   Teste: J. T. Austin

LANCASTER, Josiah   Sarah P. RANSONE
M.B. 21 October 1815   Surety: Henry Ransone

LANCASTER, Robert   Sally MADDOX
M.B. 19 July 1806   Surety: Josiah Maddox

LAND, John   Mary ISBELL
M.B. 15 December 1830   Surety: John Merryman
Note: Mary signs own consent   Teste: Sally Pitts

LAND, William   Patsy MERRYMAN
M.B. 11 January 1816   Surety: John A. Allen
Note: Daughter of Thos. Merryman   Teste: James Allen, Jr.

LAND, William   Sally FARIS
M.B. 17 December 1829   Surety: John S. Ballow
Note: Sally Faris, being of lawful age, signs own consent.
Teste: Sally Ballow   Teste: Allen Jenkins

LANDRUM, Samuel   Elizabeth TAYLOR
Married 11 Feb. 1769 by Rev. William Douglas
Ref: Douglas Register, p. 30

LANDRUM, Thomas   Molly HAWKINS
Married 1 October 1759 by Rev. William Douglas
Ref: Douglas Register, p. 30

LANE, John   Sarah EPPES
M.B. 10 Sept. 1811   Surety: Jorman Baker

LANGHORNE, William B.   Elizabeth BERRY
M.B. 13 March 1834   Surety: Charles H. Womack
Consent: Austin Berry for Elizabeth - no relation stated.
                                     Teste: William Lee

LEAKE, John   Judith FORD
Prior to 3 Sept. 1753
Will of John Ford, Cum. Co. W.B. 1, p. 73

LEDBETTER, Joseph   Judith FUQUA
M.B. 7 Feb. 1806   Surety: Nathaniel Fuqua

LEE, Burwell   Ann ARNOLD
M.B. 6 Sept. 1788   Surety: Stephen Cooke
Note: Daughter of Moses Arnold   Teste: John Arnold

LEE, Charles, Jr.   Susanna PEARCE
M.B. 18 January 1786   Surety: Joseph Lee
Note: Daughter of Jeremiah Pearce   Teste: Rachel Pearce
Note: Will of Jeremiah Pearce - 1796 - names daughter
      Susanna Lee.

LEE, Charles P.   Polly L. BONDURANT
M.B. 22 Dec. 1817   Surety: Miller Woodson, Jr.
Note: Daughter of William Bondurant, Muddy Creek Mills

LEE, Henry R.   Martha J. CHRISP
M.B. 15 Dec. 1834   Surety: Sam^1 Chrisp
Note: Daughter of James Chrisp   Teste: E. Blanton

LEE, Joseph D.   Sophia T. GARRETT
Minister's return only
Married 12 December 1822 by Rev. Abner Watkins

LEE, William   Eliza C. WOMACK
M.B. 6 December 1823   Surety: Benj. Holeman
Note: Daughter of Chas Womack   Teste: Charles Womack, Jr.

LEE, William   Elizabeth SIMPSON
M.B. 14 Dec. 1829   Surety: Sam'l R. Simpson
Note: Daughter of Richard Simpson   Teste: William Jeter
Married 17 December 1829 by Rev. John T. Watkins

LEE, William   Hannah A. SANDERS
26 October 1840   Surety: Charles S. Palmore

LeGRAND, Alexander   Lucy WALKER
b. 12-25-1732   b. 12-15-1742
Married 23 November 1757 - Note: Daughter of William and
Judith Walker.   Elliott: LeGrand Family Records
Will of Judith Walker, Cum. Co. W.B. 1, p. 337

LeGRAND, Peter   Mary WOODSON
M.B. 27 November 1751   Surety: Jacob Mosby

LeSEUER, Edwin C.   Sarah L. APPERSON
M.B. 11 Nov. 1839   Surety: John R. Apperson

LEWIS, Charles   Sally GUTHREY
M.B. 19 Oct. 1807   Surety: John Caldwell
Married 25 October 1807 by Rev. Rane Chastain

LEWIS, Charles W.   Maria L. DRAPER
M.B. 27 Jan. 1834   Surety: Fontaine C. Boston
Note: Fontaine C. Boston, guardian for Maria.

LEWIS, Edmund / Jane ISBELL
M.B. 17 Feb. 1813 / Surety: Jas. Isbell
Note: Daughter of Lewis Isbell / Teste: Polly D. Isbell

LEWIS, Pleasant / Phebe PRICE
M.B. (no date) __ __ 1806 on back of bond. Surety: John Price

LEWIS, Thomas / Jedidah WHITEHEAD
M.B. 22 January 1810 / Surety: Benjamin Whitehead

LEWIS, Wiltshire M. / Nancy H. COUPLAND
M.B. 7 April 1829 / Surety: Robert H. Rose
Note: Daughter of William R. Coupland who gives consent.

LIGON, Elijah / Judith CARTER
M.B. 26 November 1789 / Surety: Thomas Bolling

LIGON, Joseph / Nancy WOODSON
M.B. 2 October 1809 / Surety: George Raine

LIGON, Joseph S. / Adaline E. PALMORE
M.B. 30 August 1820 / Surety: Elijah W. Colley
Consent: 20 Aug. 1820 - George Hobson, guardian for Adaline.
Note: Daughter of William Palmore, deceased. Wm. M. Colley

LIGON, Leonard W. / Eliza ATKINSON
M.B. 1 April 1811 / Surety: Samuel Atkinson

LIGON, Nelson / Kitty CASTLEY
M.B. 14 June 1813 / Surety: Charles Harris
Consent: Kitty Castley signs own consent. Wit: Burwell Farmer

LIGON, Peter / Patsy WARD
M.B. (not dated) / Surety: Joseph Ligon
Consent: 16 Feb. 1808 - Susanna Ward consents - no relation stated.

LIGON, Thomas / Betty POVALL
M.B. 23 April 1764 / Surety: James Hankley
Note: Betty, spinster daughter of Richard Povall of Cumberland County.

LIGON, William / Patsy WRIGHT
M.B. 27 Sept. 1794 / Surety: Saymer Wright
Consent: 24 Sept. 1794 - Elizabeth Wright for daughter Patsy.
Teste: William Wright / Teste: P. C. Wright

LIGON, William F. / Ann F. DAVENPORT
M.B. 16 November 1816 / Surety: Noton Goodman
Note: Daughter of Rebe Davenport / Teste: J. S. Hobson

LIGON, William P. / Ann EDWARDS
M.B. 28 November 1831 / Surety: Nehemiah Edwards
Note: Daughter of Nehemiah Edwards

LIGON, Woodson　　　　　　　　　　　Elizabeth M. ALLEN
M.B. 15 December 1823　　　　　　Surety: John Garrett

LINCH, Henry　　　　　　　　　　　　　　Sarah FARIS
M.B. 24 August 1789　　　　　　　Surety: Th^S Bolling

LINDSEY, John　　　　　　　　　　　Elizabeth WATKINS
M.B. 16 Nov. 1824　　　　　　Surety: Byrd G. Tucker
Note: Daughter of Abner Watkins　　Teste: Harriet S. Watkins

LINTHICUM, Edward　　　　　　　　　　Mary TERRELL
M.B. 8 Sept. 1773　　　　　　Surety: William Terrell

LINTHICUM, Thomas　　　　　　　　　　* Sarah BENNETT
* Sarah Bennett, widow
M.B. 13 October 1773　　　　Surety: George Carrington, Jr.

LIPFORD, Anthony P.　　　　　　　Elizabeth ROBINSON
M.B. 25 July 1785　　　　　　　Surety: Creed Haskins

LIPFORD, Thomas W.　　　　　　　　　Tabitha HOLT
M.B. 23 January 1827　　　　　Surety: Wm B. Murray
Note: Daughter of Philip Holt　　Teste: J. A. Merryman
Married 25 January 1827 by Rev. Joseph Jenkins.

LIPFORD, Thomas W.　　　　　　　　Martha J. STRATTON
M.B. 13 February 1832　　　　Surety: Randolph Phillips
Note: Martha Jane daughter of William Stratton who consents.
Teste: David Stratton　　　　Teste: Frances W. Stratton

LOCK, James　　　　　　　　　　　　* Susannah DePee
Married 20 Sept. 1753 by Rev. William Douglas
Ref: Douglas Register, P. 31　　* Susannah DuPuy ?

LOGAN, Caesar　　　　　　　　　　　Mary Ann BARTLETT
M.B. 9 Sept. 1818　　　　　　　Surety: Saml Bartlett

LOGAN, Chastain *　　　　　　　　　　** Judith MAYO
* ** Free persons of color.
M.B. 21 Dec. 1826　　　　　　　Surety: Scipio Mayo

LOGAN, Pleasant　　　　　　　　　　Synthia MAYO
M.B. 26 July 1820　　　　　　　Surety: William Mayo

LOOKADO, John　　　　　　　　　　Susannah SPALDEN
M.B. 24 January 1762 - Married by Rev. William Douglas
Ref: Douglas Register, p. 32

LOOKADO, Peter　　　　　　　　　　Elizabeth THOMAS
Prior to 16 July 1756
Will of David Thomas, Cum. Co. W.B. 1, p. 119
Names daughter Elizabeth wife of Peter Lookado
Executors named: Peter Lookado and William Howard

LOVING, Thomas N.   Locky L. ROBINSON
M.B. 8 February 1815   Surety: Robert Scruggs
Note: Daughter of John Robinson who gives consent.
Teste: Nancy T. Robinson   Teste: Margaret T. Merryman

LOW, David   Nancy HOLMAN
Prior to 12 November 1788   Surety: John Holman
Administration of Gov. Edmund Randolph
              11/30/1786-11/12/1788

LOWRY, James   Elizabeth WOOD
M.B. 10 January 1827   Surety: S. L. Lowry
Note: Daughter of Lucy Wood   Teste: Jesse Wood

LOWRY, Nathan   Nancy HUDGINS
M.B. 1 January 1817   Surety: Joseph S. Bradley
Note: Daughter of Holloway Hudgins   Teste: Daniel Bradley

LOWRY, Samuel L.   Polly WOOD
M.B. 8 January 1823   Surety: Robert Scott
Note: Daughter of Lucy Wood, guardian   Teste: John Smith

LUMPKIN, Moore   Anne WOODSON
M.B. 14 April 1773   Surety: John Gannaway, Jr.
Note: Daughter of John Woodson   Teste: John Woodson, Junr.

LUNSFORD, John   Mary SMITH
M.B. 21 January 1828   Surety: Robert P. Jordan
Note: Daughter of Thomas Smith   Teste: J. A. Wilson

LYLE, James   Ann MORTON
M.B. 1 June 1837   Surety: H. P. Irving
Note: Daughter of Thomas A. Morton   Teste: CHarles A. Morton

LYLE, Samuel   Martha MORTON
M.B. 29 Sept. 1823   Surety: S. D. Morton
Note: Daughter of Thomas A. Morton   Teste: Mary A. Morton

LYNCH, Benjamin W.   Frances K. WALTHALL
M.B. 22 February 1831   Surety: John Holman
Note: Daughter of Katharine Walthall who gives consent.
Teste: Eliza M. Yancey   Teste: Frances Walthall

McASHAN, John T.   Catharine ANDERSON
M.B. 6 February 1835   Surety: R. H. Montague
Consent: Fountain C. Boston for his ward Catharine Anderson
Teste: N. J. McAshan

McCALVEY, William   Mary MASON
M.B. 13 Dec. 1789   Surety: John Boatright
Consent: Caty Mason consents for her daughter to marry Wm.
         McKalvara. ?   Teste: Milly Huganes   ?   Hudgins

83

McCORMACK, Daniel S.   Mary Jane WATKINS
M.B. 20 January 1823   Surety: William B. Hobson
Note: Wm B. Hobson makes oath that Mary Jane Watkins is above
      age 21 years.

McCORMACK, Thomas   Lucy OSBORNE
M.B. 27 October 1840   Surety: William S. Armistead

McCORMACK, William   Polly CLARKE
M.B. 27 March 1816   Surety: Richard Clarke
Note: Daughter of William Clarke   Teste: William Minter

McCORMACK, William   Mary CHRISP
M.B. 22 December 1835   Surety: Samuel Chrisp
Married 24 December 1835 by Rev. John T. Watkins.

McCRAW, Francis   Mary WOODSON
M.B. 18 Sept. 1752   Surety: Thompson Swann

McDONALD, James   Mary LIGON
M.B. 26 Nov. 1822   Elijah Ligon
Note: Daughter of Elijah Ligon

McELLIOTT, John R.   Elizabeth SHELTON
M.B. 27 August 1816   Surety: William P. Bradley
Note: Daughter of Pheby Shelton   Teste: Joseph L. Bradley

McGEHEE, Abner   Gracy GLENN
M.B. 29 Sept. 1789   Surety: William Glenn

McGEHEE, Elijah   Virginsia WALKER
M.B. (not dated)   Surety: John S. Walker
Date on back of bond - <u>27 May 1816</u>   Daughter of Wm. Walker

McGEHEE, Thomas B.   Lucy A. ARMISTEAD
M.B. 1 Sept. 1837   Surety: James Blanton

McKIM, John S.   Catherine L. HARRISON
M.B. 18 October 1831   Surety: Nelson Page
Note: Daughter of Randolph Harrison   Teste: Henry P. Irving
Married 20 October 1831 by Rev. Wiley F. Lee

McKOWIN, Archibald Scott   Mary LYLES
M.B. ____ October 1795   Surety: John Lyles

McPHAIL, George Wilson   Mary Cary PAGE
M.B. 18 Dec. 1840   Surety: S. W. Blain
Consent: Henry Page - no relation stated.

MACON, Henry   Frances NETHERLAND
Prior to 12 Nov. 1773   Daughter of Wade Netherland
Cumberland County Will Book 2, page 124.

MADDOX, Samuel   Milly ROBINSON
M.B. 23 Sept. 1793   Surety: Christopher Robinson

MADDOX, William C.   Ann CARTER
M.B. 17 August 1820   Surety: Nicholas Ware
Note: Daughter of Hezekiah Carter   Teste: Thomas Carter

MADDOX, William G.   Agnes BROWN
M.B. 16 October 1816   Surety: Clement Brown

MANN, William F., Sr.   Susannah PARKER
M.B. 10 July 1819   Surety: William F. Mann, Jr.
Consent: Susannah writes own consent.   Teste: Ann B. Mann

MANN, William F., Jr.   Frances MEADOR
M.B. 24 August 1809   Surety: Ben. W. Napier
Consent: Frances writes own consent.   Teste: James Cheatham

MANN, William F., Jr.   Nancy HOLT
M.B. (not dated)   Surety: Maurice L. Hobson
Consent: Dated 9 July 1816 - John Holt gives consent for his
daughter. Teste: Philip Holt   Teste: Polly Holt

MANN, William H.   Elizabeth STEGAR
M.B. 13 Jan. 1834   Surety: John F. Cox
Note: Daughter of Hanse Stegar who gives consent.
Teste: Thomas E. Stegar   Teste: Benjamin H. Mann

MANSFIELD, Samuel   Ann SMITH
M.B. 19 Feb. 1752   Surety: James Smith

MARKHAM, Barnard   Mary HARRIS
Married 14 May 1767 by Rev. William Douglas.
Ref: Douglas Register, p. 33

MARROW, John M.   Elizabeth CORSON
M.B. 13 March 1820   Surety: Archibald McLaurine

MARSHALL, Francis, Jr.   Phebe HATCHER
M.B. 27 June 1774   Surety: Royal Lockett

MARSHALL, Thomas   Catharine THORNTON
M.B. 11 June 1822   Surety: James H. Fitzgerald
Note: Daughter of F. Thornton   Teste: Rob't E. Thornton
Married 11 June 1822 by Rev. Abner Watkins

MARSHALL, William   Phebe FARMER
Prior to 1 March 1759 - Deed of gift from John Farmer, Sr.,
to his daughter Phebe Marshall, wife of William Marshall.
Cumberland County Order Book 4

MARTIN, Anderson   Elizabeth DAVENPORT
M.B. 15 July 1828   Surety: Satterwhite Davenport
Note: Satterwhite Davenport certified as to ages of parties.

MARTIN, Anthony   Sarah HOLMAN
M.B. 15 Dec. 1758   Surety: Tho. Prosser
Note: Daughter of James Holman   Teste: Jn° Martin
Married 21 December 1758 by Rev. William Douglas

MARTIN, Archer   Elizabeth WALDEN
M.B. 24 Dec. 1840   Surety: Samuel Hobson
Note: Daughter of Mary Walden   Teste: John Duncom
Married 24 December 1840 by Rev. Henry D. Wood

MARTIN, Benjamin   Ann BARTEE
M.B. 25 May 1789   Surety: Thos. Bartee

MARTIN, Daniel   Ann THOMAS
M.B. 13 Jan. 1817   Surety: David Snoddy
Note: Daughter of Frances Thomas

MARTIN, Henry   Elizabeth BOWLES
M.B. 18 February 1761   Surety: William Hambleton

MARTIN, Henry   Elizabeth SOUTHALL
M.B. 14 Feb. 1812   Surety: Turner Southall
Consent: Elizabeth writes her own consent.   : James Southall

MARTIN, Henry, Jr.   Lucy F. ORANGE
M.B. 11 Dec. 1805   Surety: Joshua Orange

MARTIN, Hezekiah   Sarah HARRIS
M.B. 26 May 1828   Surety: William Hambleton

MARTIN, James   Ann OGLESBY
M.B. 29 May 1762   Surety: Isaac Crews
Note: Daughter of Thomas Oglesby   Teste: Obadiah Martin

MARTIN, Jefferson   Elizabeth MARTIN
M.B. 8 July 1833   Surety: Thos. H. Brackett

MARTIN, Jesse   Betsy BARRETT
Prior to 11 December 1819   Surety: Shadrack OAKLEY
Administration of Gov. James Patton Preston
                   12/11/1816-12/11/1819

MARTIN, John   Elizabeth BOATRIGHT
M.B. 2 March 1789   Surety: James Boatright
Note: Daughter of Daniel Boatright
Teste: James Boatright, Senr.   Teste: Stephen Martin, Junr.

MARTIN, John, Jr.   Frances FARIS
M.B. 15 November 1822   Surety: B. J. Sandige
Note: Daughter of Martin Faris, Senr.   Teste: James Sandige

MARTIN, Moses   Hannah BOWLES
M.B. 7 July 1794   Surety: Benja. Martin
Note: Hannah daughter of Hezekiah Bowles

MARTIN, Orson   Judith BOATWRIGHT
M.B. 4 October 1813   Surety: Reuben Davidson
Note: Daughter of James Boatwright, Sr.   Teste: Daniel Smith
Teste: William Price   Teste: Beverly J. Sandidge

MARTIN, Valentine   Ann SCOTT
Married 28 January 1767 by Rev. William Douglas
Note: Both parties from Cumberland County
Ref: Douglas Register, p. 33

MARTIN, Valentine   Levena YANCEY
M.B. 24 Oct. 1825   Surety: Geo. C. Walton
Consent: Levena writes own consent. Teste: Zachariah Sandige

MARTIN, William   Jane HOLEMAN
M.B. 26 November 1759   Surety: Thomas Prosser
Note: Daughter of James Holeman
Married 20 December 1759 by Rev. William Douglas

MASON, Joseph, Jr.   Sarah WALKER
M.B. 28 July 1785   Surety: Joseph Mason

MASON, William   (   ) GUTHREY
M.B. 23 April 1804   Surety: Bernard Guthrey
               Teste: Miller Woodson

MASTERS, Edward   * Betty FURCRAN
* Betty Fourqurean - Both parties of Cumberland County
Married 12 March 1761 by Rev. William Douglas
Ref: Douglas Register, p. 34

MATTHEWS, John A.   Maria DAVIS
M.B. 21 August 1828   Surety: William Jones

MATTHEWS, Thomas   Elizabeth TONEY
M.B. 25 August 1824   Surety: James Anderson
Note: James Anderson made affidavit that Elizabeth was of age

MAUCK, Henry   Keturah BROWN
M.B. 12 December 1826   Surety: James Sutphin
Note: Thomas H. Walton swears that Miss Keturah Brown was
      born 8 Sept. 1804. Source Family Bible in father's
      handwriting.   Teste: William Smith

MAXEY, John   * Marianne Fforsey
* Mary Ann Forsee - Will of John Forsee Cum. Co. W.B. 1,p.317
Married 19 January 1758 by Rev. William Douglas
Ref: Douglas Register, p. 34

MAXEY, Sylvanus   Mary WORLEY
Prior to 22 March 1757
Will of John Worley, Cum. Co. W.B. 1, p. 149

MAY, William   (See next page)   Polly NORRIS

87

M.B. (not dated)   Surety: Jn⁰ NAPIER
Consent: Dated <u>1 Nov. 1810</u>
Note: Daughter of Thomas Norris who gives consent.
Teste: John Dunn   Teste: Sam¹ Dunn

MAYES, Daniel W.   Luritta CHRISTOPHER
M.B. 7 August 1809   Surety: Samuel Allen
Note: Luritta states she is a resident of this county and of
      lawful age.   Teste: John Woodson

MAYO, Billy *   * Eliza MAYO
* Free people of color ?
M.B. 18 Dec. 1833   Surety: Scipio Mayo
Married 20 December 1833 by Rev. Lewis Chaudoin, Jr.

MAYO, Scipio *   * Judy JENKINS
* Free people of color
M.B. 16 July 1840   Surety: Scipio Mayo, Jr.

MAYO, Henry *   * Harriett MAYO
* Free people of color
M.B. 4 June 1840   * Surety: Finley Cousins

MAYO, James C.   Mary A. PAYNE
M.B. 19 November 1827   Surety: Robert Daniel
Consent: Robert Spears, guardian for Mary Payne
Teste: Edward W. Spears   Teste: Joseph Mayo

MAYO, James C.   Sarah MARTIN
M.B. 8 April 1829   Surety: Robert Mayo

MAYO, John   Betsy WOMACK
M.B. (not dated)   Surety: James Ellison
Date: 27 July 1816 on back of bond
Note: Daughter of Sampson Womack who gives consent.

MAYO, Joseph   Susan JENKINS
M.B. 28 August 1837   Surety: James L. Carrington
Note: Daughter of Stephen Jenkins   Teste: Morman Jenkins

MAYO, Peter   Rebecca MAYO
M.B. 15 August 1812   Surety: Jeffrey Mayo

MAYO, Robert H.   Maria L. MAYO
M.B. 22 October 1838   Surety: E. W. Spears
Note: Daughter of William Mayo.

MAYO, William   Chloe CARRINGTON
M.B. 12 October 1809   Surety: James Boatwright
Note: Daughter of Tiller Carrington   Teste: John G. Daniel

MAYO, William H.   Harriet P. CARRINGTON
M.B. 4 October 1823   Surety: Codrington Carrington
Note, Daughter of William Carrington Wit: Benjamin Carrington

MEADOR, Albert   Sarah TALLEY
M.B. 23 Nov. 1840   Surety: Albert Meador, Sr. ?

MEADOR, Daniel B.   Martha BROWN
M.B. 12 Dec. 1826   Surety: Samuel Brown

MEADOR, Gideon   Rhoda MEADOR
M.B. 8 December 1828   Surety: Thomas Anderson
Consent: Rhoda, of age, signs own consent. James Meador, Jr.

MEADOR, Hubbard   Mary M. BRADLEY
M.B. 11 Nov. 1820   Surety: John Anderson
Consent: Mary M. Bradley signs own consent Wit: Eliz. Ballow

MEADOR, Jackson G.   Lucy ROBERTSON
M.B. 21 December 1840   Surety: Jesse Robinson

MEADOR, James   Fanny ANDERSON
M.B. 4 December 1809   Surety: Gross Robinson
Consent: Catherine Anderson - relation not stated
Teste: Shirley Anderson

MEADOR, Jesse   Elizabeth WINFREY
M.B. 13 July 1824   Surety: John Winfree
Note: John Winfree made oath that Elizabeth was above age 21
      and a resident of this county.

MEADOR, Jonas   Polly ROBINSON
M.B. 4 January 1806   Surety: William Bond

MEADOR, Jonas   Mary OAKLEY
M.B. 26 Nov. 1832   Surety: Shed Oakley

MEADOR, Robert   Mary RICHARDSON
M.B. 12 December 1837   Surety: Frederick H. Booker
Note: Granddaughter of John Brown   Teste: B. B. James

MEADOR, Swann   Susan A. PARKER
M.B. 14 Nov. 1824   Surety: William Anderson
Note: Daughter of John H. Parker   Teste: Jane A. Parker

MEADOR, Thomas L.   Obediance B. ROBERTSON
M.B. 13 Nov. 1838   Surety: Gross Robinson

MEADOR, Valentine   Harriet E. PARKER
M.B. 23 November 1833   Surety: William D. Austin
Note: Daughter of John H. Parker   Teste: Frances W. Dunkum

MEADOR, William M.   Catherine C. MERRYMAN
M.B. 10 Dec. 1830   Surety: Isham Bradley
Note: Daughter of Elizabeth H. Merryman Wit: Martha Merryman

MEREDITH, Pleasant   Ann LEE
M.B. 29 June 1793   Surety: Curtis Haynes

MEREDITH, Pleasant W.   Harriett BRADLEY
M.B. 17 December 1813   Surety: Ja^s Hobson
Note: Daughter of Eliza Bradley who gives consent
Teste: Martha Bradley   Teste: Carter H. Bradley

MEREDITH, Warren W.   Martha W. ALLEN
M.B. 4 Sept. 1818   Surety: James Blanton, Jr.

MERIWETHER, Joseph M.   Judith C. SHIELDS
M.B. 1 June 1833   Surety: Geo. C. Walton
Note: Daughter of David Shields   Teste: Mary C. Shields

MERIWETHER, William W.   Anne H. W. SHIELDS
M.B. 12 April 1825   Surety: Alfred G. W. Shields
Consent: 12 April 1825 - D. Shields of "Mt. Elba" gives con-
         sent for his daughter to marry Dr. William W. Meri-
         wether of Amelia County.

MERRYMAN, Edward   Elizabeth SCRUGGS
M.B. 22 May 1815   Surety: Benj. Bransford
Consent: Elizabeth signs own consent.
Teste: T. Bransford   Teste: R. Merryman

MERRYMAN, Jesse D.   Judith HOLT
M.B. 28 July 1823   Surety: Robert Scruggs
Note: Daughter of Philip Holt

MERRYMAN, John   Mary FLIPPEN
M.B. ___ June 1781   License 10/
Cumberland County Fee Book - 1779-1781
Note: Will of John Merryman (1785) names wife Mary and
       father-in-law Ralph Flippen and wife Martha.
Note: Mary (Flippen) Merryman married (2) (   ) Hix
       Will of Martha Flippen (1794)

MERRYMAN, John   Susan MERRYMAN
M.B. 14 Sept. 1819   Surety: Thomas H. Brackett
Consent: Susan Merryman signs own consent being of lawful age
Teste: James Hobson   Teste: Mary J. Merryman

MERRYMAN, Peter   Patsy WARD
M.B. 19 May 1808   Surety: Joseph Ligon

MERRYMAN, Pleasant   Susanna BURTON
M.B. 19 May 1808   Surety: William A. Burton
Note: Susanna daughter of Nancy Burton who consents.

MERRYMAN, Thomas   Phebe JAMES
M.B. 17 January 1752   Surety: Jacob Mosby
Note: Phebe daughter of Francis and Mary James.
Teste: Ruby James - Richard James and John Harris, Junr.

MERRYMAN, Thomas   Mariah SOUTHALL
M.B. 8 December 1818   Surety: Turner Southall
Note: Daughter of John Southall   Teste: Thos Meador

MICHAUX, Daniel   Eliza F. CARY
M.B. 6 Sept. 1797   Surety: Jos. Michaux
Consent: Eliza Cary signs own consent.   (Catharine Francisco
                                  Teste (Polly Peek

MICHAUX, Jacob   Sally NEVILS
Married 21 March 1765 by Rev. William Douglas
Ref: Douglas Register, p. 34   Both of Cumberland County

MICHAUX, Jacob   Mary Ann Elizabeth Miller WOODSON
M.B. 23 Oct. 1788   Surety: William DeGraffenreidt

MICHAUX, Jesse   Rebecca COOPER
M.B. (not dated) *   Surety: Joseph A. Royall
* On back of bond ___ Oct. 1807   Consent dated 20 Oct. 1807
Note: "Please to issue a license for Mr. Jesse Michaux
      to intermarry with Miss Rebecca Cooper of this
      County, for which this shall be your sufficient
      Warrant".   Signed teste: Jos. A. Royall

MICHAUX, Paul   Judith WILLMORE
M.B. 25 July 1768   Surety: George Carrington
Note: Daughter of Daniel Willmore

MICKLE, James   America SEAY
M.B. 24 Feb. 1819   Surety: James M. Smith
Note: Daughter of John Seay   Teste: Gabriel H. Jennings

MILES, Charles   Susan T. STOKES
M.B. 4 March 1817   Surety: Frederick Stokes
Note: Daughter of Rhoda Jones   Teste: Henningham Jones

MILES, Drury   Catherine T. TYREE
M.B. 15 Nov. 1827   Surety: John Oakley
Consent: Rhoda Tyree for Catherine - no relation stated
Married 15 November 1827 by Rev. Joseph Jenkins

MILES, Thomas   Nanny PATTERSON
M.B. 15 February 1774   Surety: John Brown
Note: Daughter of Gideon Patterson   (William Miles
                                    Teste (John Miles

MILLER, Dabney P.   Martha J. WOMACK
M.B. 9 August 1833   Surety: Arch'd M. Webster
Note: Daughter of Charles Womack   Teste: James M. Eanes

MILLER, James S.   Elizabeth A. S. WALKER
M.B. 12 Nov. 1812   Surety: James Hobson
Consent: William Walker - no relation stated   (John Walker
                                           Teste (William A. Miller

MILLER, Jesse   Elizabeth WALTON
Prior to 1 March 1758 - Cum. Co. O.B. 3, page 516-D.B.2 p.356
Daughter of Thomas Walton - Cum. Co. W.B. 2, p. 54

MILLER, John   Hanna ARMISTEAD
M.B. 27 June 1785   Surety: Thomas Walton
Consent: William Armistead - no relations stated
Teste: Thomas Miller - 27 June 1785

MILLER, Thomas   Joana ARMISTEAD
M.B. 22 Nov. 1784   Surety: William Miller
Consent: William Armistead - no relation stated.
                                          Teste: William Miller

MILLER, William   Martha C. STREET
M.B. (not dated) On back ___ Oct. 1808   Surety Dudley Street
Married 1 November 1808 by Rev. Samuel Woodfin

MILLER, William A.   Lucy W. DANIEL
M.B. 11 Nov. 1806   Surety: Henry H. Woodson
Note: Daughter of William Daniel   Teste: Jos. Woodson

MILLER, William Jr.   Lucy WOODSON
M.B. 14 May 1812   Surety: John Leake
Consent: Ch^s Woodson   Teste: John M. Leake

MIMMS, Drury   Ann RIDGWAY
M.B. 2 April 1750   Surety: Samuel Ridgway

MINNOCK, William   Eliza Duval YARRINGTON
M.B. 14 April 1821   Surety: Jno L. Bondurant
Note: Daughter of Arana Yarrington   Teste: Jesse S. Holt
Married 24 April 1821 by Rev. Joseph Jenkins

MINOR, John W.   Phebe HARRIS
M.B. (not dated) *   Surety: Albert G. Taylor
Listed on back of bond - 12 Jan. 1819   (John Carter
Consent: Phebe signs own - 11 Jan. 1819   Wit(Mary A. Carter

MINTER, Billy   Liszea BRADLEY
M.B. 8 Sept. 1794   Surety: John Bradley

MINTER, James   Lucy BOATRIGHT
M.B. 30 August 1815   Surety: Valentine Boatright
Consent: Lucy signs own consent   Teste: William F. Mann, Jr.

MINTER, John   Elizabeth MORGAN
Prior to 1 February 1760 - Chancery Suit, Cum. Co. O.B. 4,
page 158.

MINTER, John   Martha SCRUGGS
M.B. 6 Dec. 1806   Surety: Elijah Scruggs

MINTER, John E.   Mary S. BAIRD
M.B. 3 Nov. 1834   Surety: Thomas Adcock
Note: Daughter of P. Baird   Teste: John B. Bradley

MINTER, William   Polly JENKINS
M.B. 1 November 1813   Surety: Edward Jenkins

MINTON, Drury   Mary GLOVER
M.B. 27 July 1807   Surety: Robert Glover
Married 16 August 1807 by Rev. John Pollard

MINTON, William   Ann SCRUGGS
M.B. 1 Nov. 1773   Surety: Drury Scruggs, Jr.
Note: Daughter of Drury Scruggs, Senr.   Teste: John Huse

MITCHELL, Robert   Judith HUGHES
Married 11 March 1776 by Rev. William Douglas
Note: Robert Mitchell of Richmond
Note: Judith Hughes of Cumberland County
Ref: Douglas Register, p. 35

MITCHELL, William M.   Elizabeth EDWARDS
M.B. 16 Sept. 1835   Surety: John Creasy
Consent: Elizabeth signs own consent   Teste (Edward England
John Creasy makes affidavit she is of age   (John Mitchell

MONROE, David W.   Mahala C. DOWDY
M.B. 12 Jan. 1824   Surety: Richard Dowdy
Note: Daughter of Richard Dowdy

MONROE, Lewis   Adaline SMITH
M.B. 28 January 1824   Surety: William W. Jones
Note: Daughter of Thos Smith   Teste: Maurice Langhorne, Jr.

MONTAGUE, Peter   Lucy POLLARD
M.B. _____ 1780   License 10/
Cumberland County Fee Book - 1779-1781

MONTAGUE, Rice D.   Ann RANSONE
M.B. 4 Dec. 1815   Surety: William Ransone
Consent: Ann signs own consent   Teste: Thomas Ransone

MONTAGUE, Rice D.   Ann ADAMS
M.B. 5 October 1830   Surety: Francis Armistead

MONTAGUE, John N.   Emaline E. TANNER
M.B. 12 Dec. 1834   Surety: John F. Tanner
Consent: Emaline signs own consent   Teste: Frances A. Tanner

MONTAGUE, Thomas   Sarah S. DANIEL
M.B. 12 March 1821   Surety: William W. Montague
Note: Daughter of Leonard Daniel   Teste: William Faris
Married 15 March 1821 by Rev. Joseph Jenkins

MONTAGUE, William W.   Mary MONTAGUE
M.B. 22 March 1824   Surety: John T. Austin
Note: Mary Montague over age 21 years   Teste: R. M. Montague

MONTGOMERY, Alexander   Joanna DUNKUM
M.B. 2 December 1829   Surety: Alonza Robertson
Note: Daughter of Phebe Robertson   Teste: Matthew Robertson

MONTGOMERY, Alexander   Frances MANN
M.B. 14 March 1832   Surety: Daniel Boatright
Note: Daughter of William F. Mann, Jr.   Teste: Ann B. Mann

MOORE, Robert   Ann McGEHEE
M.B. 8 January 1759   Surety: Thompson Swann

MOORE, Robert   Martha ALLEN
M.B. 13 April 1814   Surety: Maurice Langhorne, Jr.
Note: Daughter of Benjamin S. Allen who gives consent.

MOORE, William   Martha BOWLES
M.B. 4 December 1788   Surety: Martin S. Davenport
Note: Daughter of John Bowles   Teste: Marshall Booker

MOORE, William   Mary HUDSON
M.B. 10 October 1793   Surety: Jesse Davenport
Note: Daughter of William Hudson   Consent 30 Sept. 1793

MORGAN, Edward   Polly Scott FLIPPEN
M.B. 24 May 1811   Surety: Matthew Bagley
Polly signs own consent 22 May 1811   Teste: John Robinson
                                    Teste: Lockey L. Robinson

MORGAN, John   * Mary BARNES
* Mary Barnes, widow
M.B. 26 July 1755   Surety: John Woodson

MORGAN, John   Mary ROGERS
M.B. 28 November 1755   Surety: John Woodson

MORGAN, Meredith   Martha CREASY
M.B. 23 May 1825   Surety: Isaac Cooper
Consent: Martha signs own consent 16 April 1825

MORGAN, Morman   Betsy JENKINS
M.B. 28 March 1836   Surety: Philip Holt
Note: Philip Holt makes affidavit that Betsy is of age.

MORRIS, John   Mary ENGLAND
M.B. 24 March 1817   Surety: John England

MORROW, Ewing   Dorothy GORDON
M.B. 23 April 1821   Surety: Abraham Cock
Note: Daughter of Richd Gordon   Teste: A. T. Gordon

MORTON, Richard M.   Elizabeth F. PHAUP
M.B. 17 December 1838   Surety: John Daniel
Note: Daughter of William Phaup who gives consent.
Teste: William R. Phaup   Teste: Thomas Hobson

MOSBY, Alfred D.   Virginia J. McLAURINE
M.B. 19 October 1831   Surety: James McLaurine
Note: Daughter of James McLaurine
Married 20 October 1831 by Rev. Joshua Leigh

MOSBY, Benjamin   Polly McLAURINE
M.B. 29 October 1828   Surety: Alfred D. Mosby
Note: Daughter of James McLaurine   Teste: Elbert Mosby

MOSBY, Daniel   Elizabeth MOSBY
M.B. 26 Sept. 1774   Surety: (None given)
Note: Daughter of Joseph Mosby

MOSBY, Edward   Patty WALTON
Prior to 1 March 1758   - Cum. Co. D. B. 2, p. 355
Deed of Gift - Cum. Co. O.B. 3, p. 516   March Court 1758
Will of Thomas Walton - Cum. Co. W.B. 2, p. 54

MOSBY, Hezekiah   Elizabeth MERRYMAN
M.B. 21 December 1807   Surety: Chas. A. Merryman
Consent: Jesse Merryman - no relation stated.

MOSBY, Jacob   Nancy CLARKE
M.B. 22 December 1817   Surety: Richard Clarke
Note: Daughter of Gater Clarke (?)   Teste: Frederick Stokes

MOSBY, Jacob G.   Apphia C. WOODSON
M.B. 11 Feb. 1833   Surety: William B. Hobson
Note: Daughter of Jos. R. Woodson   Teste: Stephen W. Allen

MOSBY, Joseph   Sarah BEDFORD
M.B. 29 August 1753   Daughter of Stephen Bedford
Will of Elizabeth Flippen, Cum. Co. W.B. 1, p. 144
Names: Son-in-law Stephen Bedford   See also W.B. 1, p. 156

MOSELEY, Arthur   Harriet P. MEADOR
M.B. 1 October 1838   Surety: Henry L. Meador
Note: "Jonas Meador certifies that Harriet P. Meador is will-
      ing to marry Arthur Moseley". (Not dated or witnessed

MOSELEY, Charles   Mary POVALL
M.B. 23 Nov. 1772   Surety: Arthur Moseley

MOSELEY, Edward   Hinson Wager HARRIS
24 Sept. 1770   Surety: Edmond Logwood
Note: Daughter of Benj^a Harris   Teste: Tho. Harris
Note: Benjamin Harris of Manakin Town.

MOSELEY, John   Patty POVALL
M.B. 21 December 1772   Surety: Thos Childrey

MOSELEY, Robert   Magdalene GUERRANT
Married 23 Sept. 1756 by Rev. William Douglas
Ref: Douglas Register, p. 35

MOSELEY, Robert   Sarah M. LEWIS
M.B. 29 March 1815   Surety: George F. M. Payne
Note: Woodlawn - 27 March 1815 - Gilley Lewis consents for
      his daughter, who is of age, to marry Maj^r R. Moseley.

MOSELEY, Thomas   Jane STONER
M.B. 4 December 1759   Surety: Jacob Woodson
Note: Daughter of Daniel Stoner   Teste: John Wright

MOSELEY, Thomas   Polly WALTON
M.B. 28 June 1790   Surety: Thomas Walton

MOSELEY, William   Mary WATKINS
M.B. 4 February 1755   Surety: Edward Watkins
Note: Daughter of John Watkins   Teste: Benjamin Otey ?

MOSS Ray   Elvira W. WILLIAMS
M.B. 28 October 1828   Surety: William F. Davis
Note: Daughter of Drury Woodson   Teste: Thomas N. Johnson

MOSS, William   Mary CRIDDLE
M.B. 24 Jan. 1792   Surety: Finch Criddle
Note: Daughter of Ann Criddle   Teste: William Burton
Teste: Jesse Thomas   Teste: Jesse W. Thomas

MOULTRY, James   Sally Ann WOOD
M.B. 28 October 1840   Surety: John F. Wood

MULLINS, John   Anne D. JOHNS
M.B. 15 December 1815   Surety: Jno. A. S. Johns
Note: Daughter of Thomas Johns

MUNFORD, Dan   Judith ROBINSON
M.B. 12 Nov. 1780   License 10/
Cumberland County Fee Book - 1779-1781

MURRAY, Alexander   Rhoda MELTON
M.B. 22 Feb. 1806   Surety: John Farmer
Note: Daughter of Nathan and Rhoda Melton
Teste: Alex^r Murray   Teste: E. Richardson

MURRAY, Anthony   Elizabeth AMMONETTE
M.B. 5 Dec. 1826   Surety: Thomas W. Lipford
Note: Daughter of William Ammonette Teste: William B. Murray

MURRAY, James   Phebe HUDGINS
M.B. 4 Nov. 1787 ? (or 1788)   Surety: William Anderson ?
Bond mutilated - Marked: Administration of Gov. Edmund
    Randolph which was 11/30/1786-11/12/1788.

MURRAY, Reuben B.   Judith POWERS
M.B. 14 Dec. 1814   Surety: William Powers
Note: Daughter of Judith Powers who consents.
      "Her daughter being of age". Teste: Henry Lipford

NASH, Thomas   Lucy L. HOBSON
M.B. 8 June 1807   Surety: Joseph Hobson
Note: Daughter of Caleb Hobson
Consent: 8 June 1807 - Teste: Jo Brackett   Teste: Sam^1 Hobson

NEAL, Joseph   Sally BROWN
M.B. 13 March 1813   Surety: Josiah Ward

NELSON, Humphrey   Judith WATSON
M.B. 26 Sept. 1788   Surety: Abner Watson
Note: Daughter of Drury Watson   Teste: John Watson, Sr.

NESBIT, Richard B.   Elizabeth W. JORDON
M.B. 11 October 1839   Surety: William N. England

NETHERLAND, John   Mary Ann MOSBY
M.B. 1 February 1750   Surety: James Claiborne

NEWTON, Isaac   Martha S. MERRYMAN
M. B. 27 Sept. 1824   Surety: Charles A. Merryman
Note: Daughter of Edward Merryman   Teste: J. D. Merryman

NICE, William George   Lucy TURPIN
M.B. 17 Dec. 1816   Surety: Thomas J. Turpin
Note: Daughter of William Turpin

NICHOLAS, John S.   Ann H. TRENT
M.B. 18 May 1833   Surety: Carter H. Trent
Note: Daughter of Stephen W. Trent   Teste: P. H. Nunnally

NOELL, Stephen   Judith PALMORE
M.B. 5 August 1806   Surety: Bernard Sims
Married 7 August 1806   Witness (?) : J. B. Woodson

NORRIS, David   Nancy WEBBER
M.B. 27 June 1809   Surety: Miller Woodson, Jr.
Consent: Polly Webber, mother 25 June 1809

NORRIS, Jesse   Nancy COUSINS
M.B. (not dated)   Surety: Thos. Hobson
On back of bond - 7 April 1808
Note: Daughter of Jane Cousins who consents - 6 April 1808
Teste: John Cousins   Teste: Thomas Norris

NORRIS, Reuben (recorded as Rubin)   Jane BANKS
M.B. (not dated)   Surety: Michael Lawson
On back of bond - 6 January 1814
Consent: Jane signed own consent 5 Jan. 1814
Teste: Robert Banks   Teste: Jesse Norris

NORTH, Elijah   Elizabeth ANDERSON
M.B. (not dated) 27 Jan. 1817 on back   Surety: Jacob Anderson

NORTH, John   Susanna BIRD
M.B. 25 Jan. 1808   Surety: John Richardson
Note: Daughter of William Bird who gives consent
Married 27 January 1808 by Rev. William Walker

NORTH, Thomas   Rosamond C. TALLEY
M.B. 2 August 1830   Surety: Carter H. Trent
Note: Daughter of Daniel C. Talley who gives consent
Married 5 August 1830 by Rev. Poindexter P. Smith

NORTH, William   Mary DUNKUM
M.B. 6 Feb. 1829   Surety: Richard A. Booker

NORTH, William   Jenetta CHENAULT
M.B. 11 October 1836   Surety: Ephraim Self

NOWELL, John   Mary SMITH
M.B. 23 October 1775   Surety: Robert Smith
Note: Daughter of Robert Smith of this county.

NUNNALLY, John A.   Elizabeth GAULDIN
M.B. 26 Feb. 1809   Surety: John Nunnally
Note: Daughter of Susannah Gauldin who consents
Teste: William A. Burton   Teste: John Gordon

OAKLEY, Erasmus   R(ebecca) ALDERSON
M.B. 21 October 1780   License 10/
Cumberland County Fee Book - 1779-1781

OAKLEY, Shadrack   Elizabeth DONAHOE
M.B. 24 Sept. 1792   Surety: John Jones

OAKLEY, Thomas G.   Judith J. MEADOR
M.B. 19 January 1836   Surety: William Meador

OGLESBY, Daniel   Frances SHARPE
M.B. (not dated)   Surety: Joseph Blankenship
On back of bond - 17 December 1811

OLD, Philip J.   Judith Maria BRANSFORD
M.B. 16 August 1823   Surety: Thos. H. Brackett
Consent: Jacob Bransford - no relation stated - John Daniel
Note: Judith, daughter of Jacob and Elizabeth H. Bransford.
      Granddaughter of John and Judith A. Bransford.

OLIVER, Hezekiah   Frances BOSHER
M.B. 23 Feb. 1832   Surety: Maurice Oliver
Frances, over age 21, signs own consent Teste: Maurice Oliver

OLIVER, John   Martha NORTH
M.B. 7 May 1833   Surety: Fleming Cayce

OLIVER, Pleasant   Sally WHITLOW
M.B. 24 Feb. 1829   Surety: Elmer Brown
Note: Daughter of Jackson Whitlow   Teste: John Harris
     Elmer Brown swears that Sally is above age 21 years.

ORANGE, Cozby D.   Nancy W. MONTGOMERY
M.B. 13 February 1838   Surety: John Melton
Note: Nancy says she is 21 years old and signs own consent
Teste: Mary Boatright   Teste: Hubbard Meador

ORANGE, Joel   Ailsey PRICE
M.B. 28 October 1820   Surety: Miller Woodson, Jr.
Note: Daughter of Charles Price who consents.
Teste: James Blanton, Jr.   Teste: Thos. Price

ORANGE, Lewis   Rhoda MARTIN
M.B. 23 Oct. 1806   Surety: Henry Martin, Jr.
Note: Daughter of Henry Martin who consents
Married 23 October 1806 by Rev. John Shurrey of Amelia County

ORANGE, William   Elizabeth MELTON
M.B. 26 Sept. 1785   Surety: James Farmer

ORANGE, William A.   Stiry WADE
M.B. 30 June 1807   Surety: Claiborne Wade
Married 9 July 1807 by Rev. John Pollard

ORANGE, Zephaniah   Elizabeth R. MELTON
M.B. 24 February 1813   Surety: Nathan Melton

OSBORNE, Davis   Sally WHEELER
M.B. 20 October 1812   Surety: Saml Wheeler

OSBORNE, John   Polly WHITE
Prior to 1 Dec. 1794   Surety: Micajah Minter
Administration of Gov. Henry Lee   12/1/1791 - 12/1/1794

OSBORNE, Richard   Lucy MORGAN
M.B. 12 March 1814   Surety: John Robinson
Note: Daughter of Samuel Morgan who consents.

OSBORNE, William   Mary F. ALLEN
M.B. 28 Dec. 1837   Surety: Fleming Cayce

OSLIN, James   Mary MINTER
Prior to 3 June 1785
Will of John Minter, Cum. Co. W.B. 4, p. 242
Note: See division of estate recorded June Court 1813.

OSLIN, John A.   Frances ANDERSON
M.B. 25 August 1823   Surety: Edward Bradley

OSLIN, Samuel   Ann MOSS
Prior to 30 Sept. 1753 - Will of William Moss - W.B. 1, p. 84
          Recorded 23 Sept. 1754 - Cumberland County

OVERTON, Thomas   Sarah WOODSON
Prior to 1 January 1793
Will of John Woodson - Cum. Co. W.B. 3, p. 16

PACE, George W.   Catharine P. LIPFORD
M.B. 30 Jan. 1832   Surety: William B. Murray
Note: Daughter of Henry Lipford   Teste: Thomas Lipford

PACE, James   Elizabeth LIPFORD
M.B. 18 Nov. 1820   Surety: John Lipford
Note: Daughter of Henry Lipford   Teste: Robert Walton

PACE, James   Martha R. TOLER
M.B. 27 Jan. 1830   Surety: James Snoddy
Consent: Martha, being of lawful age, signs own consent.
Note: Daughter of Frances Toler who says her daughter Martha
      is more than 21 years old.   Teste: John D. Garrett

PAGE, Alexander T.   Martha E. HENDERSON
M.B. 16 December 1840   Surety: B. B. Woodson
Note: Daughter of Robert Henderson of "Northfield" Cumberland
      County.
Married 16 December 1840 by Rev. William H. Kinkle

PAGE, Henry   Jane Browne DEANE
M.B. 23 Dec. 1813   Surety: Miller Woodson, Jr.
Note: Daughter of T. W. Deane who consents 22 December 1813
Teste: E. H. Deane   Teste: P. W. Deane

PAGE, Henry   Aurilla YARRINGTON
M.B. 19 December 1827   Surety: Albert Yarrington
Note: Daughter of Alfred Yarrington who consents

PAGE, John C.   Marianna F. TRENT
M.B. 18 October 1808   Surety: Thomas Hobson
Consent: W. Wilson consents 8 October 1808 for his ward,
         Marianna Trent.

PAGE, Nelson   Lucia C. HARRISON
M.B. 10 March 1829   Surety: William F. Randolph
Note: Daughter of Randolph Harrison who consents 7 March 1829
Nelson Page appoints W. F. Randolph to act for him.
                                           Teste: T. J. Harrison

PAGE, Robert T.   Amanda COOKE
M.B. 21 December 1835   Surety: James E. Cooke
Note: Stephen Cooke consents for Amanda - no relation stated.

PALMORE, Benjamin   Elizabeth CARTER
M.B. 27 April 1840   Surety: John S. Holland
Note: Daughter of Polly Evans who consents. Wit: T. T. Womack
Consent dated 25 April 1840.

100

PALMORE, Charles — Jane CALDWELL
M.B. 17 October 1785   Surety: William Gadbery
Note: Daughter of Thomas Caldwell who consents fo^r Jane.
Teste: Jesse Flippen   Teste: William Starkey

PALMORE, Fleming — Fanny WALTON
M.B. 23 August 1824   Surety: Alex^r Cheatwood
Consent: James A. Armistead, uncle, consents for Fanny Walton
"whom I have management of since her birth".
Teste: Anderson H. Armistead   Teste: James Richardson

PALMORE, John — Diannah PALMORE
M.B. 24 March 1806   Surety: William Colley

PALMORE, John R. — Maria SMITH
M.B. 3 February 1827   Surety: William B. Hobson

PALMORE, John R. — Susan DANIEL
M.B. 24 Feb. 1827   Surety: William W. Montague
Note: Daughter of Leonard Daniel   Teste: A. Cheatwood

PALMORE, Joseph — Sally PRICE
M.B. 5 January 1774   Surety: Edmund Price
Note: Daughter of Joseph Price who consents. Wit: Mary Flippen

PALMORE, Joseph S. — Lucy Ann ALLEN
M.B. 8 July 1826   Surety: Benj^a Allen
Note: Daughter of Elizabeth Allen   Teste: Lucy Ann Jeter

PALMORE, Miletus — * Maria S. BOSHER
M.B. 5 Nov. 1838   Surety: J. A. Caldwell
* Or Margaret S. Bosher - name indistinct
Note: Daughter of Maria R. Bosher   Teste: Fleming Cayce

PALMORE, William — Judy CARTER
M.B. (not dated)   Surety: Hezekiah Carter
On back of bond - 1816, but no day and month.

PALMORE, William P. — Patsy BROWN
M.B. (not dated) *   Surety: James Brown
* 22 December 1813 on back of bond.

PALMORE, William P. — Elizabeth A. HOBSON
M.B. 5 Sept. 1831   Surety: Patrick R. Lewis
Consent: Elizabeth being of lawful age signs own consent.

PANKEY, Edward — Nancy B. PANKEY
M.B. 13 January 1818   Surety: Thomas Pankey

PARK, John K. — Margaret H. ADAMS
M.B. 2 March 1830   Surety: Robert P. Jordon
Consent: Ed(ward) J. Carrington consents for the marriage of
    Margaret H. Adams, his ward, 1 March 1830
Teste: Samuel C. Hooton   Teste: William S. McAshan

PARKER, Charles   Mary A. E. HIX
M.B. 28 Nov. 1839   Surety: Royal W. Blacker
Note: Daughter of Samuel Hix   Teste: Jesse D. Parker

PARKER, Isham   Judith MANN
M.B. 23 January 1826   Surety: William F. Mann, Jr.

PARKER, Jesse D.   Elizabeth M. WALTON
M.B. 8 March 1840   Surety: John B. Robinson
Note: Daughter of Sarah F. Walton   Teste: Isham Parker

PARKER, John Alex^r   (Mary) Polly NORTH
M.B. (not dated) *   Surety: John Richardson
* 16 January 1805 on back of bond
Consent: Lucy Garrott consents for her daughter and says
         "Mary North is upwards of 21 years old"
Teste: John Richardson   Teste: Thos. Cooper

PARKER, John H.   Elizabeth MANN
M.B. 13 January 1806   Surety: William Mann, Jr.
Consent: William Mann for Elizabeth - no relation stated.

PARKER, John H.   Jane DUNCUM
M.B. 10 August 1829   Surety: Philip Snoddy

PARKER, Thomas   Harriet BURTON
M.B. 5 December 1815   Surety: George T. Wright
Consent: Felixville - 4 December 1815 - N. Ford consents for
         his ward Harriet Burton   Teste: Hezekiah Ford

PARRISH, Peter   Sophia THOMAS
M.B. 27 March 1775   Surety: James Thomas
Note: Daughter of James Thomas of this county.

PARRISH, Valentine   Jane F. T. ANDERSON
M.B. 11 November 1820   Surety: William A. Howard

PARROT, Robert   Patsy PHILLIPS
M.B. (date incomplete)   Surety: John Blanton
Consent dated 16 June 1794
Patsy, being of lawful age, signs own consent.
         Witness: Miller Woodson, Cl. Ct.

PATTERSON, Charles C.   Judith Ann SCRUGGS
M.B. 31 December 1806   Surety: John Scruggs
Consents: Dated 29 December 1806
   Charles Patterson for his son Charles C. Patterson
   Edward Scruggs for his daughter Judith Ann Scruggs

PATTERSON, Henry C.   Mary BRANSFORD
M.B. 7 November 1839   Surety: R. H. Gilliam
Note: Daughter of Benjamin Bransford Teste: Henry Bransford
Married 7 December 1839 by Rev. John Ayres

PATTERSON, John C.   Jane T. SCRUGGS
M.B. 20 August 1816   Surety: Edward Scruggs, Jr.

PAYNE, George F. M.   Susan M. LEWIS
M.B. 10 October 1815   Surety: Benajah Brown
Note: Daughter of Gilley Lewis   Teste: Ambrose Baber

PAYNE, Robert A.   Ann C. ARMISTEAD
M.B. 26 Sept. 1832   Surety: Thos. D. Armistead
Consent: Ann signs own consent.   Teste: Susan B. Holeman

PAYNE, Robert B.   Elizabeth DANIEL
M.B. 20 Dec. 1806   Surety: Joseph McLaurine
Note: Daughter of Mary Daniel who gives consent
Teste: William Daniel   Teste: Drury Woodson

PAYTRIM, William *   Lucy FOSTER
M.B. 27 October 1834   Surety: E. W. Spears
Note: Daughter of Roderick Foster   Teste: John G. Thurston
* Paytrim on bond, but Tranham on minister's return.
Married 28 October 1834 by Rev. F. C. Lowry

PEA, Balfor ?   (Balfor Pearce ?)   Sarah Jane HIX
Consent only - dated 23 July 1838   Teste: F. Womack
Note: Daughter of Lavinia King who consents - Thomas Carter

PEARCE, Edmund   Eliza W. ALLEN
M.B. 16 Sept. 1826   Surety: George H. Matthews

PEASLEY, Gabriel   Judith DAVIDSON
M.B. 14 July 1809   Surety: Thos. Taylor
Judith, being of age, signs own consent
                                Teste: Philemon Davidson

PECK, John   Mary MELVILLE
M.B. 17 August 1832   Surety: P. H. Nunnally

PEMBERTON, Richard   Frances BRADLEY
Married 1 September 1757 by Rev. William Douglas
Ref: Douglas Register, p. 38

PEMBURTON, William   Joanna HOWARD
Married 12 May 1771 by Rev. William Douglas
Ref: Douglas Register, p. 38

PENICK, John   Martha WALKER
Consent only dated 31 August 1787   Teste (Moses Sharp
Daughter of John Walker who gives consent. (Samuel Williams

PENICK, Josiah   Elizabeth S. ALLEN
M.B. 25 Nov. 1811   Surety: Nathaniel Penick
Note: Daughter of Charles Allen   Teste: Nathl Penick

PERKINS, William R.   Sally AMOS
M.B. 22 December 1834   Surety: James Amos

PERRY, Collin M.   Mary DONNELL
M.B. 23 December 1805   Surety: John Donnell

PETTUS, Washington   Sarah W. EGGLESTON
Minister's Return only
Married 16 October 1822 by Rev. Abner Watkins

PHAUP, Ellis   Mary AMONETT
M.B. 26 Jan. 1830   Surety: John H. Stratton
Note: Daughter of William Amonett   Teste: William P. Stratton

PHAUP, Joseph   Elizabeth MURRAY
M.B. 26 Jan. 1839   Surety: George W. Murray
Note: Daughter of William Amonett   Teste: John Murray
Note: Elizabeth Ammonette married Anthony Murray 5 Dec. 1826

PHAUP, William   Julia B. ALLEN
M.B. 30 June 1824   Surety: William Dinwiddie
Married 8 July 1824 by Rev. Abner Watkins

PHAUP, William   Judith ARMISTEAD
M.B. 2 April 1833   * Surety: A. Baldwin
* Archer A. Baldwin

PHELPS, Samuel   Elizabeth HUGHES
Prior to 24 April 1760   Daughter of Anthony Hughes
Will of Anthony Hughes, Lunenburg Co. W.B. 2, p. 191
See also Mecklenburg County D.B. 1, p. 149
Will of Samuel Phelps, Cumberland Co. W.B. 2, p. 482

PHILLIPS, Benjamin A.   Harriet HAZLEGROVE
M.B. 5 December 1825   Surety: Pleasant Hazlegrove

PHILLIPS, Peter T.   Mary Jane ALLEN
M.B. 23 December 1833   Surety: Joseph S. Palmore
Note: Daughter of Elizabeth Allen   Teste: P. H. Nunnally

PHILLIPS, Richard J.   Eliza W. BLANTON
M.B. 14 December 1837   Surety: John Blanton

PHILLIPS, Richard M.   Martha MURRAY
M.B. 28 January 1833   Surety: George W. Murray
Note: Daughter of John Murray   Teste: Richard Murray

PHILLIPS, William A.   Mary BLANTON
M.B. 24 October 1836   Surety: John Blanton

PIGG, Josiah W.   Judith COLLEY
M.B. 20 April 1829   Surety : William W. Colley
Married 21 April 1829 by Rev. John T. Watkins

PITTS, Ambrose   Sarah THOMPSON
M.B. (not dated)   Surety: Robert Wright
Consent dated 3 April 1810   Teste: Henry Lipscombe

PLEASANTS, Isaac   Susan R. BRADLEY
M.B. 27 Sept. 1819   Surety: Allen Wilson

PLEASANTS, Jesse   Elizabeth SMITH
M.B. 2 May 1769   (no surety given)
Note: Daughter of William Smith

PLEASANTS, John   Ann RANDOLPH
Married 14 June 1759 by Rev. William Douglas
Note: John Pleasants of Cumberland County
Note: Ann Randolph of Goochland County

PLEASANTS, John Jr.   * Anne SCOTT
M.B. 12 June 1750   Surety: John Scott
* Anne Scott, widow
Will of John Pleasants, Jr. - Cumberland Co. W.B. 1, p. 300

PLEDGE, Absalom S.   Eliza TALLEY
M.B. 14 December 1836   Surety: Miller Woodson
Consent: Jackey Talley consents for Eliza no relation stated
Teste: Nelson Talley - Caleb Anderson Teste: Edward Bradley

POINDEXTER, Thomas   Susanna HUGHES
M.B. 23 June 1755   Surety: Joseph Hughes

POLLARD, John W.   Mary D. KERR
M.B. 13 January 1818   Surety: Daniel W. Kerr
Consent: 12 Jan. 1818 - Charlotte County - Dabney Kerr who
    says his daughter lives in Cumberland County.
Teste: Wiley Featherston

POLLARD, Thomas   Julia B. NELSON
M.B. 25 Nov. 1822   Surety: John Pollard
Note: Daughter of Andrew Nelson   Teste: David Hambleton
Married 5 December 1822 by Rev. Abner Watkins

POLLOCK, William   Ann BALLEW
Married 23 March 1770 by Rev. William Douglas
Both parties residents of Cumberland County
Ref: Douglas Register, p. 40

PORTER, John, Jr.   Sarah WATKINS
M.B. 5 November 1759   Surety: William Porter
Note: Daughter of John Watkins

PORTER, William   Magdalene CHASTAIN
Married 13 February 1765 by Rev. Douglas   in Manakin Town
Ref: Douglas Register, p. 40

POVALL, Richard   Tabitha HUDSPETH
M.B. 16 October 1751   Surety: Benj^a Childrey
Consent: Tabitha signs own consent   Teste: Mary Childrey

POWELL, Benjamin H.   Martha Ann HATCHER
M.B. 3 January 1821   Surety: Edward Walton
Married 11 January 1821 by Rev. Joseph Jenkins

POWELL, Nathaniel R.   Sophonesba A. CARRINGTON
M.B. 14 Feb. 1835   Surety: Lawrence Carrington
Note: Daughter of Benjamin Carrington - Joseph N. Carrington

POWELL, Thomas R.   Lucy V. CARRINGTON
M.B. 16 November 1837   Surety: James Miller
Consent: William E. Carrington for his ward Lucy Carrington

POWELL, William   Martha COX
M.B. 1 October 1774   Surety: William C. Hill
Consent: Dated 28 Sept. 1774 - Martha Cox states she is of
         lawful age and asks that license be issued.
Teste: Tho. Smith   Teste: Mary Smith

POWELL, William   Mary D. LANGHORNE
M.B. 15 Sept. 1824   Surety: George H. Matthews
Note: Daughter of William B. Langhorne of Cumberland County.

POWELL, William   Mary H. WOODSON
M.B. 6 November 1826   Surety: Joseph R. Woodson

POWERS, John   Lurena ATKINSON
M.B. 29 April 1835   Surety: Ja^S D. Weymouth
Note: Lurena Atkinson, ward of James Weymouth

POWERS, Julius   Nancy BAGBY
M.B. 17 April 1820   Surety: John Murray

POWERS, Thomas   Ellen FARMER
M.B. 24 March 1828   Surety: Henry Hatcher

POWERS, William   Ann LIPFORD
M.B. 9 February 1812   Surety: Henry Lipford
Note: Daughter of Henry Lipford who gives consent
Teste: Abraham Cardoza   Jas. M. Cullen   Henry Lipford, Jr.

PRICE, James   Elizabeth DUNNAVANT
M.B. 24 April 1834   Surety: Thos. Stinson
Note: Elizabeth Price makes affidavit that Elizabeth Dunna-
     vant is of age.

PRICE, John   Nancy H. WILSON
M.B. 18 Nov. 1819   Surety: John W. Wilson
Note: Daughter of Richd Wilson   Teste: W. W. Wilson

PRICE, Thomas W.   Amanda COLEMAN
M.B. 27 March 1838   Surety: John Guthrey
Consent: Benja. H. Price for his son who is under age 21.
Consent: Gulielmus Coleman for his ward Amanda Coleman.
Teste: John M. Price   Teste: John DANIEL

PRICE, William D.   Mary A. WRIGHT
M.B. 15 October 1839   Surety: James DeJarnett
Note: James DeJarnett makes affidavit that Mary is of age.

PRINCE, William H.   Judith BAGBY
M.B. 23 August 1819   Surety: Robert S. Robinson

PRYOR, Banister S.   H. Rebacca EGGLESTON
M.B. (not dated)   Surety: George Eggleston
Married 24 March 1808 by Rev. William Walker

PRYOR, William   Elizabeth HUGHES
Married 16 May 1776 by Rev. William Douglas
Note: William Pryor of Goochland County
Note: Elizabeth Hughes of Cumberland County
Ref: Douglas Register, p. 40

PUCKETT, Josiah   Prudence LIPFORD
M.B. (not dated)   Surety: Amos Lipford
Prior to 30 November 1786
Administration of Gov. Patrick Henry (1) 7/5/1776 - 6/1/1779
                                (2) 11/30/1784 - 11/30/1786

PUGH, Thomas   Nancy TILLER
Married 22 January 1769 by Rev. William Douglas
Ref: Douglas Register, p. 41   Both of Manakin Town
Note: Thomas Pugh removed to Charlotte County.

PULLIAM, Samuel G.   Mary H. MATTHEWS
M.B. 24 December 1817   Surety: John B. Boatwright

PURYEAR, William   Polly SCRUGGS
M.B. 15 January 1813   Surety: Richard Anderson
Note: Daughter of Edward Scruggs who gives consent.

PUTNEY, Samuel   Sally BRYANT
M.B. 14 December 1810   Surety: Daniel Bryant
Note: Daughter of Mary Bryant   Teste: Richard E. Putney

QUARLES, Allen   Polly WILLIAMS
M.B. 7 October 1820   Surety: Daniel Taylor
Consent: Polly Williams signs her own consent.
Teste: James Quarles   Teste: Balona Taylor

QUARLES, Allen   Drucilla NEWTON
M.B. 18 August 1828   Surety: William Jones
Note: James Poore makes oath that Drucilla is above age 21.

QUARLES, James   Sarah DAVIS
M.B. 27 Sept. 1830   Surety: William D. Peasley
Married 28 September 1830 by Rev. Poindexter P. Smith

RAILEY, John   Elizabeth RANDOLPH
M.B. 29 January 1750   Surety: Stephen Hughes

RAINE, Hugh   Ann E. VAUGHN
M.B. 16 August 1825   Surety: Miller Woodson

RAINE, John   * Keziah COCKE
M.B. 23 December 1761   Surety: Chesley Daniel
Consent: 22 December 1761 - Keziah Cocke signs own consent
* Keziah Cocke, widow Teste: Charles Anderson - Ayres Hodnett

Raine, John   Eliza WOODSON
M.B. 13 December 1819   Surety: Miller Woodson

RAMSEY, James   Frances Anne SELF
M.B. 31 August 1785   Surety: William Russell
Note: Daughter of William Self who gives consent.

RANDOLPH, William F.   Jane C. HARRISON
M.B. 10 Sept. 1817   Surety: John W. Nash
Note: Jane Cary Harrison, daughter of Randolph Harrison

RANSONE, Ambrose   Ann ANDREWS
M.B. 30 December 1793   Surety: John F. Ransone

RANSONE, Henry P.   Elizabeth BAGBY
M.B. 25 May 1825   Surety: John Garrett
Consent: Elizabeth signs own consent   Teste: Ann W. Ransone

RANSONE, James A.   Martha Ann WALKER
M.B. 29 Dec. 1835   Surety: Fleming Cayce
Note: Daughter of James Walker   Teste: Thomas J. Ransone

RANSONE, John   Nancy C. MADDOX
M.B. 9 February 1810   Surety: William W. Barker
Consent: Thomas Maddox - no relation stated - Josiah Maddox

RANSONE, Robert   Elizabeth A. ARMISTEAD
M.B. 25 Feb. 1793   Surety: Jacob L. Abraham
Consent: Daughter of Francis Armistead who gives consent.
Teste: John Armistead   Teste: David Johnson

RANSONE, Robert   Martha P. GUTHREY
M.B. 29 May 1836   Surety: John Ransone

REDD, John W.   Lockey H. WOODSON
M.B. 22 November 1823   Surety: John Garrett
Consent: Lockey signs own consent   Teste: Mary M. Garrett
Married 26 November 1823 by Rev. M.M. Dance

REDD, Joseph   Elsie WRIGHT
M.B. 24 August 1807   Surety: Richd Michaux
Married 24 September 1807 by Rev. Abner Watkins

REDD, Thomas   Rebecca M. MACON
M.B. 11 August 1804   Surety: Jn° F. Redd
Consent: Richard Michaux, guardian for Rebecca Mayo Macon,
        gives consent.   Teste: Henry Macon
Note: Thomas Redd of Prince Edward County.

REEVES, Marcus   Martha C. WILLARD
M.B. 23 July 1830   Surety: S. H. Parrack ?

REYNOLDS, James W.   Nancy COOPER
M.B. 30 April 1827   Surety: Thos. Cooper
Married 3 May 1827 by Rev. Joseph Jenkins

REYNOLDS, James W.   Julia A. CARTER
M.B. 3 December 1840   Surety: Albert G. Sanderson
Consent: George W. Carter consents for his ward Julia A.
         Carter   Teste: Champe Carter

REYNOLDS, Seymour   Mary Frances BLANTON
M.B. 16 July 1839   Surety: Alexander Blanton
Consent: Anderson Blanton consents for Mary Frances Blanton -
         no relation stated.   Teste: William M. Cooke
Married 18 July 1839 by Rev. John T. Watkins

RHODES, William H.   Mary V. MERRYMAN
M.B. 28 May 1838   Surety: Edward Merryman

RICE, C. O.   America M. ANDERSON
M.B. 3 March 1835   Surety: William B. Hobson
Consent: Daughter of John Anderson   Teste: M. Woodson
Married 18 March 1835 by Rev. John T. Watkins

RICE, John   Amanda NANCE
M.B. 8 June 1821   Surety: Francis W. Venable
Consent: "This is to certify that Amanda Nance is the
         daughter of Frederick Nance of Washington County,
         Kentucky, which is her usual place of residence.
         Capt. Rice whom she has chosen to marry has been
         to see her father on the subject and was bearer of
         a letter to me giving his consent to marriage pro-
         vided I had no objections. You will grant same."
         /s/ William L. Venable   Teste: Jno. R. Cook

RICHARDSON, John   Ann Branch BURTON
Prior to 1 Dec. 1791   Surety: Jesse Hill
Administration of Gov. Beverly Randolph 11/12/1788-12/1/1791

RICHARDSON, John H.   Mary A. BROWN
M.B. 22 Sept. 1817   Surety: Benj. Hatcher
Note: Daughter of John Brown who gives consent.

RICHARDSON, John P.   Catharine PRICE
M.B. 13 Nov. 1820   Surety: William G. Price
Note: Bond signed Tho. P. Richardson

RICHARDSON, John R.   Nesbit Ann POWELL
M.B. 7 December 1822   Surety: Sam[l] Irvine
Consent: William Woodson for his ward John Richardson
Consent: Robert K. Dabney of "Red House" for his ward Nesbit

RICHARDSON, Richard   Susanna PRICE
M.B. 27 May 1793   Surety: Jesse Thomas

RICHARDSON, Robert   Patsy BRADLEY
M.B. 26 Sept. 1808   Surety: Jesse Criddle
Consent: Patsy signs her own consent
Married 28 September 1808 by Rev. William Walker.

RICHARDSON, William   Phebe SCRUGGS
M.B. 25 Sept. 1775   Henry Scruggs

RIDDLE, James   Mary MORTON
M.B. 24 Feb. 1826   Surety: Francis W. Venable
Note: Daughter of Thos A. Morton   Teste: Charles Morton
Note: Fras W. Venable makes affidavit that Mary is of age.

RIDGWAY, Samuel   Phebe SEAY
M.B. 1 May 1751   Surety: Jacob Mosby
Consent: Phebe Seay signs own consent as she is age 21 years.
Teste: Patience Coleman   Teste: Lucy Coleman

RIVES, Henry   Ann A. ALLEN
M.B. 17 December 1810   Surety: Peter T. Phillips

ROBINSON, Joseph   (or Robertson)   Jane HENDRICK
Prior to 25 January 1758
Will of Adolphus Hendrick, Cum. Co. W.B. 1, p. 149
See also Deed of Gift - Cum. Co. O.B. 4, p. 44 - Court 1759

ROBERTSON, Alonza   Amanda C. DOWDY
M.B. 20 Dec. 1830   Surety: Littleberry Amos
Note: Daughter of Richard Dowdy   Teste: John Matthews

ROBERTSON, Charles   Phebe DUNKUM
M.B. 12 April 1821   Surety: Daniel C. Talley
Consent: Phebe signed own consent to marry Charles Robertson.
Married 12 April 1821 by Rev. Joseph Jenkins.

ROBERTSON, Henry M.   Martha Jane BROWN
M.B. 23 Nov. 1836   Surety: Chesley Brown

ROBERTSON, John   Jane FERGUSON
Prior to 1 June 1793   Daughter of William Ferguson
Cum. Co. W.B. 3, p. 24   Cum. Co. O.B. 18, p. 137

ROBERTSON, John   Anne TRENT
M.B. 26 April 1819   Surety: Henry Skipwith

ROBINSON, Christopher   Elizabeth HOBSON
M.B. 26 Sept. 1791   Surety: William Hobson
Consent: Elizabeth of lawful age signs her own consent.
Teste: Martin S. Davenport

ROBINSON, Davis   * (   ) DAVIS?
M.B. 24 December 1811   Surety: Jesse Davis
* Name not given on bond.

ROBINSON, Field   Keziah SCRUGGS
M.B. 9 December 1784   Surety: Edwd Robinson

ROBINSON, Gross   Sarah ANDERSON
M.B. 30 October 1809   Surety: Jackey Talley
Consent: Catherine Anderson consents - no relation stated.

ROBINSON, Jonas   Nancy TALLEY
M.B. 22 March 1825   Surety: John A. Hall
Note: Daughter of Jackey Talley   Teste: John P. Talley
John A. Hall made affidavit that Nancy Talley is of age.

ROBINSON, Joseph   Sally ROBINSON
M.B. 24 February 1807   Surety: Joseph McLaurine

ROBINSON, Norvell Hill *   Elizabeth M. CRIDDLE
M.B. 25 February 1813   Surety: Daniel C. Talley
Consent: Elizabeth Criddle signs her own consent.
* Name on bond "Robinson", but signature "Robertson".

ROBINSON, Robert S.   Martha BAGBY
M.B. 14 December 1811   Surety: Jesse S. Street
Consent: John Murray, Executor, for Martha Bagby.
Teste: Hatcher Robinson

ROBINSON, Samuel   Frankey BROWN
M.B. 22 August 1788   Surety: William Robinson
Consent: James Douglas, guardian for Frankey Brown, gives
        consent.   Teste: Isom Parker

ROBINSON, Stephen   Martha MEADOR
M.B. 23 December 1812   Surety: Shirley Anderson
Note: Daughter of Martha Meador, Senr.   Teste: John Hatcher

ROBINSON, Thomas   Mary BAUGHAN
M.B. 4 Nov. 1806   Surety: Isaac Butler
Consent: Mary signs own consent.   Teste: Jos. Butler

ROBINSON, William   Frankey WINFREE
M.B. 24 Oct. 1785   Surety: Jesse Parker
Note: Daughter of Charles Winfree who gives consent.
Teste: Isom Parker   Teste: Samuel Robinson

ROBINSON, William A.   Mary H. ENGLAND
M.B. 19 March 1835   Surety: Zach S. Goodman
Note: Daughter of W. England   Teste: Gross Robinson

ROBINSON, William   Mildred FOSTER
M.B. 30 July 1823   Surety: Edward Bolling, Jr.
Note: Daughter of Roderick Foster who gave consent.
Teste: David Barker   Teste: John Harris

ROBINSON, Wiltshire   Sally ROBINSON
M.B. 1º December 1826   Surety: Thos H. Isbell
Note: Daughter of Levina Robinson   Teste: Sally Robinson
Thomas H. Isbell made affidavit that Sally is of age.

ROPER, James   Molly SIMS
M.B. 28 January 1793   Surety: Henry Smith
Note: Daughter of Benjamin Sims who gave consent.
Teste: Judith Sims   Teste: Randolph Roper

ROY, Pleasant   Susanna CHARLTON
M.B. 12 October 1809 *   Surety: John Charlton
* Bond not dated, but date on back of bond.
Witness: Rebecca Woodson

ROY, Richard D.   Sarah PALMORE
M.B. 5 August 1826   Surety: Thos. W. Lipford
Note: Daughter of Fleming Palmore. Thos. W. Lipford makes
affidavit that Sarah is of age. Consent: Fleming Palmore
who says Sarah was born in Cumberland County, and "is of an
age full sufficient to choose a companion for herself".

ROYSTER, Charles   Elizabeth MOSELEY
M.B. 22 May 1760   Surety: Thomas Moseley
Consent: Arthur Moseley signs consent - no relation stated.
Teste: William Moseley   Teste: Richard Moseley

RUCKER, Joshua   Anne BOATRIGHT
M.B. 7 June 1812   Surety: John Martin
Note: Daughter of James Boatright   Teste: Benjamin Toler
Teste: Leonard Daniel   Teste: Daniel Boatwright

SADLER, Benjamin   * Elizabeth QUALLS
* Elizabeth Quarles ?   Surety: James Quarles
M.B. 8 August 1826   Consent: John Qualls consents to
marriage - both being of lawful age.

SALLE, Isaac   Elizabeth BRYAN
Married 6 May 1759 by Rev. William Douglas
Ref: Douglas Register, p. 42

SALLE, Jacob   Kerrenhappuck MAXEY
Prior to 5 May 1771 - Will of William Maxey, W.B. 1, p. 356
Will of Mary Maxey - Cumberland County   Maxey Family Records

SALLE, Joseph   Jemima MAXEY
Prior to 5 May 1771 - Will of Mary Maxey C. Co. W.B. 2, p. 46
Will of Richard C. Epperson, Cum. Co. W. B. 2, p. 180

SAMPSON, Charles   Ann PORTER
Married 3 Nov. 1767 by Rev. William Douglas
Note: Charles Sampson of Goochland County
Note: Ann Porter of Manakin Town   Ref: Douglas Register, p.42

SANDERS, James B.   Mary E. ALLEN
M.B. 1 June 1830   Surety: Peter B. Foster
Consent: Wm. Wright for Mary E. Allen - no relation stated.
Teste: Eliza R. Garrett

SANDERSON, Daniel   Elizabeth C. MITCHELL
M.B. 10 May 1819   Surety: William H. Prince
Note: Daughter of Cary Mitchell   Teste: John M. Bagby

SANDERSON, Daniel   Edith WOOD
M.B. 18 August 1838   Surety: William S. Armistead
Consent: Edith Wood signs own consent   Teste: John F. Wood

SANDERSON, Daniel G.   Sally Ann SANDERSON
M.B. 30 Sept. 1834   Surety: William Sanderson
William Sanderson makes affidavit that Sally Ann is of age.

SANDERSON, John, Jr.   Lucy WORD
M.B. 10 March 1810   Surety: Thos. H. Word

SANDERSON, Robert   Sarah H. MERRYMAN
M.B. 22 Sept. 1823   Surety: Thos. B. Sanderson
Thos. B. Sanderson makes affidavit that Sarah is of age.

SANDERSON, Robert   Elizabeth R. SANDERSON
M.B. 12 October 1840   Surety: J. W. Reynolds
J. W. Reynolds makes affidavit that Elizabeth is of age.
Married 12 October 1840 by Rev. Henry D. Wood

SANDERSON, Thomas B.   Mary BURCH
M.B. 12 Dec. 1816   Surety: William Sanderson
Consent: Mary signs own consent   Teste: Jane M. Burch

SANDERSON, William   Elizabeth RICHARDSON
M.B. 28 October 1839   Surety: Robert J. Meador
Note: Granddaughter of John Brown, who is her guardian.
Teste: Thos. Booker - John T. Johns   Teste: William N. Booker

SANDERSON, Willis   Elizabeth B. REYNOLDS
M.B. 16 Nov. 1819   Surety: George G. Sanderson
Consent: J. J. Raynolds - no relation stated
                                      Teste: Daniel Sanderson

SANDIDGE, Beverly J.   Elizabeth HOLT
M.B. (not dated)   Surety: James Pittman
Consent: Dated 3 January 1808   Teste: Nancy Davidson
        "This is to certify that I am willing Beverly J.
        Sandidge shall obtain license to marry us".
                                      /s/ Elizabeth Holt
Married 9 January 1808 by Rev. Rane Chastain

SANDIDGE, John — Polly DAVIDSON
M.B. 12 December 1811   Surety: Gabriel Peasley
Consent: Polly signs own consent   Teste: Ja. N. Cardozo

SANDIDGE, Zachariah A. — Susan BIRCH
M.B. 13 August 1829   Surety: William W. Meriwether
Note: Daughter of Littleberry Birch   Teste: Edwin W. Woodson
Married 13 August 1829 by Rev. Poindexter P. Smith

SASSEEN, Alexander — Sally BANTAM
Married ____ 1767 by Rev. William Douglas
Ref: Douglas Register, p. 43

SASSEEN, David — Elizabeth PARRISH
Married 10 December 1768 by Rev. William Douglas
Ref: Douglas Register, p. 43

SCOTT, Charles — Frances SWEENY
M.B. 22 February 1762   Surety: John Scott

SCOTT, Edward — Jenny SMITH
M.B. 10 Sept. 1806   Surety: James Anderson
Consent: Jenny signs own consent   Teste: Charles Anderson
Married 18 September 1806 (minister not named)

SCOTT, Robert — Judith CHASTAIN
M.B. 25 October 1762   Surety: John Chastain
Consent: Judith signs own consent   Teste: David LeSeuer
Married 30 October 1762 by Rev. William Douglas

SCOTT, Samuel — Elizabeth K. PANKEY
M.B. 27 August 1823   Surety: Thomas A. Pankey
Note: Daughter of Thomas Pankey
Thomas A. Pankey makes affidavit that Elizabeth is of age.

SCOTT, Thomas — Lucy SCRUGGS
M.B. 5 Nov. 1805   Surety: Thomas H. Ward
Consent: Lucy signs own consent   Teste: Jnº Scott

SCOTT, William — Mary WILKERSON
Married 21 October 1773 by Rev. William Douglas
Both parties of Cumberland County.   Douglas Register, p. 43

SCRUGGS, Charles — Martha NEWTON
M.B. 14 May 1821   Surety: Thomas Scruggs
Note: Daughter of Charles Newton   Teste: Thomas McCormack
Married 18 May 1821 by Rev. Joseph Jenkins

SCRUGGS, Drury — Frances AMOS
M.B. 27 October 1788   Surety: Charles Amos

SCRUGGS, Edward — Jane DUNKUM
M.B. 13 May 1818   Surety: Valentine Scruggs
Note: Daughter of Phebe Dunkum   Teste: Norvell H. Robertson
Note: Son of Elizabeth Wheeler, who is his guardian.

SCRUGGS, Henry P.   Mary B. GAULDIN
M.B. 14 February 1832   Surety: Josiah Gauldin
Note: Daughter of Josiah Gauldin

SCRUGGS, John   Molly MINTER
M.B. 23 July 1793   Surety: John Scruggs

SCRUGGS, John   Elizabeth MINTON
Prior to 1 Dec. 1794   Surety: John Puckett
Administration of Gov. Henry Lee   -   12/1/1791 - 12/1/1794

SCRUGGS, Nathaniel H.   Martha BRADLEY
M.B. 19 January 1824   Surety: Thos. B. Sanderson
Consent: Martha signed own consent 18 January 1824.

SCRUGGS, Robert   Maria ATKINSON
M.B. 13 January 1813   Surety: Daniel A. Wilson
Note: Daughter of Samuel Atkinson who gives consent.
Teste: R. Austin   Teste: Leonard W. Ligon

SCRUGGS, Samuel   Sally MEADOR
M.B. 8 Sept. 1818   Surety: Valentine Scruggs
Consent: Sally signs own consent   Teste: Cubb Anderson

SEAY, Abner   Mary STRATTON
M.B. 2 April 1795   Surety: Reuben Seay

SEAY, Isham   Sarah W. WALTON
M.B. 17 May 1834   Surety: Branch H. Ellington
Note: Daughter of William S. Walton   Wit: Elizabeth Ann Walton

SEAY, John   Mary RICE
M.B. 6 October 1789   Surety: Booker Woodson

SEAY, John B.   Rebecca G. MAYO
M.B. 4 January 1839   Surety: Thos. P. Allen
Thos. P. Allen makes affidavit that Rebecca is of age.

SEAY, Leonard   Lucy HOLT
M.B. 22 Nov. 1824   Surety: Philip Holt

SEAY, Reuben   Mary B. SCRUGGS
M.B. 7 April 1834   Surety: James S. Gauldin
Note: Mary signs her own consent, and states that she is a
      widow, and "Clerks know that all widows are of age".
Teste: Joseph R. Hill

SEAY, Selden A.   Maria L. EGGLESTON
M.B. a8 August 1839   Surety: James A. Seay
Note: Daughter of Edm^d Eggleston who consents.

SEAYRES, John, Jr.   Elizabeth Ann CLARKE
M.B. 25 Oct. 1819   Surety: George W. Bondurant
Consent: Dated 23 Oct. 1819, Cartersville.
Note: Daughter of Gater Clarke

SELF, John E.   Mary G. HOLMAN
M.B. 14 December 1830   Surety: Edmund T. Self
Note: Mary George Holman, daughter of George Holman
Teste: George T. Holman   Teste: William T. Holman
Married 16 December 1830 by Rev. John T. Watkins

SHAW, Timothy   Sarah D. SANDERSON
M.B. 14 May 1839   Surety: Robert Sanderson
Robert Sanderson makes affidavit that Sarah is of age.
Consent: Sarah signs own consent. Wit: Caroline J. Sanderson

SHEFFIELD, Collin   Frances H. DAVENPORT
M.B. 18 January 1825   Surety: Timothy Tyree
Note: Daughter of Elizabeth Davenport   Wit: Benjamin P. Tyree

SHELTON, John W.   Elizabeth DOWDY
M.B. 19 December 1825   Surety: Richard Dowdy

SHEPARD, James   Elvira WARRINER
M.B. 18 July 1824   Surety: Thomas Johns, Jr.
Consent: Elvira signs her own consent.
Married 22 July 1824 by Rev. Abner Watkins

SHEPHERD, John M.   Catharine A. BOATWRIGHT
M.B. 7 December 1840   Surety: Gabriel B. Peasley
Note: Daughter of Leonard Boatwright

SHEPHERD, Nathaniel J.   Elizabeth SPEARS
M.B. (not dated)   Surety: George T. Thomas
Consent: Dated <u>1 April 1835</u>
Note: Daughter of Elizabeth Spears   Teste: Nathl Walton

SHEPPARD, Samuel   Susanna HOLMAN
M.B. 2 Nov. 1788   Surety: John Holman

SHORES, Chasteen   Elizabeth W. STEGAR
M.B. 3 August 1822   Surety: Edward Stegar
Note: Daughter of Thomas H. Stegar   Teste: Edward Walton

SHOOTT, Bartholomew *   Tabitha MOSS
M.B. 4 December 1753   Surety: Pat. Shoott
* It is not certain whether this is "Shoott" or "Shortt".

SHORT, John   Olive SASSEEN
Married 18 Sept. 1766 by Rev. William Douglas
Ref: Douglas Register, p. 43

SHORT, Samuel   Elizabeth LeSEUER
M.B. 28 February 1774   Surety: Peter LeSeuer

SHORT, Thomas   Ann PAYNE
Married 10 January 1762 by Rev. William Douglas
Ref: Douglas Register, p. 44

SHORT, Young Mary BILBO
Married 3 February 1756 by Rev. William Douglas
Ref: Douglas Register, p. 44

SIMMONS, John Keturah King Mariana STEGAR
Prior to 28 Nov. 1774
Daughter of Francis George Stegar - Cum. Co. O.B. 11, p. 297
Cumberland County Will Book 3, page 442.

SIMS, Edward W. Polly S. HOBSON
M.B. 16 August 1824 Surety: Benj. E. Scruggs
Note: Daughter of John Hobson, Junr., deceased.
Consent: Maurice Langhorne, guardian for Polly Hobson.
Married in "Month August" 1824 by Rev. George C. Chesley.

SIMS, Matthew Mary COLEMAN
Prior to 29 August 1763
Will of Daniel Coleman - Cum. Co. W.B. 2, p. 4

SIMS, Reuben F. Nancy M. FRAYSER
M.B. 17 February 1817 Surety: E(dward) Walton

SLADE, Jonah Mary L. BOWLER
M.B. 15 December 1819 Surety: Peter Stratton
Consent: Mary signed her own consent. Teste: P. Stratton

SLAUGHTER, George Martha SMITH
M.B. 16 February 1789 Surety: Harry Smith

SLAUGHTER, Martin Rebeccah ALLEN
M.B. 20 Nov. 1789 Surety: Larkin Smith
Note: Daughter of William Allen Teste: Edward England

SMITH, Benjamin * Sally FAWWELL
M.B. 22 March 1806 Surety: Thaddeus Armistead
* Sally Falwell ?

SMITH, Berry * Mahala JOHNSON
M.B. 20 December 1818 Surety: Henry L. Eggleston
* Bond signed "Littleberry Smith"

SMITH, Bird Gillea ARNOLD
M.B. 15 Sept. 1789 Surety: John Arnold
Note: Daughter of Moses Arnold

SMITH, Bird Sally DOWDY
M.B. 14 January 1822 Surety::James Dowdy

SMITH, Bowker Judith COX
M.B. 22 May 1749 Surety: Jacob Mosby
Note: Daughter of Judith Cox Teste: Abraham Spiers

SMITH, Daniel * (Presilla Goff) * Presilla GOUFF
M.B. 3 May 1808 Surety: Henry Goff

SMITH, Daniel (D.) — Druscillah BOATWRIGHT
M.B. 22 August 1815 — Surety: Drury Boatwright
Consent: Drucilla signs her own consent to marry Daniel D.
    Smith. — Teste: Skipp H. Stegar
Teste: Austin Martin, Junr. — Teste: Leonard Boatwright

SMITH, Edward — Nancy ROGERS
M.B. 7 Nov. 1815 — Surety: Leonard Boatwright
Note: Daughter of Martha Rogers who gives consent.
Teste: Daniel Martin — Teste: John Garrott

SMITH, Francis, Jr. — Sarah SEAY
M.B. 7 May 1821 — Surety: James M. Smith
Note: Daughter of John Seay who gives consent - Hugh Raine

SMITH, George — Caroline TRABUE
Married 4 June 1758 by Rev. William Douglas
Ref: Douglas Register, p. 44

SMITH, George Stovall — Frances SANDEFER
M.B. 26 July 1773 — Surety: John Dupie
Note: Daughter of Abra^m Sandefer — Teste: Stephen Forsee

SMITH, Guy — Martha T. SHEPHERD
M.B. 28 December 1818 — Surety: William Wade
Note: Daughter of Nancy Shepherd — Teste: James Shepherd

SMITH, James — Mary HAISTIE
M.B. 16 November 1759 — Surety: James Aiken
Note: Daughter of Thomas and Elizabeth Haistie who consent to
    the marriage. — Teste: Holcraft Povall

SMITH, James — Mary WORLEY
Married 2 October 1760 by Rev. William Douglas
Ref: Douglas Register, p. 44

SMITH, James — Susanna SELF
M.B. 6 July 1793 — Surety: Joseph Walston

SMITH, James Miller — Mary SEAY
Prior to 11 Dec. 1816 — Surety: William Seay
Administration of Gov. Wilson Cary Nicholas
    12/11/1814 - 12/11/1816

SMITH, Jesse — Sarah Miller BELLAMY
M.B. 23 March 1835 — Surety: James A. Bellamy
Note: Daughter of Richard and Martha Bellamy.

SMITH, John — Sally ROWTON
Prior to 7 Nov. 1785
Will of William Rowton, Charlotte County, Will Book 2, p. 305
Note: John Smith removed to Lawrence County, Georgia.
    Charlotte County Deed Book 11, p. 158

SMITH, John   Nancy MATTHEWS
M.B. 25 March 1793   Surety: Lewis Lowry
Consent: Elizabeth Matthews consents - no relation stated

SMITH, John   Elizabeth BOSHER
M.B. 18 October 1815   Surety: Ro(bert) Smith

SMITH, John   Sophia W. PRICE
M.B. 10 April 1821   Surety: William D. Price

SMITH, John   Sarah MERRYMAN
M.B. 15 June 1840   Surety: James W. Reynolds
Note: Daughter of Edward Merryman   Teste: J. W. Reynolds
Married 17 June 1840 by Rev. M. A. Dunn

SMITH, Lawrence   Martha THOMPSON
M.B. 24 November 1755   Surety: Robt. Thompson

SMITH, Lawrence   Catherine MONTAGUE
M.B. 5 Sept. 1774   Surety: Thomas Montague

SMITH, Miller *   * Julia BROWN
M.B. 1 June 1825   Surety: Man S. Hebson
* Free persons of color.

SMITH, Peter F. T.   Mary J. TURPIN
M.B. 16 December 1807   Surety: Henry Randolph
Note: Daughter of William Turpin

SMITH, Robert   Elizabeth JAMES
M.B. 20 May 1763   Surety: William Smith

SMITH, Robert   Polly DOWDY
M.B. 28 January 1823   Surety: James Dowdy
James Dowdy makes oath before John Daniel, Junr., Dep. Clerk,
that Polly Dowdy is above age 21 years and resident of this
County.

SMITH, Robert P.   Sally SMITH
M.B. 2 October 1809   Surety: Thos Wilkinson

SMITH, Stark   Tabitha COX
M.B. 24 October 1774   Surety: Robt. Smith
Note: Daughter of Stephen Cox, deceased.

SMITH, Thomas   Magdalene GARRETT
Married 15 October 1756 by Rev. William Douglas
Ref: Douglas Register

SMITH, Thomas J.   Susanna C. STEGAR
M.B. 13 December 1830   Surety: Henry J. Harris
Note: Daughter of Hanse Stegar who gives consent for Susanna
      to marry Thomas Jefferson Smith. Wit: James A. Harris

SMITH, William   Nancy FARISS
M.B. 22 November 1805   Surety: Edward Walton, Jr.
Note: Daughter of Martin Fariss   Teste: Jn⁰ Hardin

SMITH, William   Polly AUSTIN
M.B. 16 Sept. 1817   Surety: James H. Austin
Note: Daughter of Judith Austin

SNODDY, David   Nancy THOMAS
Consent only - Dated 29 December 1806
Consent: Frederick Jones, Guardian, for Nancy Thomas
                                                        Teste: Samuel Snoddy

SNODDY, David   Elizabeth FARIS
M.B. 26 May 1817   Surety: Charles Faris
Note: Daughter of Martin Faris. Teste: William and James Faris

SNODDY, James C.   Eliza BURCH
M.B. 24 October 1836   Surety: Henry Wheeler
Note: Daughter of Littleberry Burch   Teste: Robert Wheeler

SNODDY, Philip   Jane Ann PARKER
M.B. 30 March 1830   Surety: Swann Meador
Note: Daughter of John H. Parker   Teste: William Minter

SNODDY, Samuel   Sally ALLEN
M.B. 8 November 1794   Surety: Danl Allen

SOUTHALL, Cary   Polly E. MADDOX
M.B. 11 November 1816   Surety: Thomas Maddox

SOUTHALL, Furney   Polly RICHARDSON
M.B. 18 November 1808   Surety: James Southall
Note: Daughter of Robert Richardson who consents.

SOUTHALL, Turner   Patsy BROWN
M.B. 10 January 1811   Surety: Turner Brown
Note: Daughter of Clement Brown   Teste: James Southall

SOUTHALL, William   Paulina HIX
M.B. 28 December 1830   Surety: Jourdan Salmon
Note: Daughter of Josiah Hix   Teste: Jn⁰ Miller

SOUTHERN, Henry   Elizabeth FARLEY
M.B. 25 January 1833   Surety: Miller Woodson

SPEARS, Edward W.   Catharine MAYO
M.B. 13 June 1825   Surety: Z. Wilkinson
Note: Daughter of William Mayo who gives consent.
Teste: William H. Mayo   Teste: James C. Mayo

SPEARS, Jesse   Sally SPEARS
M.B. 23 February 1795   Surety: William Spears, Jr.
Note: Daughter of William Spears   Teste: Jn⁰ Woodson

SPEARS, Robert   Betsy YARRINGTON
M.B. 1 November 1804   Surety: William Hobson
Note: Daughter of Mary Yarrington

SPEARS, Robert   Elizabeth PAYNE
M.B. 24 March 1817   Surety: Samuel Stegar
Consent: Elizabeth Payne signs own consent Wit: Samuel Stegar

SPEARS, William   Polly DANIEL
M.B. 26 Sept. 1791   Surety: Jn^e Woodson
Note: Daughter of Abraham Daniel who gives consent for his
      daughter to marry Mr. William Spears, Jr. - A. Daniel

SPENCER, John   Betsy PRICE
M.B. 24 July 1809   Surety: Chas. Womack

SPENCER, John   Elizabeth GUERRANT
M.B. _____ 1815 (mutilated)   Surety: Richmond Allen
Consent: Elizabeth signs own consent.
Note: John Spencer of Charlotte County.

SPENCER, Sion   Mary HARRISON
Married 20 May 1769 by Rev. William Douglas
Note: Mary Harrison of Manakin Town.
Note: Sion Spencer of Charlotte County
Ref: Douglas Register, p. 44

STANFORD, David   Elizabeth FOURQUERAN
Married 16 December 1759 by Rev. William Douglas
Ref: Douglas Register, p. 45

STAPLETON, Benjamin   Agnes MORGAN
M.B. 3 June 1755   Surety: Alexander Moss

STARKEY, Abraham   Elizabeth CAYCE
M.B. 22 December 1795   Surety: Shadrach Cayce
Note: Daughter of Nancy Cayce who consents. - Fleming Cayce
Teste: William Shepherd   Teste: Elijah Chastain

STARKEY, John   Obedience COX
M.B. 22 June 1789   Surety: Francis Cox

STARKEY, Joseph   Elizabeth JONES
M.B. 16 August 1753   Surety: Thomas Prosser

STEGAR, Edward   Louisa A. GOODMAN
M.B. 12 July 1830   Surety: Edwd Walton
Note: Daughter of Elizabeth Goodman who gives consent for her
      daughter Louisa Ann Goodman.   Teste: Z. Wilkinson

STEGAR, Francis George   Anna Barbara TSCHIFFLY
Prior to 1 February 1760
Chancery Suit - Cumberland County Order Book 4, page 161.

STEGAR, Francis George   (Ann) Janet STEVENSON
After 23 January 1764
Janet Stevenson late relict and widow of John Stevenson.
Cumberland County Will Book 1, page 269 - Deed Book 4, p. 369

STEGAR, Giles   Sally M. JONES
M.B. 17 Dec. 1829   Surety: Thomas Alderson
Consent: Sarah M. Jones signs own consent. Wit: Thomas Oakley

STEGAR, Hanse   Jane FLIPPEN
M.B. ___ June 1794   (Mutilated)   Surety: Francis Flippen
Note: Bond signed "Hanse Stegar, Junr."

STEGAR, Isham   Lockey BOATWRIGHT
M.B. 10 October 1803   Surety: John Martin
Note: Jane and Lockey Boatwright authorize clerk to issue
      license - no relation stated.   Teste: James Boatwright
Teste: Samuel Boatwright   Teste: John Tuggle

STEGAR, Isham   Frances MERRYMAN
M.B. 24 November 1823   Surety: Thomas Merryman
Note: Daughter of Thomas Merryman.

STEGAR, Jefferson   Ann CREWS
M.B. 23 December 1828   Surety: Peachy Crews
Married 24 December 1828 by Rev. Samuel D. Tompkins.

STEGAR, Littleberry   Eliza NUNNALLY
M.B. 29 March 1830   Surety: John Robinson, Jr.
Note: John Robinson swears that Eliza Nunnally is above
      age 21 years.

STEGAR, Samuel   Polly Coleman SIMS
M.B. (not dated)   Surety: Bernard Sims
Note: Date 7 December 1812 on back of bond.

STEGAR, Skipp H.   Anne BOATWRIGHT
M.B. 3 December 1805   Surety: Drury Boatwright
Note: Consent by her parents is signed James Boatwright.
Teste: William Boatwright   Teste: Isham Stegar

STEGAR, William C.   Mary V. McLAURINE
M.B. 26 Sept. 1836   Surety: Jerman Stratton
Consent: John H. Stegar for his ward William Stegar.
                                          Teste: John O. Stegar
Note: Daughter of Robert McLaurine   Teste: W. Stratton

STEPHENS, Isaac *   Mary WRIGHT
M.B. 12 May 1788   Surety: Thomas Wright
* Bond signed "Isaac Stevens".

STEPHENS, James   Elizabeth MORELAND
M.B. 29 November 1814   Surety: James Bryant

STEVENS, Absolam T.   Elizabeth RIDDLE
M.B. 11 Sept. 1815   Surety: James Bryant
Consent: Elizabeth "being of lawful age" signs own consent.
                                           Teste: Mary Bryant

STEVENS, William   Martha MOSELEY
M.B. 25 April 1774   Surety: Richard Moseley

STEWART, James   Sarah HARRIS
M.B. 26 October 1773   Surety: John Cox
Note: Daughter of Charles Harris   Teste: Jnº Jefferson
Teste: William Irby   Teste: Robert Haskins

STOKES, Frederick   Elizabeth ANDERSON
M.B. 6 November 1826   Surety: John Anderson
Consent: Elizabeth T. Anderson for daughter Elizabeth Ann.
                                          Teste: James Anderson

STOKES, Samuel   Mary T. BEAVER
M.B. 28 October 1811   Surety: John Jordan

STOKES, Sylvanus   Catherine HICKS
Married 21 September 1755 by Rev. William Douglas
Ref: Douglas Register, p.
Note: Sylvanus Stokes of Cumberland County.
      Catherine Hicks of Goochland County.

STOKES, William   Mary M. BRACHER
M.B. 25 August 1814   Surety: Benj. Bransford
Consent: Mary M. Bracher "of lawful age" signs own consent.
                                        Teste: Judith Bransford

STONE, William   Lucy Lockett
M.B. 27 February 1767   Surety: Caleb Stone

STOVALL, Bartholomew, Jr.   Tabitha MOSS
M.B. 4 Sept. 1750   Surety: Robt McLaurine
Note: Son of Batt Stovall who gives consent   Wit: Henry King
                                          Teste: Paul Michaux
Consent: William and Elizabeth Moss consent for daughter.
Teste: James Moss   Teste: William Naish

STOVALL, Landis   Anna ISBELL
M.B. 13 February 1806   Surety: Peter T. Phillips

STRATTON, David   Susanna NORRIS
M.B. (not dated see below)   Surety: Beverly J. Sandidge
Consent: Thomas Norris gives consent for daughter 7 May 1808
Married 10 May 1808 by Rev. Rane Chastian.

STRATTON, Edward   Polly FLIPPEN
M.B. 17 August 1807   Surety: Thos. Hobson
Note: Daughter of Philip Flippen   Teste: William Flippen

STRATTON, Edward   Jane B. B. SANDERSON
M.B. 1 May 1826   Surety: Geo. W. Sanderson

STRATTON, Henry, widower   Sarah HAMPTON
Married 26 December 1753 by Rev. William Douglas
Note: Henry Stratton of Cumberland County
      Sarah Hampton of Goochland County
Ref: Douglas Register, p. 45

STRATTON, James   Dinah RUSSELL
M.B. 20 Sept. 1797 - Married in Cumberland County.
Ref: Stratton Book, Vol. II, p. 373

STRATTON, John   Anne DOUGLAS
Prior to 1 April 1785   Daughter of Robert Douglas
Will of Robert Douglas - Cum. Co. Will Book 2, p. 411.

STRATTON, Peter   Polly STREET
M.B. 21 April 1807   Surety: Dudley Street

STRATTON, Peter   Nancy BONDURANT
M.B. 28 February 1815   Surety Geo. W. Bondurant
Consent: William Bondurant for his daughter Ann T. Bondurant
Consent dated 11 February 1815   Teste: John L. Bondurant

STRATTON, Peter B.   Jane E. SWANN
M.B. 1 June 1838   Surety: Jnº C. Trent
Consent: Thˢ T. Swann for Jane - no relation stated
                                         Teste: R. A. Booker

STRATTON, Richard   Jane DANIEL
M.B. 5 July 1814   Surety: William Stratton
Note: Daughter of Leonard Daniel   Teste: James Daniel

STRATTON, Richard B(augh)   *   Elizabeth M(ichaux) McLAURINE
M.B. 10 February 1836   Surety: W. C. Stegar
Note: Daughter of Robert McLaurine   Teste: Burleigh Trent
*Full names given in Stratton Book

STRATTON, Robert   Drucilla S. STREET
M.B. 13 January 1837   Surety: Geo. C. Walton
Drucilla Street signs own consent   Teste: Henry Bagby

STRATTON, William *   * Nancy STRATTON
M.B. 18 December 1805   Surety: William Stratton
Consent: William Stratton (uncle) and guardian "signed her
          marriage license:.
* Cousins - Ref: Stratton Book, Vol. II, p. 366.

STREET, David A.   Mary D. WOODSON
M.B. 25 October 1828   Surety: Tscharner Woodson
Note: Daughter of Tscharner Woddson who gives consent.
Note: David A. Street of Lunenburg County.

STREET, Dudley
M.B. 17 October 1809
Consent: <u>Maryan</u> signs own consent

Mary Ann WOODSON
Surety: Blake B. Woodson
Teste: James V. Bagley

STREET, Jesse S.
M.B. (not dated)
Consent dated <u>22 September 1810</u>
Note: Daughter of John Murray

Drusilla S. MURRAY
Surety: Robert S. Robinson
Teste: Robert Robinson

STRONG, Christopher B. *
M.B. 28 April 1808
* Christopher B. Strong of Georgia.
Married 28 April 1808 by Rev. Conrad Speece.

Lucy Ann WOODSON
Surety: Miller Woodson

SWANN, Thomas Thompson
M.B. 13 December 1789
Consent: "Sir: You will grant a license of marriage to
Thos T. Swann and Judith Ligon. She is now in
Cumberland County. She is of age and also signs
the same"
/s/ Wm Ligon, Jr.

Judith LIGON
Surety: Reuben Sims

/s/ Judith Ligon
Teste: Bernard Sims

SWANN, Thomas T.
M.B. 16 July 1806

Sally W. MACON
Surety: Geo. T. Swann

SWOOPE, Washington
M.B. (not dated)
Consent dated <u>25 May 1818</u>
Note: Jno Trent signs consent - no relation stated.

Elizabeth A. TRENT
Surety: William A. Trent

TABB, Langhorne
M.B. 19 Nov. 1771
Note: Daughter of Henry Cox who gives consent.
Note: Langhorne Tabb son of Thomas Tabb of Cumberland County
Teste: Jesse Merryman   Teste: William Allen Burton

Judith COX
Surety: Thomas Tabb

TALLEY, Daniel Carter
M.B. 18 January 1814 *
* Date on back of bond - bond not dated.
Note: Daughter of Jeffrey Robertson   Teste: Frederick Hatcher

Sally Norvell ROBERTSON
Surety: Fre^d Hatcher

TALLEY, James
M.B. 16 March 1833
Note: Daughter of Lewis Jones who gives consent.
Teste: Nancy Jones

Ava JONES
Surety: William Jones
Teste: Elizabeth Jones

TALLEY, Nelson
M.B. 15 January 1838
Note: Daughter of John Minter who consents.
Teste: John J. Bradley

Sarah MINTER
Teste: John D. Jenkins
Teste: John Sanderson

TALLEY, Samuel H.   Sarah H. HILL
M.B. 11 March 1834   Surety: John Hatcher
Consent: John Hatcher, Senr., grandfather of Sarah Hill,
        consents for Sarah.   Teste: Samuel Hatcher

TALLEY, William A.   Polly Ann DOWDY
M.B. 5 December 1821   Surety: Chesley Anderson
Consent: Thomas Dowdy gives consent - no relation stated.
                                          Teste: Shirley Anderson
Married 8 December 1821 by Rev. Joseph Jenkins.

TALLEY, Zachariah   Permely TALLEY
M.B. 13 February 1805   Surety: James Baughan
Note: Daughter of William Talley who consents.
Teste: John Baughan   Teste: Garland Talley

TALLEY, Zachariah   Nancy OSBORNE
M.B. 5 March 1823   Surety: Joseph Jenkins

TANNER, John F.   Harriet L. JORDAN
M.B. 23 October 1833   Surety: William E. Tanner
Married 23 October 1833 by Rev. F. C. Lowry.

TARLTON, Fleming   Lucy E. COCKE
M.B. 23 November 1821   Surety: William A. Cocke
Note: William Cocke consents for his daughter Lucy Elenor.
                                          Teste: Henry M. Dandridge

        Note: This name apparently reversed, and should
              correctly be Tarlton FLEMING.

TATUM, Jeter J.   Mary B. GLOVER
M.B. 10 April 1827   Surety: James W. Reynolds
Note: Daughter of Elijah Glover   Teste: William Price
Married 12 April 1827 by Rev. Joseph Jenkins.

TATUM, William P.   Sarah H. HARRIS
M.B. 5 May 1827   Surety: Lewis McLaurine
Note: Daughter of Benjamin Harris   Teste: Allen H. Harris

TAYLOR, Archibald   Letitia CUNNINGHAM
M.B. ___ ___ 1811 (mutilated)   Teste: Richard Cunningham

TAYLOR, Creed   Lucy A. M. WOODSON
M.B. 7 February 1839   Surety: B(lake) B. Woodson

TAYLOR, James M.   Louisa FORD
M.B. 19 December 1831   Surety: Alfred Wood
Consent: Louisa signs own consent.   Teste: John W. Minor

TAYLOR, Joseph   Judith GILLIAM
M.B. 30 November 1768   Surety: Michel Rowland
Note: Daughter of James Gilliam   Teste: Thomas Fearn

TAYLOR, Joseph   Sary MOSELEY
M.B. 27 August 1770   Surety: Richard Moseley
Note: Daughter of Richard Moseley of Cumberland County.

TAYLOR, Rd (Richard)   Susan CARTER
M.B. 1 February 1780   License 20/
Cumberland County Fee Book - 1779-1781

TAYLOR, Thomas   Mila MARKHAM
M.B. 28 December 1785   Surety: John Charlton

TAYLOR, Thomas   Nancy DAVIDSON
M.B. 6 November 1810   Surety: Gabriel Peasley

TAYLOR, Thomas   Tabertha ARMISTEAD
M.B. 16 April 1811   Surety: John Armistead

TAYLOR, Thomas   Lucinda HENSON
M.B. 24 January 1820   Surety: William P. Boatwright
Note: Daughter of Charles Henson   Teste: John D. Garrett

TAYLOR, Zachariah   Elizabeth M. ARMISTEAD
M.B. 28 October 1807   Surety: Jesse Michaux
Note: Daughter of James A. Armistead who gives consent.
Teste: Jacob Johnson   Teste: Obadiah Johnson
Married 5 November 1807 by Rev. Lewis Chaudoin.

TERRY, Rollin   Mary MERRYMAN
M.B. 22 December 1823   Surety: Hardiman Crews
Note: Daughter of Thomas Merryman who gives consent.
Teste: Rhoda A. Stegar/Susan Y. Merryman/ Thos. Merryman, Jr.

THAXTON, William   Lucy CLAY
M.B. ___mber 1770 (mutilated)   Surety: Charles Clay
Note: Daughter of Charles Clay of this county.

THOMAS, Benjamin   Terecy RUSSELL
M.B. (not dated)   Surety: James Farmer
Date 15 June 1817 on back of bond.
Consent: Dated 14 June 1817 - Buckingham County
Note: Daughter of Tabitha Russell   Teste: Thos. B. Drake

THOMAS, Gideon *   Hannah CLAY
M.B. 15 July 1762   Surety: Chas McKinnie
Note: Daughter of William Clay   Teste: Thomas Spaldin
* Gideon Thomas of Raleigh Parish, Amelia County

THOMAS, James A.   Mary PEASLEY
M.B. 15 January 1826   Surety: Z(achariah) A. Sandidge
Note: Daughter of Gabriel B. Peasley   Teste: Wm. D. Peasley

THOMAS, Jesse L.   Sarah G. FARMER
M.B. 8 December 1834   Surety: Gus E. Farmer
Note: Daughter of Elam Farmer   Teste: William L. Boatright

THOMAS, Joseph S.   Sarah G. FARMER
M.B. 28 April 1834   Surety: Elam Farmer

THOMAS, Phinetas   Ann PRICE
Prior to 3 October 1779   Daughter of Joseph Price
Will of Joseph Price - Cumberland County Will Book 2, p. 312

THOMAS, Thomas   Rebecca LOOKADO
Prior to 5 November 1767   Daughter of Peter Anthony Lookado
Will of Peter Anthony Lookado - Cum. Co. W.B. 1, p. 355

THOMPSON, Alexander A.   Nancy NEWTON
M.B. 21 April 1827   Surety: Zach A. Sandidge
Zach A. Sandidge makes affidavit that Nancy is of age.
Note: Daughter of Nancy Newton who gives consent.
Teste: James Newton   Teste: Polly Newton
Montgomery County - 17 April 1827
    "This day Mary Thompson personally appeared before me,
    J.P. of said County, and made oath that Alex A. Thompson
    is above age 21 years".   /s/ Isaac A. Ford, J.P.

THOMPSON, Bart *   Ann HAMBLETON
M.B. 7 March 1781   License 10/
Cumberland County Fee Book - 1779-1781
* Bartlett Thompson - Cum. Co. Deed Book 6, p. 541

THOMPSON, George   Mahala BROWN
M.B. 9 April 1811   Surety: John Thompson

THOMPSON, John   Sarah S. ANDERSON
M.B. 12 July 1827   Surety: William M. Thornton
Note: Wm M. Thornton certifies that Sarah is above age 21.

THOMPSON, Josiah   Mary SWANN
M.B. 30 August 1757   Surety: Thompson Swann

THOMPSON, Josiah   Polly COLQUITT
M.B. 1 January 1827   Surety: Thos H. Brackett
Note: Daughter of John Colquitt   Teste: Benjamin L. Burton
Married 4 January 1827 by Rev. Joseph Jenkins.

THOMPSON, Robert   Catherine LeSEUER
Prior to 24 May 1769   Daughter of David LeSeuer, Sr.
Will of David LeSeuer, Jr. - Cum. Co. W.B. 1, p. 453
Names sister Catherine LeSeuer
Will of David LeSeuer, Sr. - Cum. Co. Will Book 2, p. 48
Names son-in-law Robert Thompson

THORNTON, Anthony   Mary Jane IRVING
M.B. 18 December 1839   Surety: Edwd Hubbard
Note: Daughter of Charles Irving   Teste: R. K. Irving

THURSTON, John G.   Melinder FOSTER
M.B. 27 October 1834   Surety: E. W. Spears
Note: Daughter of Roderick Foster   Teste: William Paytrim

128

John G. Thurston - Melinder Foster, Cont'd
Married 28 October 1834 by Rev. F. C. Lowry.

TIGER, John L.   Frances A. SEAY
M.B. 29 June 1839   Surety: Isham Seay
Isham Seay makes affidavit that Frances Seay is of age.
Consent: Frances Seay signs own consent. Teste: Susan Woodson

TOLER, Simeon   Nancy E. TOLER
M.B. 27 January 1823   Surety: George Stratton
Note: Daughter of Benjamin Toler who gives conssnt.
Teste: Peter Johnson   Teste: Decker Johnson

TOLER, William L.   Sarah M. CARTER
M.B. 18 March 1839   Surety: Gabriel B. Peasley, Jr.
Note: Daughter of Elizabeth Carter   Teste: John G. Daniel

TOMPKINS, Samuel D.   Martha CURTIS
M.B. 21 January 1828   Surety: Edward Walton
Edward Walton swears that Martha is above age 21 years.

TONEY, Edmund   Catharine TYREE
M.B. 2 December 1817   Surety: David Tyree

TONEY, William A.   Clarkey JONES
M.B. 18 Sept. 1807   Surety: Jesse Michaux

TOTTY, Thomas T.   Mary D. PRICE
M.B. 9 March 1831   Surety: George R. Jeffries

TOWLER, John   Martha JOHNSON
M.B. 28 December 1780   License 10/
Cumberland County Fee Book - 1779-1781

TOWLER, John   Elizabeth G. LEE
M.B. 23 Sept. 1805   Surety: Joseph D. Lee

TOWLER, Lemuel   Nancy JOHNSON
M.B. 19 May 1807   Surety: Joseph Thomas
Note: Daughter of Isaac and Nancy Johnson   Wit: Joseph Thomas
Married 22 May 1807 by Rev. Rane Chastain

TOWERS, Rodger   Ann B. FOWLER
M.B. 5 June 1818   Surety: Wm. H. Prince
Cartersville - 5 June 1818
Consent: Elizabeth Fowler for daughter   Teste: James Baughan

TRABUE, David   Mary SALLE
Married 7 May 1760 by Rev. William Douglas
Ref: Douglas Register, p. 47

TRENT, Alexander, Junr.   Frances SCOTT
M.B. 27 Sept. 1750   Surety: John Dobie

TRENT, Carter H.   Maria A. WILSON
M.B. 28 April 1834   Surety: William Howard
Consent: Elizabeth Wilson for daughter Maria Alexander Wilson
Daughter of Matthew Wilson, deceased. Teste: Benjamin Wilson
Division of estate of Matthew Wilson - Cum. Co. W.B. 9, p.240
One of legatees: Carter H. Trent and wife.

TRENT, John   Lucy CUNNINGHAM
M.B. 10 August 1812   Teste: Miller Woodson, Jr.
Consent: John Cunningham for his daughter to marry Dr. John
        Trent.   Test : Charles P. Lee

TRENT, John   Kitty SOUTHALL
M.B. 10 April 1819   Surety: Henry Martin

TRENT, John   Judith STARKEY
M.B. 25 March 1828   Surety: F. Brook

TRENT, Richard B.   Eliza L. HOBSON
M.B. 3 Sept. 1838   Surety: C. D. Coleman

TRENT, William A.   Judith C. ANDERSON
M.B. 25 October 1819   Surety: David O. Coupland

TRENT, William A.   Eliza Sumner DEANE
M.B. 24 April 1826   Surety: Francis B. Deane, Jr.
Francis B. Deane, Jr., swears that Eliza is over age 21.

TUCKER, Thomas   Frances WOOD
M.B. 20 March 1837   Surety: John F. Wood

TURNER, F. W. Spencer   Mary HARRIS
M.B. 11 March 1811   Surety: Benjamin Harris
Note: Daughter of Rebekah Harris   Teste: Jos. Harris

TURNER, William   Mary BROWN
M.B. 25 February 1811   Surety: Thos. Brown

TURNER, William A.   Eliza A. BOATWRIGHT
M.B. 18 December 1839   Surety: Henry J. Harris
Note: Daughter of Lucy A. Boatwright   Teste: Rom. M. Layne

TURPIN, Thomas   Martha Ward GAINES
Married 9 April 1767 by Rev. William Douglas
Ref: Douglas Register, p. 47

TURPIN, William   Sary HARRIS
M.B. 28 June 1773   Surety: John Archer, Jr.
Consent: Daughter of William Harris who gives consent.
Teste: Mary Gaines   Teste: John Pointer

TYREE, David, Jr.   Patsy TYREE
M.B. 11 January 1815   Surety: David Tyree, Sr.

TYREE, Timothy   Polly K. MELTON
M.B. 19 May 1824   Surety: John Melton
Note: Daughter of John Melton of Cumberland County.

UTZ, Morgan   Mary L. JAMES
M.B. 14 Sept. 1827   Surety: John Daniel, Jr.
Consent: John R. B. Eldridge as guardian for Mary L. James
         No relation stated.   Teste: Edwin H. Jordan

VAUGHAN, Craddock   P. Mary WILKINSON
M.B. __ February 1793 (mutilated)   Surety: Fred^k James
Consent dated 9 Feb. 1793
Note: Thos Wilkinson consents for his daughter Mary.
Teste: Carter Wilkinson   Teste: Daniel Jones

VAUGHAN, Edmund   Sally MICHAUX
M.B. 6 March 1775   Surety: John Woodson

VAUGHAN, Joseph   Henrietta Rochet MICHAUX
Prior to ____ 1803
Will of Joseph Michaux - Cum. Co. Will Book 3, p. 347
Names son-in-law Joseph Vaughan and daughter Henriette Rochet
Vaughan. Henrietta Rochet Michaux, born 15 February 1782,
daughter of Joseph and Judith (Woodson) Michaux.
QV. V.M.H. Vol. XLV. No 2, p. 221.

VAUGHAN, Patrick   Martha ROBINSON
M.B. 18 October 1837   Surety: Geo. C. Walton
Consent: Martha signs own consent.   Teste: William Baughan

VAWTER, Clement   Sarah JOHNSON
M.B. 17 Sept. 1788   Surety: James A. Spencer
Note: Daughter of William Johnson   Teste: Edwd Vawter

VAWTER, Ludwell   Frances ROBINSON
M.B. 20 March 1809   Surety: John Robinson

VAWTER, Wyatt L.   Eliza R. HARRISON
M.B. 26 August 1816   Surety: Nathl Penick
Consent: Zadock Lackland, guardian for both of his wards
                                          Teste: James Lackland

VENABLE, Samuel S.   Virginia BRANSFORD
M.B. 20 Sept. 1833   Surety: Henry Bransford
Note: Daughter of Benjamin Bransford   Teste: John Bransford

WADE, Charles   Elizabeth ANDERSON
M.B. 27 Sept. 1773   Surety: James Holloway
Daughter of Charles Anderson who gives consent.
Teste: John Chambers   Teste: Linus Chambers

WADE, Nathaniel   Mary Ann BROWN
M.B. 4 May 1779   Surety: Thos Sanderson
Note: Daughter of John Brown who consents Teste: Charles Lee

WADE, William   Franky SIMS
M.B. 27 October 1818   Surety: Sam Williams
Consent: Franky S. Sims signs own consent   Teste: Guy Smith

WAKEHAM, John   Julia Ann MERRYMAN
M.B. 17 February 1835   Surety: Robert W. Brown
Note: Daughter of Edward Merryman   Teste: F. C. Boston ?

WALDEN, John W.   Jane MARTIN
M.B. 21 Dec. 1830   Surety: Robert Hudgins
Note: Daughter of John Martin   Teste: Fleming Bagby
Married 23 December 1830 by Rev. Poindexter P. Smith

WALDEN, Richard, Jr.   Patty DAVENPORT
M.B. 3 October 1774   Surety: Henry Davenport
Note: Daughter of Henry Davenport of this county.

WALDEN, Samuel   Sarah COLEMAN
M.B. 17 December 1839   Surety: William Hubbard
Note: Daughter of Frances Coleman   Teste: James Foster
Note: Signature on bond apparently "Woldron".

WALKER, James   Agnes FOWLER
M.B. 30 November 1785   Surety: William Walker

WALKER, John M.   Clementina M. CARRINGTON
M.B. 24 March 1827   Surety: William M. Burwell
Consent: Clementina signs own consent Teste: Ed J. Carrington

WALKER, Peter   * Elizabeth HARRIS
Married 23 December 1756 by Rev. William Douglas
* Deceased before 15 February 1771
Daughter of Peter and Elizabeth Harris - Cumb. W.B. 2, p. 190

WALKER William A.   Mary W. BLANTON
M.B. 13 December 1837   Surety: Chas. S. Palmore
Note: Daughter of James Blanton

WALKER, William B.   Mary Frances A. BLANTON
M.B. 19 August 1829   Surety: Chas. B. Allen
Consent: Lindsey Blanton, guardian   Teste: Joseph Blanton
Daughter of Lindsey Blanton on bond.

WALLACE, Samuel   Ann F. BALLEW
M.B. 28 December 1819   Surety: Hez(ekiah), Ford

WALTHALL, Francis   Susanna DICKEN
M.B. 23 August 1791   Surety: Jno Chumbley
Consent dated 22 August 1791 - Richd Dicken gives consent.
Note: Daughter of Richard Dicken   Teste: Jasper Pillow

WALTHALL, Francis   Katy ANGLEA
M.B. 12 January 1807   Surety: John Holman, Jr.
Consent: Katy signs her own consent   Teste: John Holman, Sr.
Married 12 January 1807 by Rev. Abner Watkins.

WALTHALL, James D.   Elizabeth BLANTON
M.B. 10 February 1838   Surety: H. W. Caldwell
Married 15 February 1838 by Rev. John T. Watkins.

WALTHALL, John E.   Lucy A. RICHARDSON
M.B. 23 July 1827   Surety: Joseph Coleman

WALTON, A(Anthony ?) A.   Mary AUSTIN
M.B. 18 April 1829   Surety: John Austin
James H. Austin makes oath that Mary is upwards of age 21.

WALTON, Anthony   Rebecca JOHNSON
Prior to 16 January 1794
Will of Daniel Johnson, Cum. Co. Will Book 3, p. 72

WALTON, Anthony A.   Sarah J. DANIEL
M.B. 15 October 1840   Surety: B. Hancock
Note: Daughter of Abraham Daniel   Teste: William L. Toler

WALTON, Ch(arles)   Rebecca HUDSON
M.B. 22 December 1780   License 10/
Cumberland County Fee Book - 1779-1781

WALTON, Edward   Martha WRIGHT
M.B. 25 November 1820   Surety: Archer McLaurine
Consent: Lewis Isbell consents for daughter   Wit: James Isbell

WALTON, George   Martha HUGHES
M.B. 22 May 1749   Surety: Robt. Walton

WALTON, George   Margaret TABB
M.B. 25 June 1759   Surety: Thomas Tabb
Notes: George son of Thomas Walton of Cumberland County
      Margaret daughter of Thomas Tabb of Cumberland County

WALTON, John J.   Jane D. HUDGINS
M.B. 23 March 1840   Surety: Jesse D. Parker
Note: Daughter of Jane Hudgins   Teste: Robert Hudgins

WALTON, Langhorne Tabb   Elizabeth GEORGE
M.B. 24 July 1786   Surety: Jesse Thomas
Consent: Elizabeth signs own consent   Teste: Phl Thomas

WALTON, Minjam ?   Sally F. MANN
M.B. 5 February 1806   Surety: Benj. Fuqua
Consent: William F. Mann consents for Sally - no relation
      stated.   Teste: Pleasant Merryman

WALTON, Nathaniel   E(lizabeth ?) B. PAYNE
M.B. 28 February 1828   Surety: Geo. C. Walton

WALTON, Robert   Milley ARMISTEAD
M.B. 23 November 1795   Surety: William Isbell

WALTON, William   Elizabeth WALTON
M.B. (not dated)   Surety: Jesse Thomas
Consent: Dated 24 March 1794
Thomas Walton consents for daughter Elizabeth   Wit: John Baugh
Teste: William Walton   Teste: John Flippen

WALTON, William   Rebecca MURRAY
M.B. 21 August 1794   Surety: Reuben Bagby

WALTON, William S.   Julia POLLARD
M.B. 5 December 1836   Surety: Isham Seay

WARD, Josiah   Temperance BROWN
M.B. 8 October 1810   Surety: John Webber
Note: Daughter of George Brown   Teste: Tscharner Woodson

WARD, Leonard   Anne EGGLESTON
M.B. 26 Sept. 1768   Surety: Richd Eggleston
Note: Daughter of Richard Eggleston of this county.

WARE, John   Mary WATSON
Married 6 April 1762 by Rev. William Douglas
Note: John Ware of Manakin Town - Mary Watson of Henrico
Ref: Douglas Register, p. 49

WATKINS, Abner   Elizabeth GUERRANT
Prior to 13 May 1802
Will of Daniel Guerrant, Cum. Co. Will Book 3, p. 201
Executors: Son Peter Guerrant and son-in-law Abner Watkins.

WATKINS, Benjamin   Agnes HATCHER
M.B. 26 December 1774   Surety: Benj^a Hatcher
Note: Agnes daughter of Benjamin Hatcher of this county.

WATKINS, Charles   Peggy PHELPS
M.B. 28 July 1785   Surety: Alex^r Gordon
Note: Daughter of Saml Phelps   Teste: Capt. Miller Woodson

WATKINS, Edward   Rhoda THOMPSON
M.B. 17 April 1759   Surety: Robert Thompson
Wit: Richd Pringle   Wit: Frederick Hatcher

WATKINS, George   Magdaline J. GUTHREY
M.B. 24 April 1809   Surety: Saymer Wright
Married 1 May 1809 by Rev. Rane Chastain

WATKINS, George E.   Rebecca THOMPSON
M.B. 17 April 1759   Surety: Robert Thompson
Notes: George Watkins son of Edward Watkins
       Rebecca Thompson daughter of Robert Thompson

WATKINS, Henry   Temperance HUGHES
M.B. 28 January 1760   Surety: Robert Hughes

WATKINS, John   Magdaline J. MEREDITH
M.B. 25 December 1809   Surety: Miller Woodson, Jr.

WATKINS, John T.   Elizabeth R. GODSEY
M.B. 28 March 1839   Surety: * Bartlett A. Sanders
* Signature - Bartlett A. Saunders
Consent: Elizabeth of age signs own consent Teste: Ch. B. Lee

WATKINS, Moses   Mary STINSON
M.B. 9 August 1793   Surety: Samuel Freeman
Note: Daughter of Joseph Stinson   Teste: John Jones

WATKINS, Robert R.   Mary H. WALTON
M.B. 27 February 1828   Surety: Edw. S. Gay

WATKINS, Robert R.   Arianna Frances Jane ARMISTEAD
M.B. 12 December 1834   Surety: Thos. D. Armistead
Note: Daughter of Nancy Armistead   Teste: Susan B. Holman

WATKINS, Royall   Nancy S. MEREDITH
M.B. 21 August 1811   Surety: John T. Watkins

WATKINS, Royal   Delilah MAYES
M.B. 5 May 1830   Surety: John W. Wright
Consent: Delilah signs own consent   Teste: William Wright

WATKINS, Samuel   Elizabeth GOODE
M.B. 26 July 1773   Surety: John Goode

WATKINS, Silas   Phebe WATKINS
M.B. 26 April 1773   Surety: Edward Watkins
Consent: Joel Watkins gives consent for son Silas Watkins
Teste: Saml Watkins   Teste: S. Walker

WATKINS, Thomas   Mary Marshall THOMPSON
M.B. 28 October 1793   Surety: Josiah Thompson

WATSON, Abner   Polly PRICE
M.B. 22 November 1788   Surety: Archib^d Wright

WATSON, Drury   Frances RICHARDSON
M.B. 26 November 1791   Surety: Abner Watson

WATSON, Hugh   Matilda MONTAGUE
M.B. 27 Sept. 1813   Surety: Richd Cunningham
Note: Daughter of Peter Montague   Teste: J. Austin

WATSON, Josiah   Mary NELSON
M.B. 22 February 1785   Surety: Andrew Nelson
Note: Mary daughter of Matthew Nelson
Will of Matthew Nelson - Cum. Co. Will Book 2, p. 377

WATTS, John   Ann BOND
Prior to 10 October 1756
Note: Daughter of William Bond
Will of William Bond - Cum. Co. Will Book 1, p. 181
Cumberland County Deed Book 4, pp. 148, 182

WEATHERFORD, Hardin   Rebeccah DOWDY
M.B. 5 December 1780   License 10/
Cumberland County Fee Book - 1779-1781

WEAVER, Benjamin   Mary WOODSON
Married 27 April 1758 by Rev. William Douglas
Note: Benjamin Weaver of Manakin Town
Ref: Douglas Register, p. 49

WEAVER, Daniel   Sarah DURHAM
Married 11 November 1756 by Rev. William Douglas
Ref: Douglas Register, p. 49

WEBBER, John   Sally WHITEHEAD
M.B. 7 June 1809   Surety: Sherwood Fowler
Consent: Sally Whitehead signs her own consent.

WEST, John   Susanna ROBINSON
M.B. _____ 17__ (mutilated)   Surety: John Robinson
Consent: (not dated) signed Joseph Robinson
Teste: Frederick James   Teste: John Robinson

WEYMOUTH, James D.   Jane MURRAY
M.B. 19 June 1826   Surety: Anthony Murray
Note: Daughter of John Murray   Teste: William Murray

WHEELER, Archer   Emeline CHENAULT
M.B. 28 May 1832   Surety: Patrick Chenault

WHEELER, Charles   Virginia COLEMAN
M.B. 28 December 1836   Surety: William Osborne
Note: Daughter of Sarah R. Coleman   Teste: James W. Hubbard

WHEELER, John   Elizabeth BARKER
M.B. 29 December 1823   Surety: Sam[l] Wheeler
Note: Samuel Wheeler makes affidavit that Elizabeth is of age

WHEELER, John   Ann GUTHREY
M.B. 23 October 1826   Surety: Jas. Apperson
Note: James Apperson makes affidavit that Ann is over age 21.

WHEELER, Robert   Julia Ann DUNKUM
M.B. 11 June 1839   Surety: James D. Anderson
Note: Daughter of Nancy Dunkum   Teste: Willis W. Dunkum

WHEELER, Samuel   Polly OSBORNE
Prior to 29 Dec. 1802   Surety: William D. Coleman
                                       Attest: James Hobson
Administration of Gov. James Monroe - 12/19/1799 - 12/29/1802

WHEELER, Samuel   Elizabeth SCRUGGS
M.B. 5 Sept. 1814   Surety: Miller Woodson, Jr.
Consent: Elizabeth signs own consent   Teste: Thos. Hobson

WHEELER, Samuel   Nancy WHEELER
M.B. 15 December 1836   Surety: Simeon Allen

WHITE, Caleb   Susanna STERN
M.B. 23 February 1785   Surety: Jas. Anderson

WHITE, Chapman   Mary PHILLIPS
M.B. (not dated - Dec. 1832 on back) Surety:Richd M. Phillips
Consent: Dated 18 December 1832
Note: Daughter of Randolph Phillips   Teste: James M. Donnell

WHITE, Edward T.   Mary BRANSFORD
M.B. 22 December 1828   Surety: Henry Bransford
Note: Daughter of Sally Bransford   Teste: Sarah Bransford

WHITE, Hercules   Suky (Susanna) SMITH
M.B. 24 January 1814   Surety: Saml Hilton

WHITE, John   Hannah PICKETT
M.B. 23 August 1762   Surety: Alexander Walker
Note: Daughter of Henry Pickett, deceased.

WHITE, Richard   Sally SMITH
M.B. 24 August 1812   Surety: John Randolph

WHITE, Samuel   Edey ELLISON
M.B. 24 October 1825   Surety: Francis Anderson

WHITEHEAD, Benjamin   Sarah WALKER
M.B. 11 May 1789   Surety: Saymer Wright
Consent: Sally signs own consent   Teste: Henry Walker

WHITLOW, William   Patsy WARD
M.B. (not dated)   Surety: Josiah Ward
Incomplete date - ___ April 1808 on back of bond.

WHITNEY, Edward A.   Martha L. MICHAUX
M.B. (not dated)   Surety: Jacob N. Cardozo
Date: 20 January 1813 on back of bond.
Consent: Jacob N. Cardozo gives consent - no relation stated.

WHITWORTH, Jacob   Polly RAIBOURNE
M.B. 18 March 1816   Surety: * John Raiborne
Signature on bond - John Rayborne *
Consent: Polly W. Rayborne signs own consent. Wit: James Ellis

WILBOURNE, Claiborne W.   Julia F. AMONETTE
M.B. 2 December 1834   Surety: Robt. Barker
Note: Daughter of William Amonette   Teste: Henry B. Oliver
Married 4 December 1834 by Rev. F. C. Lowry

WILBOURNE, Thompson   Susanna HARRIS
M.B. 10 January 1822   Surety: Henry Martin

WILBOURNE, William H.   Eliza F. ANDERSON
M.B. 25 Sept. 1837   Surety: Nathl Penick
Note: Consent of James B. Anderson for daughter Eliza Frances
      Anderson   Teste: Winston Hazlegrove

WILKINSON, Izard *   Emaline H. SPEARS
M.B. (not dated) **   Surety: James Stratton
* Signature on bond - Z. Wilkinson
** Incomplete date - __ January 1816 on back of bond.
Consent dated: <u>15 January 1816</u>
Note: Thomas Fowler, guardian, consent^{s}for his ward.
Teste: James T. Wilkinson   Teste: William Hix

WILKINSON, Samuel C.   Ann GLOVER
M.B. 1 April 1830   Surety: Fleming Bagby
Consent: Elijah Glover consents for Ann. No relation stated.
Teste: Francis L. Wilkinson
Married 6 April 1830 by Rev. Poindexter P. Smith

WILKS, Thomas   Margaret BLACKWELDER
M.B. 26 November 1763   Surety: Poindexter Mosby

WILLARD, Gains C.   Martha C. FUQUA
M.B. 22 December 1823   Surety: Benj. Fuqua
Note: Daughter of Benjamin Fuqua.

WILLIAMS, Anderson   Mildred SHEPARD
M.B. 18 December 1786   Surety: Samuel Williams

WILLIAMS, Drury   Tabitha MARSHALL
M.B. 26 March 1770   Surety: John Todd
Note: Tabitha daughter of William Marshall, deceased.
      Drury son of William Williams   teste: Thomas Hall

WILLIAMS, James   Emaline CHRISP
M.B. 30 May 1837   Surety: Sam'l Chrisp
Married 31 May 1837 by Rev. John T. Watkins

WILLIAMS, John   Frances HUGHES
M.B. 4 January 1768   Surety: John Woodson
Consent: Joseph Williams for his son to marry Frances Hughes.
Charlotte County - 26 December 1767
   "There is a marriage intended between John Williams, son
of Joseph Williams of Lunenburg County, and Frances Hughes, daughter of Robert Hughes, deceased, now of Cumberland County. This is to certify that I, her guardian am
agreeable thereto, and a license may be granted for that

purpose". /s/ Sherwood Walton, Gdn.
Teste: John Thomason   Teste: Elizabeth Jouett

WILLIAMS, John   Polly LEE
Prior to 1 December 1794   Surety: Samuel Williams
Administration of Gov. Henry Lee - 12/1/1791 - 12/1/1794

WILLIAMS, Joseph   Elizabeth HARRISON
M.B. 11 Sept. 1805   Surety: Abraham Bransford
Consent: Elizabeth signs her own consent. Teste: John Daniel

WILLIAMS, Joseph   Susanna WOODSON
M.B. (not dated) *   Surety: William Wright
* Date on back of bond - 10 June 1815
Note: Susanna daughter of John Woodson who gives consent.
Teste: John M. Woodson, Jr.   Teste: Sally H. Woodson

WILLIAMS, William   Judith SAUNDERS
Prior to 12 November 1788   Surety: Matthias Williams
Administration of Gov. Edmund Randolph - 9/30/1786-11/12/1788

WILLIAMS, William *   Mary GANNAWAY
Prior to 1 December 1794   Surety: Samuel Williams
* Signature on bond - William Ligon Williams
Administration of Gov. Henry Lee - 1/1/1791 - 12/1/1794

WILLS, Matthew   Martha DANIEL
M.B. 13 December 1788   Surety: Leonard Daniel
Note: Martha daughter of Abraham Daniel Wit: William Garrott

WILSON, Allen   Elizabeth WRIGHT
M.B. 18 February 1806   Surety: Jesse Michaux
Note: Daughter of Saymer Wright   Teste: Jos. Vaughan

WILSON, Benjamin   Ann SEAY
M.B. 25 March 1754   Surety: Thomas Tabb
Consent: James Seay - no relation stated   Teste: Lucy Coleman

WILSON, Benjamin F.   Mary E. WILSON
M.B. 20 Sept. 1831   Surety: Chas: F. Woodson
Note: Daughter of A(llen) Wilson   Teste: John Hughes

WILSON, John   Priscilla TRENT
M.B. 14 February 1772   Surety: Ben Wilson
Note: Daughter of Henry Trent who gives consent.
Teste: George Keeling   Teste: William Kent

WILSON, John P. *   Maria WILSON
M.B. ___ Sept. 1814   Surety: John Trent
* John P. Wilson of Berkeley County - Daughter of W. Wilson

WILSON, John P.   Elizabeth W. TRENT
M.B. 16 October 1832   Surety: Stephen W. Trent

WILSON, John W.   Martha WRIGHT
M.B. (not dated)   Surety: Miller Woodson
Date on back of bond - 24 Nov. 1817

WILSON, Matthew   Betsy TRENT
M.B. 13 July 1808   Surety: Miller Woodson, Jr.
Consent: Betsy signs own consent.   Teste: Jos. Hobson

WILSON, Samuel   Susan A. JONES
M.B. 7 December 1835   Surety: Joseph V. Hobson
Note: Daughter of Mary Ann S. Jones   Teste: Harrison Jones

WILSON, William   Ann A. ALLEN
M.B. 25 October 1819   Surety: James H. Lindsey
Consent: 17 October 1819
    "I certify as guardian for Ann A. Allen, daughter of
    Benjamin Allen, deceased, I make no objection to the
    Clerk issuing marriage license".
    Teste: John C. Allen   /s/ James W. Womack

WILTSE, Edmund   Martha FLIPPEN
M.B. 25 Sept. 1826   Surety: John Flippen
Consent: Martha signs her own consent.

WINFREE, Elijah   Phebe A. OSBORNE
M.B. 27 March 1826   Surety: Chesley Anderson

WINFREE, Stephen   Mary BAILEY
M.B. _____ 1789 (mutilated)   Surety: John Winfree

WINFREY, Isaac   Sarah BROWN
M.B. 25 May 1756   Surety: Sam'l Brown
Note: Daughter of Samuel Brown

WINFREY, John   Mary WALTON
M.B. 27 April 1752   Surety: Isaac Hughes
Consent: 17 April 1752 - Application by contracting parties
        for license.
Teste: John Johnson   Teste: Mary Woodson

WINFREY, John   Martha OAKLEY
M.B. 27 October 1823   Surety: Shedrick Oakley
Note: Daughter of Shedrick Oakley

WINFREY, William H.   Sarah Y. HOLMAN
M.B. 25 November 1833   Surety: William Godsey
Consent: George Holman for his daughter who is under age of
        21 years.   Teste: John T. Watkins

WINSTON, Isaac   Martha ISBELL
M.B. 3 May 1817   Surety: Daniel Isbell

WISHAM, William   Elizabeth CHILDRESS
M.B. 17 March 1837   Surety: William Frayser
Note: Daughter of Joseph Childress   Teste: John North
Married 30 March 1837 by Rev. John T. Watkins

WITT, Benjamin   Mary CHASTAIN
Prior to 22 December 1760
Will of John Chastain - Cum. Co. Will Book 1, p. 230
Note: Marianne Chastain daughter of John Chastain.

WITT, Daniel   Mary C. COCKE
M.B. 28 January 1829   Surety: Richard R. Randolph
Consent: Mary signs own consent to marry Rev. Daniel Witt
                              Teste: Eliza J. F. Stanard
Note: Richard Randolph swears that Mary is above age 21 years

WITT, Daniel   Mary A. WOODFIN
M.B. 17 August 1836   Surety: Edmund Woodfin
Consent: Elisha Woodfin consents for his daughter to marry
        Elder Witt   Teste: Sarah Woodfin

WOMACK, James W.   Sally C. ALLEN
M.B. 28 August 1809   Surety: Danl E. Allen
Note: Daughter of Benjamin S. Allen who gives consent.

WOMACK, Thomas F.   Julia Ann FRAYSER
M.B. 9 June 1830   Surety: Anthony A. Walton
Note: Anthony A. Walton swears that Julia Ann Frayser is
      over age 21 years.

WOMACK, William L.   Judith A. MEREDITH
M.B. 27 January 1840   Surety: James B. Anderson
Guardian appointed 25 January 1840
        Judith A. Meredith says she is 18 years old and
        has the right to choose a guardian, and asks the
        Court to appoint William L. Womack.
        Teste: James A. Womack Teste: Frances Anderson

WOOD, And(rew) ?   Eliz(abeth) BOWLES
M.B. 1 June 1780   License 20/
Cumberland County Fee Book - 1779-1781

WOOD, Henry D.   Jane Frances GOODMAN
M.B. 24 November 1838   Surety: Thos. W. Crowder
Consent: Samuel Hobson consents for his ward Miss Jane
         Frances Goodman to marry Rev. Henry D. Wood
                              Teste: Samuel Simpson

WOOD, Henry W.   Phebe A. STEGAR
M.B. 25 Sept. 1834   Surety: Francis Stegar
Note: Daughter of Thomas H. Stegar   Teste: Edwd Walton
Married 2 October 1834 by Rev. Joseph A. Brown

WOOD, James   Sally RYE
M.B. 10 Sept. 1818   Surety: Samuel B. Bradley

WOOD, Jesse   Mary DUNKUM
M.B. 12 April 1834   Surety: Thomas Hobson
Note: Thomas Hobson makes affidavit that Mary is of age.

WOOD, John — Mary HUDGINS
M.B. 7 October 1818   Surety: Jesse Meador
Consent: Mary signs own consent and says she is of full age.

WOOD, John T. — Mary F. STEGAR
M.B. 6 March 1838   Surety: Francis E. H. Stegar
Note: Daughter of Thos H. Stegar who consents – Edwd Walton

WOOD, Jones — Sarah S. WRIGHT
M.B. 25 July 1836   Surety: Jno. W. Wilson
Married 10 August 1836 by Rev. John T. Watkins

WOODFIN, James — Judith HUGHES
M.B. 12 December 1829   Surety: P. H. Nunnally
Consent: Edward Hughes guardian for Judith Hughes.

WOODFIN, John — Ann S. SCRUGGS
M.B. 22 Sept. 1807   Surety: Edward Scruggs

WOODRUFF, Wilson — Frances J. GODSEY
M.B. 6 December 1836   Surety: William Godsey
Consent: 28 November 1836
Frances signs own consent and states that she is more than 21
years old.   Teste: John T. Watkins
Married 15 December 1836 by Rev. John T. Watkins

WOODSON, Booker — Elizabeth HYLTON
M.B. 7 October 1789   Surety: John Seay

WOODSON, Booker — * Betsy or Patsy STONE
M.B. 29 August 1807   Surety: M. Woodson
* Name not legible on bond.
Married 2 September 1807 by Rev. Abner Watkins

WOODSON, Charles L. — Linton G. POWELL
M.B. 19 February 1817   Surety: Tarlton Woodson
Consent: 16 February 1817
    "Chr. Woodson gives consent for license to be issued
    to Charles Woodson to intermarry with Miss Linton G.
    Powell". No relation stated. Wit: Frederick A. Woodson

WOODSON, George — Polly T. MANN
M.B. 17 January 1817   Surety: William F. Mann, Jr.
Consent: William F. Mann consents for Polly T. Mann.
       No relation stated. Teste: Patsy Robinsin

WOODSON, George B. — Sarah H. RAINE
M.B. 14 December 1814   Surety: Austin Watkins
Consent: Daughter of John Raine, Senr., who consents.

WOODSON, Henry L. — Martha V. WOODSON
M.B. 22 May 1833   Surety: Jacob G. Mosby
Consent: Jos. R. Woodson consents for his ward Martha Woodson
        daughter of Tscharner Woodson. Teste: Jacob G. Mosby
See also Cumberland County Order Book 35, page 43.

WOODSON, James B.   Gracy EDWARDS
M.B. 14 December 1813   Surety: William Edwards

WOODSON, James B.   Lockey H. McCRAW
M.B. 18 October 1818   Surety: Miller Woodson, Sr.
Consent: Lockey H. McCraw signs her own consent.

WOODSON, James G.   Minerva C. FLIPPEN
M.B. 15 October 1832   Surety: Joseph S. Palmore
Consent: Minervy signs her own consent. Wit: Lucy Ann Palmore

WOODSON, John   Anne DAVENPORT
M.B. 5 November 1772   Surety: (not stated)
Consent: Letter from her father Thomas Davenport, Jr., of
    Littleton Parish, gives consent.
        Witness: Henry Davenport - Thomas Davenport, 2nd.

WOODSON, John   Judith HUGHES
M.B. 24 November 1779   License 20/
Cumberland County Fee Book - 1779-1781

WOODSON, John   Elizabeth VENABLE
M.B. __ Oct. 17__ (mutilated)   Surety: Creed Taylor
Between 1786 and 1788
Consent: Elizabeth Venable writes own consent - illegible
Teste: Henry DeShazo   Teste: Peter Woodson

WOODSON, John   Polly B. SANDIDGE
M.B. 26 November 1804   Incomplete
Daughter of William Hobson

WOODSON, Joseph   Sarah HUGHES
Married 24 November 1779 by Rev. William Douglas
Note: Joseph Woodson of Goochland County
    Sarah Hughes of Cumberland County
Ref: Douglas Register, p. 51

WOODSON, Joseph R.   Marinda WOODSON
Married 16 May 1822 by Rev. Abner Watkins
No bond found - Minister's return

WOODSON, Joseph R.   America A. HOPKINS
M.B. 10 February 1834   Surety: Miller Woodson

WOODSON, Mathew   Elizabeth WOODSON
M.B. 16 November 1753   Surety: Jacob Woodson
Parents: Mathew Woodson   Jacob Woodson

WOODSON, Matthew   Elizabeth LeVillian
M.B. 22 November 1753   Surety: Jacob Woodson
Note: Daughter of John LeVillian who gives consent.
Teste: Samuel Branch   Teste: Thomas Porter
Married 28 November 1753 by Rev. William Douglas
Consent: See next page   See also Douglas Register, p. 51

Consent: Nov. ye 22, 1753
    "These lines are to let you know that I have given my consent to a marriage between Matthew Woodson and my daughter Elizabeth Levillian, and by seeing these lines you may grant him a license without danger".
                    From yours /s/ John Villian
   Teste: Samuel Branch   Teste: Thomas Porter

WOODSON, Patrick   Frances W. MANN
M.B. 18 October 1813   Surety: William Mann, Sr.

WOODSON, Richard O.   Susan D. A. HATCHER
M.B. 21 November 1835   Surety: John Hatcher, Jr.
Note: Daughter of Milly D. Hatcher who gives consent.
                      Teste: Obadiah R. Sanderson

WOODSON, Tucker   Mary NETHERLAND
M.B. 22 February 1762   Surety: Wade Netherland
Note: Tucker Woodson of Goochland County

WOODSON, William   Mary RICHARDSON
M.B. 2 February 1814   Surety: Maurice M. Langhorne

WOOLDRIDGE, Edmund   Elizabeth WATKINS
M.B. 22 August 1774   Surety: Sam^1 Watkins

WOOLDRIDGE, Thomas   Ann POVALL
M.B. 25 April 1774   Surety: Arthur Moseley

WRAY, Creed T.   Sally BAILEY
M.B. 23 October 1819   Surety: Matthew H. Young
Consent: 18 October 1819
    Savage Bailey writes "That Sally Bailey is at liberty to act as she will see cause". Teste: Matthew H. Young

WREN, Green L.   Mary M. JOHNS
M.B. 28 May 1834   Surety: John Daniel

WRIGHT, Archibald D.   Mary RAINE
M.B. 11 May 1813   Surety: Anderson Cocke

WRIGHT, Flemsted R.   Sintha SHARPE
M.B. 23 December 1811   Surety: Charles Roper
Consent: Sintha signs her own consent Teste: John Chrisp, Jr.

WRIGHT, Francis   Sally BAILEY
M.B. 10 January ____ Incomplete   Surety: Ja^s Bailey
Administration of Gov. William H. Cabell
           12/11/1805 - 12/12/1808

WRIGHT, Gabriel   Catherine RANSONE
M.B. 26 December 1785   Surety: Creed Taylor
Note: Daughter of Thomas Ransone who gives consent.
Teste: Henry Ransone   Patty Lee   Teste: Mildred Shapard

WRIGHT, George   Sally H. BURTON
M.B. 8 December 1815   Surety: Burwell Jeter
Consent: Felixville - 6 Dec. 1815
          N. Ford consents for his ward Sally Burton.
          Teste: Sterling Ford   Teste: Hezekiah Ford

WRIGHT, Green   Polly A. BURTON
M.B. 23 December 1808   Surety: Jno. Nunnally

WRIGHT, John Woodson   Nancy LANCASTER
M.B. (not dated)   Surety: John M. Woodson
Date - 11 December 1818 on back of bond
Consent: John Lancaster consents for his daughter
                                        Teste: William Lancaster

WRIGHT, Phineas *   Mary B. TATUM
M.B. 12 July 1833   Surety: Andrew J. Anderson
* Name on bond - Signature: Phinehas G. Wright
Consent: Mary Tatum signs own consent.   Teste: Elijah Glover

WRIGHT, Prior   Mary GLOVER
M.B. 21 March 1811   Surety: William Glover
Note: Daughter of Robert Glover, deceased.
Marriage Contract - Cum. Co. Deed Book 12, p. 387

WRIGHT, Robert   Molly MOSBY
M.B. 3 April 1775   Surety: Joseph Carrington

WRIGHT, Robert   Elizabeth CLOPTON
M.B. (not dated)   Surety: Newton Ford
Consent dated 5 June 1808
Elizabeth Clopton signs her own consent Teste: Samuel Clopton
Married 8 June 1808 by Rev. John Skurrey, Baptist Minister *
Name recorded elsewhere as John Scurrey.

WRIGHT, Samuel
                                                        Patience C. GLENN
M.B. 27 January 1794   Surety: William Glenn

WRIGHT, Saymer   Frances WILLIAMS
M.B. 11 August 1788   Surety: William Wright

WRIGHT, Thomas   Mary Ann DANIEL
M.B. 9 May 1820   Surety: James M. Daniel
Consent: Daughter of Leonard Daniel who gives consent.
Teste: B. J. Sandidge   Teste: Jesse Jeter

WRIGHT, William   Elizabeth WADE
M.B. 30 October 1785   Surety: Samuel Williams

WRIGHT, William   Elizabeth WOODSON
M.B. ___ March 1793   (mutilated)

WRIGHT, William R.   Judith A. B. MOSBY
M.B. 22 March 1830   Surety: Miller Woodson

WYLEY, Hugh   Polly HOLCOMBE
M.B. (not dated)   Surety: Phil Holcombe, Jr.
Consent dated - 7 January 1793
Polly Holcombe daughter of J. Holcombe who consents.

YANCEY, Archilus G.   Sophia FOSTER
M.B. 19 June 1832   Surety: Rowland W. Foster
Rowland W. Foster makes affidavit that Sophia Foster is of
age.

Note: Sixteen marriage records have not been included as the
      bonds are mutilated, and complete names illegible.

I N D E X E S

Index to Brides   148

Ministers   156

Index to Other Names   157

INDEX TO BRIDES

Abraham,
  Frances A. 34
Adams,
  Ann 93
  Elizabeth W. 77
  Jena 27
  Judith W. 47
  Margaret H. 101
Aiken,
  Elizabeth 29
Alderson,
  Judith 22
  T. 59
Allen,
  Anna 10
  Ann A. 110,140
  Arenatta 48
  Betty Ann 61
  E. 69
  Elizabeth 46,56,74
  Elizabeth M. 82
  Elizabeth S. 103
  Eliza W. 103
  Fanny 50
  Harriet E. 45
  Joana 13
  Julie B. 104
  Laura S. 75
  Lucy Ann 101
  Lucy Jane 25
  Martha 94
  Martha C. 16
  Martha W. 69,90
  Mary E. 113
  Mary F. 99
  Mary Jane 104
  Mary R. 37
  Mary Watson 48
  Patty Field 41
  Polly 8
  Rebeccah 117
  Sally 120
  Sally C. 141
  Sarah W. 48
Ammonette,
  Elizabeth 96
Amonette,
  Julia F. 138
Amonett,
  Mary 104
Amos,
  Frances 114
  Martha 19
  Rebecca 50
  Sally 103
Anderson,
  America M. 109
  Catharine 83
  Edith W. 56
  Elizabeth 12,36,61,97,
      123,131
  Elizabeth D. 27
  Eliza F. 138
  Fanny 8,89
  Frances 56,60,99
  Jane F.T. 102
  Judith C. 75,130
  Malinda V. 66
  Melvina 49
  Mary 31
  Mary B. 76
  Mary M. 7
  Phebe 45
  Polly 19
  Rebecca 10,98
  Rebecca E.T. 70
  Sarah 111
  Sarah J. 7
  Sarah S. 128
  Susanna 77
  Susannah 54

Andrews,
  Ann 108
Angelea,
  Sally 25
  Sarah 19
Anglea,
  Elizabeth 57
  Katy 133
  Nancy 31
  Polly 25
Apperson,
  Rebecca J. 48
  Sally 34
  Sarah Ann Thomas 25
  Sarah L. 80
Armistead,
  Ann C. 103
  Arianna Frances Jane 135
  Elizabeth 24
  Elizabeth A. 108
  Elizabeth M. 127
  Fanny 58
  Hanna 92
  Hannah H. 59
  Joana 92
  Judith 104
  Lucy A. 84
  Milley 134
  Tabertha 127
Arnold,
  Ann 9,80
  Gillea 117
  Rebecca 48
Atkinson,
  Eliza 81
  Judith 14
  Lurena 106
  Maria 115
  Mary Ann 29
  Nancy 76
Austin,
  Mary 133
  Mary Ann 62
  Polly 120
Ayres,
  Elizabeth 20

Bagby,
  Elizabeth 108
  Frances D. 39
  Judith 107
  Martha 111
  Nancy 106
Bailey,
  Mary 140
  Sally 144
Baird,
  Mary S. 92
Ballew,
  Ann 105
  Ann F. 132
Ballow,
  Elizabeth G. 52
  Judith 7
  Martha W. 22
  Sally C. 50
  Sarah H. 34
Baltimore,
  Elizabeth 78
Banks,
  Jane 97
Bantam,
  Sally 114
Barker,
  Ann 45
  Elizabeth 136
  Mary 36
  Rebecca 32
  Sally 32
Barnes,
  Mary 39,94

Barnett,
  Evaline 37
Barrett,
  Betsy
Bartee,
  Ann 86
Bartlett,
  Mary Ann 82
Baskerville,
  Polly 61
Bassett,
  Hellender 53
Bates,
  Sally 15
Battersby,
  Chloe 16
Baughan,
  Betsy 70
  Mary 111
  Mary W. 68
  Prudence 51
Beaver,
  Mary T. 123
Bedford,
  Sarah 95
Bellamy,
  Ellenor 20
  Sarah Miller 118
Bennett,
  Sarah 82
Berry,
  Elizabeth 79
  Julia 64
  Lucinda 46
Bilbo,
  Mary 117
Birch,
  Susan 114
Bird,
  Rebecca 61
  Susanna 98
Blackwelder,
  Margaret 138
Blackwell,
  Julia Ann 32
Blain,
  Hannah M. 46
Blake,
  Mary Ann 37
Blake,
  Sarah 38
Blanton,
  Elizabeth 133
  Eliza 62
  Eliza W. 104
  Judith 13,31
  Julia E. 19
  Martha 19
  Mary 104
  Mary Frances 109
  Mary Frances A. 132
  Mary W. 132
  Rebecca B. 29
  Sarah A.E. 62
Boatright,
  Anne 112
  Elizabeth 86
  Lucy 92
  Mary 23
Boatwright,
  Miss ___ 32
  Ann B. 23
  Anne 122
  Catharine A. 116
  Druscillah 118
  Eliza A. 130
  Jane 57,67
  Judith 87
  Lockey 122
  Mary 76
  Sally 21

Boles,
    Sarah 59
Bond,
    Ann 136
    Jane 69
Bondurant,
    Polly L. 80
    Nancy 124
    Sarah 67
Booker,
    Elizabeth 67
    Grace 39
    Harriet 52
    Martha J. 70
    Mary 75
    Polly 37
    Sally 53
Booth,
    Elizabeth 78
Bosher,
    Artimisia 43
    Elizabeth 119
    Frances 98
    Maria S. 101
Bowler,
    Mary L. 117
Bowles,
    Elizabeth 86,141
    Hannah 86
    Martha 94
Boyd,
    Mary 8
Bracher,
    Mary M. 123
Brackett,
    Louisa 66
    Martha H. 32
Bradberry,
    Priscilla 57
Bradley,
    Delila 71
    Elizabeth R. 11
    Elizabeth S. 45
    Frances 103
    Harriett 90
    Liszea 92
    Martha 115
    Martha A. 14
    Mary 26
    Mary M. 89
    Patsy 110
    Rachel 45
    Sally 39
    Susan R. 105
Bransford,
    Betsy 73
    Jane G. 59
    Judith 54
    Judith M. 52
    Judith Maria 98
    Martha 63
    Martha G. 39
    Mary 102,137
    Sarah M. 23
    Susanna H. 16
    Virginia 131
Brooke,
    Catherine 54
Brown,
    Agnes 85
    Elizabeth 45,74,77
    Finetta R. 46
    Frankey 111
    Julia 119
    Keturah 87
    Magary 26
    Mahala 128
    Martha 89
    Martha Jane 110
    Mary 12,79,130
Brown,
    Mary A. 109
    Mary Ann 45,132

Brown, cont'd
    Nancy 51
    Nancy B. 27
    Patsy 46,101,120
    Perlina 19
    Polly 37
    Rhoda 15
    Sally 97
    Sarah 27,140
    Susanna 57
    Temperance 37,134
Bryan,
    Elizabeth 112
Bryant,
    Mary A. 21
    Nancy 11
    Sally 107
    Susan 12
Buckston,
    Sarah 32
Bulloch,
    Minerva 15
Burch,
    Eliza 120
    Mary 113
Burner,
    Elizabeth 52
Burton,
    Ann Branch 109
    Harriet 102
    Mary 9,28
    Polly A. 145
    Sally H. 145
    Susanna 41,90

Caldwell,
    Jane 101
Cannon,
    Francinia 38
Carr,
    Eliza 26
Carrington,
    Chloe 88
    Clementina M. 132
    Elizabeth A. 18
    Elizabeth H. 64
    Ellen S. 24
    Hannah 29
    Harriet P. 88
    Henningham 18
    Louisa Ann 21
    Lucy V. 106
    Martha A. 29
    Mary Ann 29
    Nancy 12
    Sophonesba A. 106
    Susanna M. 28
Carter,
    Ann 85
    Cynthia 73
    Elizabeth 17,100
    Elizabeth A. 58
    Elizabeth M. 71
    Judith 30,81
    Judy 101
    Julia A. 109
    Mary 73
    Mary Ann 62
    Nancy 38
    Sarah M. 129
    Susan 127
Cary,
    Eliza F. 91
Castley,
    Kitty 81
Cayce,
    Elizabeth 121
    Nancy 43
    Rhoda 9
    Sarah 40
Charlton,
    Frances 12
    Nancy 11
    Susanna 112

Chastain,
    Judith 114
    Magdalene 105
    Mary 141
Cheatam,
    Thursa 75
Chenault,
    Emeline 136
    Jenetta 98
Cheshire,
    Polly 45
Childress,
    Elizabeth 140
    Nanny 9
Chrisp,
    Emaline 138
    Martha Ann Jane Taylor 47
    Martha J. 80
    Mary 84
    Nancy 20
Christopher,
    Luritta 88
Clarke,
    Elizabeth Ann 115
    Nancy 95
    Polly 84
Clay,
    Hannah 127
    Lucy 127
Clopton,
    Elizabeth 145
Cocke,
    Lucy E. 126
    Mary 11
Coleman,
    Amanda 106
    Ann 58
    Elizabeth 8,35
    Ellener T. 37
    Grisel 47
    Lucy 58
    Martha M. 15
    Mary 117
    Mary D. 8
    Mary Ligon 18
    Milly Wilson 49
    Orana 35
    Sally 34
    Sarah 62,132
    Virginia 136
Colley,
    Judith 104
    Julia A.E. 75
    Martha Jane 51
    Sarah H. 47
Colquitt,
    Catharine 39
    Nancy 38
    Polly 128
    Sarah 60
Coocke,
    Ann 35
Cooke,
    Amanda 100
    Keziah 108
    Mary C. 141
Cooper,
    Anna 9
    Eliza 43
    Elizabeth 66
    Nancy 109
    Polly 32
    Rebecca 91
Corley,
    Betsy 46
    Gilly 20
    Sarah 26
Corson,
    Elizabeth 85
Coupland,
    Nancy H. 81
    Susanna 34
Cousins,
    Nancy 97

Cox,
　Catherine A. 69
　Eliza G. 35
　Frances 47
　Jane 70
　Judith 117,125
　Martha 67,106
　Nancy 76
　Obedience 121
　Tabitha 119
Creasy,
　Martha 94
Crews,
　Ann 122
Criddle,
　Elizabeth M. 111
　Mary 96
Crisp,
　Elizabeth 20
Crison,
　Catharine 21
Crow,
　Elinor 59
Cullinge,
　Mary J. 69
Cunningham,
　Eliza M. 64
　Letitia 126
　Lucy 130
Curtis,
　Martha 129

Dagnell,
　Rhody 69
Daniel,
　Elizabeth 35,103
　Eliza M. 50
　Jane 124
　Lucy M. 92
　Martha 139
　Mary Ann 145
　Polly 121
　Sarah J. 133
　Sarah S. 93
　Susan 101
　Susannah 18
Davenport,
　Anne 143
　Ann F. 81
　Dorothea 44
　Drusilla 43
　Elizabeth 85
　Elizabeth M. 60
　Elizabeth Smith 16
　Frances H. 116
　Hannah G. 77
　Louisa Anne 36
　Mary 44
　Nancy G. 67
　Patty 132
　Rebecca 36
　Susannah 78
David,
　Ann 46
Davidson,
　Judith 103
　Nancy 127
　Polly 114
Davis,
　_____ 111
　Betsy 10
　Eliza 22
　Hannah 61
　Maria 87
　Martha Ann 42
　Mary Ann 11
　Sally 61
　Sarah 30,107
Deane,
　Ann W. 68
　Elizabeth H. 73
　Eliza Sumner 130
　Jane Browne 100
　Mary J. 74

Deppe,
　Eleanor 76
DePee,
　Susannah 82
Dicken,
　Susanna 132
Dickerson,
　Agnes 31
　Fanny 31
　Mildridge 16
Diuguid,
　Anne 63
Dodson,
　Elizabeth A. 78
Donahoe,
　Elizabeth 98
Donnell,
　Mary 104
Doss,
　Elizabeth 20
　Judith 28
　Nancy 43
　Patsy 18
Douglas,
　Anne 124
Dowdy,
　Amanda C. 110
　Elizabeth 116
　Elizabeth M. 9
　Harriot 64
　Jane 14
　Lavinia 34
　Mahala C. 93
　Nancy 10,50
　Patsy 72
　Polly 119
　Polly Ann 126
　Rebeccah 136
　Sally 117
Draper,
　Maria L. 80
Duncombe,
　Nancy 19
Duncan,
　Rebeccah 56
Duncum,
　Jane 102
Dunkum,
　Eliza 53
　Frances J. 59
　Jane 114
　Joanna 93
　Julia Ann 136
　Mary 98,141
　Phebe 110
　Sally 45
Dunnavant,
　Elizabeth 106
　Emily 44
Dupuy,
　Elizabeth 14
Durham,
　Elizabeth 77
　Frances 70
　Sally 12
　Sarah 136
　Susan 51
Duskins,
　Mary 26
Dutoy,
　Mary Ann 60

Edwards,
　Ann 81
　Elizabeth 93
　Gracy 143
　Judith 47
　Lucy C. 34
　Martha 38
　Mary F. 57
　Nancy 35,54
　Polly K. 65

Eggleston,
　Anne 134
　Elizabeth 47
　H. Rebecca 107
　Maria L. 115
　Sarah W. 104
Elam,
　Ann 59
Ellison,
　Edey 137
　Judy 78
Ellyson,
　Elizabeth 47
England,
　Anne 45
　Eliza J. 61
　Mary 94
　Mary H. 111
Eppes,
　Sarah 79
Evans,
　Elizabeth 63

Falwell,
　Elizabeth 53
　Fanny 52
Faris,
　Elizabeth 120
　Frances 86
　Mary 29
　Myrie 16
　Sally 79
　Sarah 82
Farley,
　Elizabeth 120
Farmer,
　Edith 67
　Ellen 106
　Phebe 85
　Sarah G. 127,128
Fariss,
　Nancy 120
　Rebecca 50
Farriss,
　Elizabeth R. 63
Faulkner,
　Jane 55
　Martha G. 13
Fawwell,
　Sally 117
Ferguson,
　Jane 110
　Mary A.M. 16
Fleming,
　Mary 18
Flippen,
　Amanda 27
　Arrina 21
　Elizabeth 52
　Eliza 70
　Fanny 62
　Jane 17,122
　Julian 56
　Lucinda B. 65
　Maria C. 54
　Martha 140
　Mary 43,90
　Mary B. 54
　Mary M. 65
　Minerva 143
　Nancy 41
　Nancy A. 39
　Patsy 17
　Patty 76
　Polly 123
　Polly Scott 94
　Sabra 45
Flournoy,
　Ursely 63
Ford,
　Elizabeth 50
　Eliza 62
　Judith 79
　Louisa 126

Ford, cont'd
  Mary 55
Fore,
  Elizabeth 38
Forsee,
  Judith 19
  Mary Ann 87
Foster,
  Lucy 103
  Melinder 128
  Mildred 112
  Sophia 146
Fourqueran,
  Elizabeth 121
Fowler,
  Agnes 132
  Ann B. 129
  Anne 53
  Jane 31
  Mariah 35
  Mary D. 58
  Prudence 31
Francisco,
  Polly 8
Frayser,
  Eliza W. 42
  Julia Ann 141
  Mary L. 23
  Melissa M. 14
  Nancy M. 114
Fretwell,
  Mary 29
  Susannah 21
Fritter,
  Jane 28
Fulcher,
  Mary Ann L. 41
Fuqua,
  Judith 79
  Martha C. 138
Furcran,
  Betty 87

Gaines,
  Martha Ward 130
  Mary 51
  Polly 13
Gaines,
  Catey 12
Galloway,
  Sally B. 53
Ganby,
  Nancy 65
Gannaway,
  Mary 139
Garrett,
  Fanny 75
  Magdalene 119
  Sabrine 66
  Selender Frances 42
  Sophia T. 80
Gauldin,
  Elizabeth 98
  Frances 66
  Mary B. 115
Gaulding,
  Polly 28
Gay,
  Elizabeth 18
George,
  Elizabeth 133
Ghee,
  Gazelle 47
Gilliam,
  Elizabeth 43
  Judith 126
  Patsy 30
Gills,
  Judith B. 56
Glenn,
  Ann 53
  Frances H. 25
  Gracy 84
  Patience C. 145

Glover,
  Ann 138
  Delphia B. 71
  Mary 93,145
  Mary B. 126
Godsey,
  Elizabeth R. 135
  Frances J. 142
  Lydia 66
  Nancy 26
  Rebecca 13
Goode,
  Elizabeth 135
  Martha 16
Goodman,
  Elizabeth Ann 60
  Eliza A. 59
  Eliza H. 68
  Jane Frances 141
  Louisa A. 121
  Martha 59
  Martha Ann 61
  Martha J. 27
  Mary A. 51
  Sarah J. 41
Gordon,
  Caroline 8
  Dorothy 94
  Martha G. 75
  Patience Turner 69
  Polly T. 66
Gouff,
  Presilla 117
Griffin,
  Nancy 50
Guerrant,
  Betsy 41
  Elizabeth 121,134
  Jane 29
  Magdalene 95
Guthrey,
        87
  Ann 136
  Jane 14
  Magdaline J. 134
  Martha P. 108
  Nancy 35
  Rebecca 55
  Sally 12,22,80
  Sally C. 11
Guthrie,
  Philadelphia 48

Haistie,
  Mary 118
Hambleton,
  Ann 29, 128
  Betsy 75
  Elizabeth 54
  Julia 62
  Sally 32
Hampton,
  Sarah 124
Harris,
  Alice 59
  Ann 38,49
  Elizabeth 71,132
  Eliza P. 13
  Hinson Wager 95
  Lucy A. 20
  Martha Ann 64
  Mary 74,85,130
  Nanny 38
  Phebe 51,63,92
  Rebecca H. 52
  Sarah 54,86,123
  Sarah H. 126
  Sary 130
  Susanna 138
Harrison,
  Anne 8
  Betty 24
  Catherine L. 84
  Elizabeth 139

Harrison, cont'd
  Eliza R. 131
  Jane C. 108
  Lucia C. 100
  Mary 64,121
  Rebecca 18
  Susan J. 19
  Williana M. 73
Haskins,
  Martha C. 44
  Phebe 64
  Rebekah 17
Hatcher,
  Agnes 134
  Elizabeth 54
  Judith 34
  Lucy 25
  Martha Ann 106
  Mary M. 51
  May Gay 30
  Nancy 55,60
  Phebe 85
  Polly 26
  Sally W. 68
  Sarah 25
  Sukey 59
  Susan D.A. 144
  Susannah 68
Hawkins,
  Elizabeth 51
  Lucy 25
  Molly 79
Hazlegrove,
  Charlotte Lotey 10
  Harriet 104
  Salinah 48
Henderson,
  Martha E. 100
Hendrick,
  Elizabeth 33,36
  Frances H. 41
  Jane 110
  Jemima 24
  Martha 49
  Martha Ann 57
  Sally 30
Henson,
  Lucinda 127
Hicks,
  Catherine 123
Hill,
  Joanna 7
  Sarah H. 126
Hix,
  Elizabeth 38
  Lavinia 78
  Martha A. 48
  Mary A.E. 102
  Paulina 120
  Sarah Jane 103
Hobson,
  Ann 33
  Elizabeth 41,111
  Elizabeth A. 101
  Elizabeth Maria 68
  Eliza G. 51
  Eliza L. 130
  Jane H. 55
  Judith 36
  Judith H. 55
  Lucy 22
  Lucy L. 97
  Martha H. 53
  Nancy 33
  Polly S. 117
  Sally 67,78
  Sarah 21
  Sarah A. L. 51
Holcombe,
  Polly 146
Holeman,
  Elizabeth 25
  Jane 87

Holland,
    Mary 10
Holloway,
    Elizabeth 67
    Martha 71
Holman,
    Mary G. 116
    Nancy 83
    Sarah 86
    Sarah Y. 140
    Susanna 116
Holt,
    Elizabeth 113
    Judith 90
    Lucy 115
    Nancy 85
    Pamelia 38
    Polly 43
    Tabitha 82
Hopkins,
    America A. 143
Hopson,
    Jane 72
Howard,
    Ann E. 49
    Jane C. 49
    Joanna 103
    Mary W. 17
    Rebekah 63
Hubbard,
    Anny 10
    Susanna 36
Hudgins,
    Catherine 23
    Charity 35
    Delilah 36
    Delphia B. 27
    Jane 43
    Jane D. 133
    Jenny 23
    Martha J. 15
    Mary 23,142
    Nancy 83
    Phebe 96
Hudson,
    Dianna 60
    Mary 94
    Rebecca 133
Hudspeth,
    Tabitha 105
Hughes,
    Elizabeth 104,107
    Frances 138
    Jane 36
    Judith 93,142,143
    Martha 133
    Sarah 143
    Susanna 105
    Temperance 135
Hutchardson,
    Nancy 11
Hutchinson,
    Eliza Ann 32
Hylton,
    Elizabeth 142

Irving,
    Mary Jane 128
Isbell,
    Anna 123
    Elenor B. 73
    Jane 81
    Martha 140
    Mary 79

Jackson,
    Sarah 17
James,
    Elizabeth 119
    Martha 33,77
    Mary L. 131
    Phebe 90

Jellis,
    Catharine 37
    Jane Maria 78
Jenkins,
    Ann 11
    Betsy 94
    Elizabeth Ann 50
    Jane 73
    Jane W. 10
    Judy 88
    Lucy 72
    Mary Mosby 71
    Nancy 44
    Polly 92
    Susan 88
Jennings,
    Mary 56
    Uphan 68
Johns,
    Anne D. 96
    Elizabeth 9
    Eliza 15
    Lucy Ann 44
    Martha 75
    Mary M. 144
Johnson,
    Ann R. 30
    Delilah 28
    Elizabeth 17,70
    Mahala 117
    Martha 7,13,129
    Nancy 78,129
    Nancy M. 66
    Polly 59
    Rebecca 45,46,133
    Sarah 131
Jo-ley,
    Nancy 32
Jones,
    Ann C. 78
    Ava 125
    Clarkey 129
    Elizabeth 12,121
    Louisa 30
    Mary 39
    Sally 26
    Sally M. 122
    Susan A. 140
Jordan,
    Elizabeth T. 76
    Elizabeth W. 97
    Harriet L. 126

Keeling,
    Elizabeth 43
    Sarah 12
Kerr,
    Mary D. 105

Lambert,
    Martha 17
Lancaster,
    Ann 7
    Elizabeth 37
    Judith B. 58
    Nancy 145
Langhorne,
    Elvira 47
    Judith 68
    Mary D. 106
    Polly 68
    Sarah 64
Leaker,
    Susanna 60
Lee,
    Ann 64,89
    Ann N. 23
    Chuziah 38
    Elizabeth G. 129
    Lucy W. 56
    Mildred D. 13
    Patty 13
    Polly 139
    Susannah 43

LeSueur,
    Catherine 128
    Elizabeth 116
LeVillian,
    Elizabeth 143
Lewis,
    Ann E. 24
    Emeline M. 77
    Sarah M. 95
    Susan M. 103
Ligon,
    Judith 125
    Mary 84
Lipford,
    Ann 106
    Catharine P. 100
    Elizabeth 100
    Mary 40
    Prudence 107
Lockett,
    Fanny 62
    Lucy 123
Lookado,
    Rebecca 128
Lyle,
    Harriott S. 53
    Rebecca F. 62
Lyles,
    Mary 84
Lynch,
    Adelina 22
    Margaret 54

McCormack,
    Lucy 24
McCraw,
    Lockey H. 143
McGehee,
    Ann 94
McGinnis,
    Elizabeth 75
McLaurine,
    Elizabeth M. 124
    Martha 74
    Mary V. 122
    Nancy 70
    Polly 95
    Sarah 56
    Virginia J. 94
Macon,
    Ann P. 39
    Rebecca M. 109
    Sally W. 125
Maddox,
    Nancy C. 108
    Polly E. 120
    Sally 79
Mann,
    Elizabeth 102
    Elizabeth B. 69
    Frances 94
    Frances W. 144
    Jane 74
    Polly T. 142
    Sally F. 133
Markham,
    Mila 127
    Sarah 36
Marshall,
    Tabitha 138
Martin,
    Anne C. 61
    Elizabeth 86
    Jane 20, 132
    Martha 44
    Mary 52
    Nancy 44
    Polly 60
    Rebecca 52
    Rhoda 99
    Sarah 41,88

Mason,
  Ann 29
  Mary 83
Matthews,
  Martha P. 39
  Mary H. 107
  Nancy 119
  Susan 9
Mattox,
  Mary J. 27
Maxey,
  Elizabeth A. 61
  Jemima 112
  Kerenhappuck 112
  Keziah 49
  Mary 42
Mayes,
  Delilah 135
  Elizabeth 58
Mayo,
  Betsy 75
  Catharine 120
  Eliza 88
  Harriet 88
  Judith 82
  Lucy 17
  Maria L. 88
  Martha T. 17
  Mary P. 60
  Rebecca 88
  Rebecca G. 115
  Susan 30
  Synthia 82
Meador,
  Delilah 59
  Frances 85
  Frances Ann 14
  Harriet P. 95
  Judith J. 98
  Martha 111
  Mary H. 42
  Nancy 23,71
  Rhoda 89
  Sally 115
  Susanna 17
Meginnis,
  Nancy 45
  Polly 23
Melton,
  Elizabeth 99
  Elizabeth R. 99
  Polly 7
  Polly K. 131
  Polly W. 50
  Rhoda 96
Melville,
  Mary 103
Meredith,
  Judith A. 141
  Magdaline J. 135
  Martha 33
  Martha W. 10
  Nancy S. 135
Merryman,
  Agnes 28
  Catherine C. 89
  Elizabeth 69,95
  Frances 122
  Jane 14
  Judith 36
  Julia Ann 132
  Lockey 23
  Lucy F. 52
  Martha 72
  Martha S. 97
  Mary 127
  Mary V. 109
  Nancy 31
  Patsy 79
  Polly 76
  Sarah 119
  Sarah H. 113
  Susan 90

Michaux,
  Arabella B. 57
  Elizabeth 34
  Henrietta Rochet 131
  Judith 54,66
  Judith E. 18
  Martha L. 137
  Sally 131
Milam,
  Grace 32
Miller,
  Betsy A.S. 75
  Catharine J. 40
  Mary A. 19
Minter,
  Agnes 11
  Anne 73
  Frances 24
  Mary 99
  Molly 115
  Sally 27
  Sarah 125
Minton,
  Elizabeth 115
Mitchell,
  Elizabeth C. 113
  Martha A.W. 73
Moracet,
  Judith 60
Moreland,
  Catharine 33
  Elizabeth 122
Montague,
  Catherine 119
  Cynthia 27
  Elizabeth 31
  Jane 14
  Martha 79
  Mary 93
  Matilda 135
  Polly D. 73
Montgomery,
  Elizabeth A. 20
  Harriet 62
  Lucy Ann 34
  Nancy W. 99
  Polly 20
Morgan,
  Agnes 34,121
  Elizabeth 92
  Lucy 99
Morris,
  Emily 71
Morrow,
  Elizabeth 37
  Elizabeth S.M. 65
Morton,
  Ann 83
  Betsy 68
  Martha 83
  Mary 110
Mosby,
  Elizabeth 95
  Hannah 15
  Judith A.B. 145
  Madeline 70
  Mary 69
  Mary Ann --
  Molly 72,145
  Sarah 76
Moseby,
  Hannah 47
  Nancy 58
Moseley,
  Elizabeth 112
  Martha 123
  Sary 127
Moss,
  Ann 99
  Judith 26
  Tabitha 116,123
Munford,
  Mary 68

Murray,
  Drusilla S. 125
  Elizabeth 15,104
  Eliza 72
  Jane 136
  Martha 104
  Mary 72
  Nancy 15
  Rebecca 134
Nance,
  Amanda 109
Nash,
  Lucy L. 55
Nelson,
  Dorothy 72
  Julia B. 105
  Mary 135
  Polly 55
Netherland,
  Ann 17
  Frances 30,84
  Mary 144
Nevils,
  Sally 91
Newton,
  Drucilla 107
  Martha 114
  Nancy 128
Noel,
  Polly 57
Noell,
  Elizabeth 48
Norris,
  Ann 61
  Betsy 74
  Polly 87
  Susanna 123
North,
  Martha 98
  Polly 102
Nowel,
  Nancy 57
Nunnally,
  Eliza 122
  Permaly J. 16

Oakley,
  Elizabeth 75
  Martha 7,140
  Mary 89
Oglesby,
  Ann 86
Oliver,
  Judith 60
  Maria 32
  Mary 33
Orange,
  Betsy P. 67
  Edith 50
  Lucy F. 86
Orslin,
  Mary 12
Osborne,
  Judith 11
  Lucy 84
  Nancy 126
  Phebe A. 140
  Polly 137
Oslin,
  Nancy 21
Overton,
  Maria W. 28

Page,
  Lavinia A. 51
  Lucy Jane 40
  Mary Cary 84
  Mary M. 40
  Virginia R. 68
Palmore,
  Adaline E. 81
  Diannah 101

Palmore, cont'd
  Elizabeth A. 33
  Jane C. 27
  Judith 97
  Manerva C. 52
  Nancy 18,72
  Polly 12,26
  Sally P. 66
  Sarah 112
Pankie,
  Elizabeth 71
Pankey,
  Car-line M.A. 70
  Elizabeth K. 114
  Nancy B. 101
  Polly Y. 48
Parker,
  Harriet E. 89
  Jane Ann 120
  Mary Ann 75
  Susan A. 89
  Susanna C. 27
  Susannah 85
Parrish,
  Elizabeth 114
Patterson,
  Nanny 91
Payne,
  Ann 116
  Elizabeth 121
  Elizabeth B. 133
  Mary A. 88
Pearce,
  Martha 49
  Phebe 31
  Sarah G. 10
  Susanna 80
Peasley,
  Lucy 42
  Mary 127
Penick,
  Martha 51
  Mary A. 42
Perrue,
  Mary 56
Phaup,
  Elizabeth F. 94
  Mary G. 77
Phelps,
  Peggy 134
Phillip,
  Mary 53
Phillips,
  Eliza 35
  Lucy Ann 66
  Martha J. 9
  Mary 48,137
  Patsy 102
  Polly A. 58
  Sarah H. 67
Pickett,
  Hannah 137
Pollard,
  Julia 134
  Lucy 93
Pollock,
  Hannah 73
Porter,
  Ann 113
  Elizabeth 25
  Mary 16,60
  Sarah 65
Povall,
  Ann 144
  Betty 81
  Lucy 72
  Mary 95
  Patty 95
  Rachel 33
  Sarah 68
Powell,
  Linton G. 142
  Nesbit Ann 110

Powers,
  Anne 33
  Judith 96
Price,
  Ailsey 99
  Amelia M. 21
  Ann 128
  Betsy 121
  Catharine 109
  Hannah 13
  Mary D. 129
  Phebe 81
  Polly 42,135
  Sally 101
  Sophia W. 119
  Susanna 110
Pryor,
  Frankey 53

Qualls,
  Elizabeth 112
Quarles,
  Matilda 42
  Rebecca 42

Radford,
  Agnes 21
  Susanna 49
Raiborne,
  Polly 137
Railey,
  Mary 32
Raine,
  Mary 144
  Sarah H. 142
Randolph,
  Ann 105
  Ann C. 77
  Elizabeth 108
  Harriet 61
  Susannah 64
Ransone,
  Ann 93
  Catherine 144
  Jane 16
  Lucy 41
  Martha 35
  Sarah P. 79
Reynolds,
  Elizabeth B. 113
  Frances 72
Rice,
  Mary 115
Richardson,
  Elcy 46
  Elizabeth 113
  Frances 74,135
  Lucy A. 133
  Mary 89,144
  Polly 120
Riddle,
  Elizabeth 123
Ridgway,
  Ann 92
Robertson,
  Catherine 39
  Elizabeth 69
  Judith 24
  Lucy 89
  Mary 47
  Mildred 40
  Norvell 125
  Obedience 89
  Sarah 21
Robinson,
  Elizabeth 82
  Elvira Ann 39
  Frances 131
  Judith 96
  Lockey L. 83
  Martha 131
  Milly 85
  Nancy 9,24

Robinson, cont'd
  Polly 89
  Sally 111,112
  Susanna 136
  Tabitha 22
Rodgers,
  Susanna 20
Rogers,
  Mary 18,94
  Nancy 118
Ross,
  Amanda Ann 44
Rowton,
  Mary Price 24
  Sally 118
Russell,
  Dinah 124
  Sally 76
  Terecy 127
Rye,
  Polly 24
  Sally 141

Salle,
  Mary 129
Sammons,
  Pasey 46
Sandefur,
  Frances 118
Sanders,
  Elizabeth F. 19
  Hannah A. 80
  Sarah L. 69
  Susan 8
Sanderson,
  Elizabeth Jane 11
  Elizabeth R. 113
  Eliza Ann 61
  Jane B.B. 124
  Maria B. 75
  Sally Ann 113
  Sally I. 26
  Sarah D. 116
Sandidge,
  Polly B. 143
Sasseen,
  Olive 116
Saunders,
  Judith 139
Scott,
  Ann 87,105
  Frances 129
  Judith 29
  Nancy 44
Scruggs,
  Ann 67,93
  Ann S. 142
  Elizabeth 63,90,137
  Elizabeth E. 62
  Jane T. 103
  Judith Ann 102
  Judith R. 55
  Keziah 111
  Lucy 114
  Mariah C. 8
  Martha 92
  Martha G. 11
  Mary 14
  Mary B. 115
  Molly 67
  Phebe 110
  Polly 107
  Sally C. 70
Seay,
  America 91
  Ann 139
  Frances A. 129
  Mary 118
  Phebe 110
  Sarah 118
Self,
  Frances Anne 108
  Sally Clough 15
  Susanna 118

Sharpe,
  Frances 98
  Sintha 144
Shepard,
  Mildred 138
Shepherd,
  Martha T. 118
Shelton,
  Elizabeth 44,84
Shields,
  Ann H.W. 90
  Judith C. 90
Shuffield,
  Sarah 47
Simpson,
  Elizabeth 80
  Nancy 9
Sims,
  Franky 132
  Judith 63
  Molly 112
  Nancy 63
  Polly Coleman 122
  Susanna 50
Slaughter,
  Sarah 9
Smith,
  Adaline 93
  Ann 85
  Arnah 42
  Ava 44
  Caroline E. 21
  Caty 59
  Elizabeth 28,105
  Elvira 64
  Jenny 114
  Maria 101
  Martha 43,117
  Mary 83,98
  Mary G. 68
  Nancy 67
  Nancy P. 22
  Sally 8,119,137
  Sarah 55
  Suky 137
Snoddy,
  Frances R. 15
  Mary A. 71
Southall,
  Elizabeth 86
  Hannah T. 71
  Kitty 130
  Mariah 90
  Polly 73
Spalden,
  Susannah 82
Spalding,
  Sarah 15
Spears,
  Elizabeth 116
  Emaline 138
  Hardenia A. 18
  Polly 40,53
  Sally 120
  Susan M.A. 65
Spencer,
  Jemima C. 58
  Judith E. 40
Stamps,
  Mary 72
Starkey,
  Judith 130
Stegar,
  Elizabeth 41,85
  Elizabeth W. 116
  Elmina H. 73
  Keturah King Mariana 117
  Martha 49
  Mary F. 142
  Phebe A. 141
  Susana C. 119
Stern,
  Susanna 137

Stevenson,
  Janet 16,122
Stinson,
  Mary 135
Stokes,
  Mary T. 66
  Susan T. 91
Stone,
  Elizabeth 77
  Patsy 142
Stoner,
  Jane 96
Stratton,
  Ann N. 29
  Jane 31
  Martha J. 82
  Mary 41,115
  Nancy 124
Street,
  Drucilla 124
  Martha C. 92
  Polly 124
Sutphin,
  Altzera B. 69
  Mary 65
Swann,
  Jane E. 124
  Mary 128
  Mary B. 70
Sweeny,
  Frances 114
Swilley,
  Ann 46

Tabb,
  Margaret 133
  Mary 26
Talley,
  Eliza 105
  Nancy 111
  Permely 126
  Rosamond C. 98
  Sally M. 22
  Sarah 89
Tally,
  Frances S. 10
  Milly 65
Tanner,
  Emaline E. 93
  Frances A. 14
Tatum,
  Mary B. 145
  Mary Jane 71
Taylor,
  Ann Jane 77
  Demaris 76
  Elizabeth 79
  Jane 63
  Maria A. 34
  Mary 50
  Mary Anne Jane 57
  Missouri 14
  Patsy 21
  Phaney 39
  Nancy 51
Terrell,
  Mary 82
Thacker,
  Elizabeth 7
Thomas,
  Ann 86
  Elizabeth 40,82
  Jane 22
  Nancy 120
  Sally 20
  Sophia 102
Thompson,
  Jane 23
  Martha 119
  Mary E. 42
  Mary Marshall 135
  Rebecca 134
  Rhoda 73,134
  Sarah 104

Thornton,
  Catharine 85
  C.C. 53
  Sarah A. 29
Tiller,
  Nancy 107
Toler,
  Martha R. 100
  Nancy E. 129
  Sarah C. 30
  Selinder 76
  Susanna 56
Toney,
  Elizabeth 87
  Mary 33
Tourman,
  Frances 57
Trabue,
  Caroline 118
Trent,
  Anne 110
  Ann H. 97
  Betsy 140
  Elizabeth A. 125
  Elizabeth W. 139
  Frances 57
  Marianna F. 100
  Martha 52
  Priscilla 139
  Sally W. 13
Tschefeli,
  Sally 60
Tschiffly,
  Anna Barbara 121
Turpin,
  Elizabeth 74
  Lucy 97
  Mary 74
  Mary J. 119
  Obedience 63
Tyree,
  Catharine 129
  Catherine T. 91
  Patsy 130

Vaughan,
  Judith 37
Vaughn,
  Ann E. 108
Vawter,
  Mary 64
Venable,
  Elizabeth 143
Wade,
  Elizabeth 145
  Stiry 99
Wager,
  Priscilla 62
Walden,
  Elizabeth 86
  Sarah 22
Walker,
  Ann 18
  Drucilla 56
  Elizabeth A.S. 91
  Lucy 80
  Martha 103
  Martha Ann 108
  Mary Ann 67
  Nancy 19,23
  Rebecca B. 20
  Sarah 63,87,137
  Susanna S. 19
  Virginia 84
Waller,
  Sally 38
Walthall,
  Frances K. 83
Walton,
  Agnes 52
  Elizabeth 91,134
  Elizabeth M. 102

Walton, cont'd
  Fanny 101
  Jane W.S. 67
  Lucy 55
  Martha 21,28
  Mary 140
  Mary H. 135
  Mary S. 47
  Mildred A. 14
  Nancy 73
  Nancy L.H. 26
  Patty 95
  Polly 96
  Sarah W. 115
  Susan 7
Ward,
  Patsy 81,90,137
Warriner,
  Elvira 116
Watkins,
  Ann Jane 40
  Elizabeth 31,82,144
  Maria L. 65
  Mary 96
  Mary Jane 84
  Phebe 135
  Sarah 105
  Susanna 33
Watson,
  Judith 97
  Mary 134
Weaver,
  Mary 44,76
  Sarah 31
Webber,
  Elizabeth 48
  Nancy 97
  Sarah 53
Webster,
  Mary S. 11
Wheeler,
  Elizabeth 71
  Fanny 35
  Jane 50
  Nancy 137
  Sally 99
  Sally C. 62
White,
  Polly 32,99
  Sarah 35
Whitehead,
  Jedidah 81
  Sally 136
Whitlow,
  Sally 99
Wilkerson,
  Mary 114
Wilkinson,
  Caroline M. 49
  P. Mary 131
  Willian 79
Willard,
  Martha C. 109
Williams,
  Elvira W. 96
  Frances 145
  Keziah 43
  Polly 107
Williamson,
  Phebe 38
Willmore,
  Judith 91
Wilson,
  Ann A. 22
  Maria 139
  Maria A. 130
  Martha 7
  Mary E. 139
  Nancy H. 106
  Sally 7
Winfree,
  Elizabeth 50
  Frances 15

Winfree, cont'd
  Frankey 111
  Mary 23
  Susan J. 70
Winfrey,
  Elizabeth 89
Winger,
  Jenny 30
Womack,
  Anne 52
  Betsy 88
  Eliza C. 80
  Judith 33
  Martha J. 91
  Sally P. 46
Wood,
  Edith 113
  Elizabeth 46,83
  Frances 130
  Lucy 19,48
  Polly 13,83
  Sally Ann 96
Woodfin,
  Mary A. 141
  Nancy 72
Woodruff,
  Molly 36
Woodson,
  Anne 83
  Anne F. 22
  Anne S. 52
  Apphia C. 95
  Charity 28
  Elizabeth 58,78,143,145
  Eliza 108
  Jemima G. 40
  Judith 56,76,77
  Lockey H. 108
  Lucy 92
  Lucy A.M. 126
  Lucy Ann 125
  Marinda 143
  Martha 55
  Martha V. 142
  Mary 80,84,136
  Mary Ann 125
  Mary Ann Elizabeth
     Miller 91
  Mary D. 124
  Mary H. 106
  Mary J. 40
  Nancy 78,81
  Polly 56,78
  Polly W. 55
  Sarah 65,100
  Susanna 139
Worley,
  Christian 7
  Elizabeth 58
  Mary 87,118
Word,
  Lucy 113
Wright,
  Elizabeth 58,139
  Elsie 108
  Martha 133,140
  Mary 122
  Mary A. 107
  Nancy 35
  Patsy 81
  Sally A. 8
  Sarah 40
  Sarah S. 142
  Susanna 30

Yancey,
  Levena 87
Yarrington,
  Aurilla 100
  Betsy 121
  Eliza Duval 92

* * *

MINISTERS

John Ayres
Joseph A. Brown
Joseph H. Brown
Robert J. Carson
Rane Chastain
Lewis Chaudoin, Sr.
Lewis Chaudoin, Jr.
J.M. Cofer
Matthew M. Dance
William Douglas
M.A. Dunn
Hiram R. Howe
Joseph Jenkins
William H. Kinckle
Drury Lacy
Wiley F. Lee
Joshua Leigh
F.C. Lowry
John Pollard
John Skurrey
Poindexter P. Smith
Conrad Speece
Samuel D. Tompkins
William Walker
Abner Watkins
John T. Watkins
Henry D. Wood
Samuel Woodfin

INDEX TO OTHER NAMES

Abraham, Jacob L. 34,108
  Jacob L. Jr. 34
Adams, James 47
  Jane 27
  Judith F. 47
  Thomas 77
Addams, Thomas 7
Adcock, Thomas 92
Agee, Pleasant F. 70
Aiken, George L. 52
  James 29,39,118
  James V. 13
  John 54
Alderson, James 54
  John 22
  Thomas 22,59,122
Alexander, Rice 23
Allen, Ann 50
  Benjamin 8,25,101,140
  Benjamin A. 58
  Benjamin S. 94,141
  B. R. 55
  Charles 10,48,103
  Charles B. 19,69,132
  Daniel 10,120,141
  Elizabeth 13,101,104
  E. N. 15
  James 43
  James Jr. 67,79
  John A. 8,10,79
  John C. 10,45,48,140
  Richmond 121
  Samuel 40,43,74,88
  Samuel C. 45
  Simeon 46,137
  Stephen W. 95
  Thomas P. 115
  William 66,117
  William A. 8
Amonnett, Elizabeth 104
  William 27,69,96,104,138
Amos, Charles 114
  Henry 19
  James 19,103
  Littleberry 110
  Robert 19
Anderson, Andrew J. 145
  Betsey 11
  Caleb 11,105
  Catherine 83,89,111
  Charles 10,11,49,108,
    114,131
  Chesley 12,126,140
  Chisley 45
  Cubb 115
  Elizabeth T. 123
  Elva H. 62
  Frances 16,141
  Francis 9,37,137
  George 45
  Jacob 46,51,66,77,97
  James 8,87,114,123,137
  James B. 20,138,141
  James D. 136
  Jane 70
  Jenny 12
  Jesse 10,56,57
  John 10,62,77,89,109,
    123
  John T. 70
  Jonas 77
  Lawrence 10
  Mary 10,75
  Nancy 60,61
  Peter F. 47
  Philemon H. 49
  Richard 70,107
  Richard J. 7,27,76
  Robert 41
  Robert N. 70
  Shirley 10,111,126

Anderson cont.
  Thomas 89
  William 76,89,96
  William Jr. 12
Anglea, Andrew 31
  Archd. E. 12
  Bartlett 70
  James 31,46
  William 26,46,57
  William Jr. 26
Apperson, Elizabeth Ann 25
  Jacob, Sr. 34
  James 48,136
  John R. 80
  Sterling G. 48
  Thomas 25
Applebury, Absolam 61
Archer, John, Jr. 130
Armistead, Anderson H. 101
  Andrew H. 64
  Frances 58,59
  Francis 93,108
  Francis, Jr. 59
  Hannah 58
  James A. 101,127
  Jesse M. 28
  John 24,108,127
  Nancy 135
  Rebecah 26
  Robert 11
  Thaddeus 117
  Thomas D. 103,135
  William 13,92
  William H. 26
  William S. 84,113
Arnold, John 80,117
  Moses 48,80,117
  William 9
Atkinson, John 78
  Mary Anne 14
  Samuel 14,76,81,115
  Thomas 8
Austin, A. 14
  J. 135
  James H. 120,133
  James M. 42,65,69
  John 133
  J. T. 79
  John T. 93
  Judith 120
  R. 115
  Reuben 11
  Sarah H. 62
  William 11,14,23
  William D. 14,39,89
Ayres, Rev. John 11,102

Baber, Ambrose 103
Bagby, Bennett 7,43
  Fleming 15,132,138
  Henry 124
  John 78
  John M. 113
  M. M. 13
  Matthew 78
  Reuben 39,134
  William T. 71
Bagley, James V. 125
  Matthew 94
Bailey, Arminadab Monroe
    15
  James 144
  Parke 11,22,70,75
  Savage 144
Baird, Charles W. 44
  P. 92
Baker, Jerman 79
Baldwin, Archer A. 104
Ballow, Charles 7
  Charles A. 22
  Elizabeth 11

Ballow cont.
  Elizabeth S. 52
  Elizabeth Smith 16
  Eliza 89
  John 52
  John S. 16,36,52,79
  Sally 79
  Thomas 38
  William, Sr. 16
  William B. 52
Baltimore, Benjamin P. 74
  Christopher 78
Banks, Robert 97
Barker, Anney 32
  David 112
  Patrick H. 34,71
  Robert 138
  William W. 108
Barley, William 54
Barnes, James 39
Barnett, Tarlton 37
Bartlett, Samuel 82
Baskerville, George 61
  John, Jr. 16
  Richard 61
Bass, Richard W. 17
Bates, Daniel 57,74
Battersby, Cloe 16
Baugh, John 134
Baughan, James 51,70,126,
    129
  John 22,41,46,51,55,70,
    126
  Peyton 17
  Tucker 68
  William 17,70,131
Bedford, Stephen 95
Bell, John 15
Bellamy, James A. 118
  Martha 118
  Richard 118
  William 20
Belt, Benjamin L. 65
Bennett, Coleman D. 18
Bernard, Joshua M. 58,59
  William 36
Berry, Austin 79
Bevill, Archer 11
Birch, Littleberry 114
Binford, William C. 56
Bird, William 98
Blacker, Royal W. 102
Blain, S.W. 84
  Samuel W. 46
Blake, Charles H. 64
  James 37,46
Blankenship, Henry 19
  Joseph 98
Blanton, Alexander 62,109
  Anderson 62,109
  David 13,64
  E. 80
  Edward 13
  Elisha 31
  James 19,84,132
  James Jr. 13,90,99
  John 102,104
  Joseph 69,132
  Lawrence 36
  Lindsey 132
  Meredith 31
  Polly 62
Boatright, Daniel 86,94
  James, Jr. 86
  James 86,112
  Joel M. 20
  John 83
  Mary 99
  Mary A. 34
  Valentine 20,92
  William L. 127

157

Boatwright, Daniel 112
  Drury 118,122
  Jesse 57,76
  Joel M. 67
  James, Sr. 87
  James 122
  James A. 56
  Jane 122
  John 23
  John B. 107
  Leonard 116,118
  Lucy A. 130
  Pryor 32
  Samuel 122
  Thomas 12,21
  Thomas T. 57
  Valentine 23
  William 122
  William L. 56
  William P. 127
Boles, Sarah 59
Bolling, Edward, Jr. 12
  Thomas 57,81,82
Bond, William 16,26,69,
  89,136
Bondurant, George W. 115,
  124
  John L. 91,124
  Jerome 16
  William 40,80,124
Booker, Edward 10,37,55,
  65,75
  Frederick H. 89
  Marshall 44,94
  Merret N. 39
  Merit 59
  R. A. 124
  Richard A. 32,70,98
  Thomas 51,55,65,75,113
  William N. 59,113
Bosher, Gideon 43
  John 43
  Leonard 43,78
  Maria R. 101
Boston, F. C. 132
  Fontaine C. 80,83
Bowker, John 70
Bowles, Hezekiah 86
  John 94
Brackett, Anne E. 66
  Jo 97
  L. 32
  Ludwell 49
  Thomas 68
  Thomas H. 32,44,64,66,
    73,86,90,98,128
Bradley, Benjamin 11
  Carter H. 14,90
  Clement 45
  Daniel 83
  Edward 99,105
  Eliza 90
  Hezekiah 23
  Isham 11,72,89
  John 23,92
  John B. 92
  John J. 125
  Joseph L. 84
  Joseph S. 83
  Martha 90
  Samuel B. 141
  William 14
  William P. 84
Branch, Samuel 143,144
Bransford, Abraham 139
  Benjamin 23,54,63,73,
    90,102,123,131
  Elizabeth H. 98
  Francis 23,73
  Henry 54,63,102,131,137
  Jacob 98
  John 131

Bransford cont.
  John H. 59
  Judith 123
  Judith A. 98
  Sally 137
  Sarah 137
  T. 90
Brightwell, J. M. 42
Brook, F. 130
Brooke, Gov. Robert 18,30,
  48,52,68
Brooks, Humphrey 54
Brown, Archer 19
  Archer J. 46
  Archibald, Sr. 26
  Archibald 12,26,37,46
  Ben 27
  Benajah 103
  Chesley 45,110
  Clement 51,85,120
  Daniel 40
  Elmer 99
  George 12,26,37,134
  James 16,27,37,101,111
  John 16,27,45,57,89,91,
    109,113,132
  Joseph A. Rev. 8,54,141
  Ludwell 26,37
  Robert W. 132
  Samuel 51,89,140
  Thomas 27,77,130
  Turner 24,51,120
  William 20
  William S. 27
Browning, William 77
Bryant, Charles 12,21
  Daniel 107
  James 122,123
  Mary 107,123
Buchanan, Neill, Jr. 57
Buckston, Jacob 32
Burch, Jane M. 113
  Littleberry 120
Burton, Allen 28
  Benjamin L. 128
  John 28
  Nancy 90
  William 96
  William A. 90,98
  William Allen 28,125
  Wiltshire 41
Burwell, William M. 29,132
Butler, Isaac 111
  Joseph 111
  Joshua 64
  Robert 28

Cabell, Gov. William H.
  27,57,144
Caldwell, Albert 58
  H. W. 133
  John 22,26,62,80
  J. A. 101
  John A. 33,67
  Joseph 38
  Robert 14,45
  Thomas 67,70,101
Cannon, Benjamin 38
  Benjamin B. 38
Cardozo, Abraham 106
  Jacob W. 114,137
Carpenter, M. 59
Carrington, Benjamin 21,88,
  106
  Codrington 88
  Edward J. 101,132
  George, Sr. 18
  George 30,53,91
  George, Jr. 7,18,82
  James L. 88
  Joseph 29,72,145
  Joseph N. 24,64,105
  Lawrence 64,106

Carrington cont.
  Paul I. 28
  Robert H. 28,30
  Tiller 88
  William 24,88
  William E. 24,106
Carson, Rev. Robert J. 72
Carter, Champe 109
  Charles 30
  Elizabeth 58,71,129
  George W. 109
  Hezekiah 85,101
  Jane 17
  John 50,62,73,92
  Mary A. 92
  Susannah 63
  Thomas 85
  William A. 17
Cayce, Fleming 48,61,98,
  99,101,108,121
  Nancy 121
  Josiah 31
  Shadrack 40,43,121
Chamberlin, Mary 37
Chambers, Elizabeth 49
  John 131
  Linus 131
Charlton, John 112,127
  Samuel 12
Chastain, Elijah 121
  John 114,141
  Rane, Rev. 18,23,24,32,
    39,51,58,76,80,113,
    123,129,134
Chaudoin, Lewis Rev. 14,
  59,72,74,127
  Lewis Jr. 88
Cheatham, Alfred C. 52
  James 85
Cheatwood, A. 17,101
  Alexander 63,101
Chenault, Patrick 136
Cheshier, Hezekiah 75
Chesley, Rev. George C.
  74,117
Childress, Francis 39
  John M. 62
  Joseph 140
  William 50
Childrey, Benjamin 28,105
  Mary 105
  Thomas 95
Chrisp, James 80
  John, Sr. 20
  John 19,32
  John, Jr. 20,144
  Samuel 80,84,138
  Samuel C. 47
  William 20
Chumbley, John 132
Claiborne, James 97
Clarke, Francis J. 22
  Gater 95,115
  Joseph 38
  Richard 84,95
  William 33,75,84
Clay, Charles 127
  Henry 33
  William 127
Clements, Sally 26
Clopton, Samuel 145
Cocke, Anderson 144
  Chastain 18
  Thomas 11
  William 126
  William A. 126
Cofer, Rev. J. M. 47,64
Coleman, Burril 47
  C. D. 130
  Daniel 8,58,117
  Daniel, Jr. 35
  Elizabeth 8

Coleman cont.
  Elliott 35
  Elliott C. 8
  Elliott R. 8
  Frances 132
  Grisel 47
  Gulielmus 34,37,106
  Henry, Sr. 34
  James 35
  James W. 34
  John S. 49
  Joseph 133
  Lucy 110,139
  Patience 47,110
  Samuel A. 34
  Sarah 8
  Sarah R. 136
  W. 8
  William 35
  William D. 32,34,137
  Wyatt S. 62
Colley, Elijah W. 81
  Pleasant 26
  William 101
  William M. 81
  William W. 51,104
Colquitt, Henry 38
  Henry, Jr. 38
  James 60
  John 30,36,39,60,128
  Robert 36
  William 60
Coock, James 35
  Stephen 35
Coocke, John 35
Cook, Abraham 37,94
  John 71
  John R. 109
Cooke, James E. 56,100
  Stephen 80,100
  William M. 109
Cooper, Isaac 94
  James 9,32,43,66
  Thomas 9,26,102,109
  Thomas S. 66
Corley, Valentine 26
  William 20
Coupland, David, Sr. 34
  David O. 34,74,130
  William R. 81
Cousins, Finley 88
  Isham 37
  Jane 97
  John 97
Cox, Bartlett 16,67
  Francis 35,121
  Henry 63,74,125
  Henry, Jr. 63
  John 41,47,123
  John F. 67,85
  Judith 117
  Mary 67
  Stephen 119
  William 64,76
Creasy, John 93
  William 38
Crews, Hardiman 127
  Isaac 86
  Peachy 122
Criddle, Ann 96
  Finch 96
  Jesse 110
  Smith 13
Crowder, Thomas W. 141
Crump, Richard 41
Cullen, James M. 106
Cunningham, John 130
  Richard 126,135

Dabney, Robert K. 110
Dagnell, Richard 69
Dance, Rev. Matthew M.
    52,65,108

Dandridge, Henry M. 126
Daniel, A. 121
  Abraham 121,133,139
  Chesley 108
  George W. 68
  James 18,56,124
  James M. 50,76,145
  John 40,94,98,106,139,
    144
  John, Jr. 55,77,119,131
  John G. 53,88,129
  Leonard 30,50,93,101,112,
    124,139,145
  Mary 103
  Micham 50
  Robert 88
  William 35,92,103
  William P. 21
Davenport, Ann 77
  Elizabeth 116
  Henry 44,78,132,143
  Jesse 20,94
  Martin S. 44,94,111
  Rebe 81
  Satterwhite 85
  Stephen 58
  Thomas 53,78
  Thomas, Jr. 143
  Thomas, 2nd 143
  Thomas F. 77
  William 16,53,78
Davies, Nicholas 9
Davis, Beverly 42
  James 42
  Jesse 30,61,111
  Levi 30
  Morton 59
  Nicholas E. 27
  Peyton P. 41
  Samuel 22
  Shelton 34
  Stephen W. 41,42
  William F. 96
  Zachariah 41,42
Davidson, Joseph 24
  Nancy 113
  Philemon 103
  Reuben 87
  Reuben F. 28
Dame, George W. 19
Deane, Anne H. 74
  E. H. 100
  Francis B. 78
  Francis B., Jr. 130
  M. J. 68
  Mary J. 74
  P. W. 100
  T. B. 73,76
  T. M. 69
  T. W. 100
Deaton, Burwell 60
DeGraffendreidt, William
    91
DeJarnett, James 107
DeShazo, Henry 143
Dicken, Richard 132
Dickenson, William 26
Dickerson, Bartlett 46
  Clemons 46
  David 16
  William 16
Dinwiddie, William 104
Dobie, John 129
Dodson, Edith 78
  John 78
Donnell, James M. 137
  John 104
Doss, James 43
  Parker 43
  Susannah 43
Douglas, James 111
  Robert 124
  Rev. William 16,18,30,

Douglas cont.
  Rev. William cont. 32,
    33,46,47,49,51,52,53,
    56,57,59,60,63,64,65,
    66,70,76,79,82,85,86,
    87,91,93,95,103,105,
    107,112,113,114,117,
    118,119,121,123,124,
    129,130,132,134,136,
    143
Dowdy, Albert 44
  Albert J. 44
  James 34,44,72,117,119
  Lucy 50
  Richard 93,110,116
  Thomas 9,10,14,43,64,126
  Thomas, Jr. 67
Drake, Thomas B. 127
Drew, F. H. 64
Duffield, John 44,61
Duncan, Mathias 45
Duncom, John 86
Dungan, George 45
Dunkum, Frances W. 89
  Moses 45
  Nancy 53,136
  Phebe 114
  Savery 26
  Willis W. 53,136
Dunn, John 88
  M. A. Rev. 39,42,71,119
  Samuel 88
Dunnavant, John 44
  William 76
  W. H. 42
Dupie, John 18
Dupuy, James 14
  Susannah 82
Durham, Frances 51,77
  Jacob 25
  Jacob A. 51
  James 12,25
  John 25
  Nicholas 12,37,46
Durrum, James 26
Dutoy, Isaac 60

Eanes, James M. 91
Edwards, Arthur 18
  Daniel C. 47
  Flemstead 34,54
  John E. 47
  Nehemiah 81
  Polly 38
  William 47,143
Eggleston, Edmund 115
  George 107
  Henry L. 117
  Richard 134
  Richard B. 47
  Richard S. 29,50,73
Elam, Joel 57
Eldridge, R. B. 131
Ellington, Branch H. 115
Ellis, James 137
Ellison, David 78
  James 88
Emanuel, William 37
England, Benjamin A. 44
  Edmund L. 12
  Edward 93,117
  John 61,94
  W. 48,111
  William 48
  William C. 42
  William N. 97
Epperson, James 12
  Richard 49
  Richard C. 112
Eubank, George 53
Evans, Polly 100
  William 66

Falwell, John 42,53
Faris, Charles 120
  Jacob 16,29
  James 120
  Martin, Sr. 66
  William 93,120
Fariss, Jacob 63
  Martin 120
Farmer, Burwell 81
  Cary 71
  Cary A. 50
  Elam 127,128
  Gus E. 127
  James 99,127
  John, Sr. 85
  John 50,96
Fearn, Thomas 126
Featherston, Wiley 105
Ferguson, William 16,110
Fisher, Edward W. 68
Fitzgerald, James H. 85
Fleming, John 18
Flippen, Archibald 65
  Daniel B. 39,54
  Elizabeth 95
  Frances 54
  Francis 62,122
  Francis J. 54
  James W. 54
  Jesse 21,52,101
  John 70,76,134,140
  John M. 26,65
  John W. 35
  Martha 90
  Mary 101
  Philip 123
  Ralph 90
  Robert 52
  Robert W. 27
  Thomas 17,41,43,45
  Thomas D. 27
  William 21,65,123
Ford, Isaac A. 128
  Hezekiah 50,102,132,145
  John 52,55,79
  Mattie 50
  N. 102,145
  Newton 62,145
  Sterling 62,145
  William A. 78
Forsee, John 19,87
  Stephen 118
Foster, A. M. 53
  James 132
  Melinder 129
  Peter B. 8,51,113
  Roderick 103,112,128
  Rowland W. 72,146
  W. H. 53
Fowler, Alexander 31
  Elizabeth 15,129
  Holeman 53
  John B. 53
  Osborne L. 58
  Sherwood 31,53,136
  Thomas 138
Francisco, Catharine 91
Frayser, John R. 42
  Roderick 69
  William 23,29,54,67,140
  William, Jr. 14
Freeman, Samuel 135
French, Hugh 52
Fretwell, James 12
  William 21,29
Fuqua, Benjamin 133,138
  Joseph 15,63
  Nathaniel 79

Gadbery, William 101
Gaines, B. 12
  Mary 130
Galloway, Frederick 13,21

Galloway cont.
  Rhoda H. 53
Gannaway, John Jr. 83
Garrett, Eliza R. 113
  John 75,82,108
  John, Jr. 71
  John D. 42,100,127
  Mary M. 108
Garrott, John 118
  Lucy 102
  William 139
Garth, D. C. 56
  Garland A. 74
Gauldin, Jacob 13
  James S. 115
  John L. 19
  Josiah 18,35,41,66,115
  Susannah 98
Gaulding, Susannah 28
Gay, Edward S. 135
  William 57
Gentry, Simon 36
Gholson, William G. 57
Gibson, Robert F. 25
Gilliam, James 126
  R. H. 102
  Richard J. 40
Glenn, Alexander H. 43
  Gideon 41,53
  William 25,84,145
  William, Jr. 25
Glover, Bradley S. 7,71
  Elijah 27,71,126,138,145
  Robert 93,145
  William 145
Godsey, Drucilla 13
  Henry 66
  William 140,142
Goff, Henry 117
Goode, Bennett 16
  Bennett, Jr. 16
  John 135
Goodman, C. J. 59
  Elizabeth 59,121
  Josiah 59
  Mary 51
  Noton 41,81
  R. J. 51,59
  Thomas A. 23,51
  Thomas J. 21,68
  Zachariah 36,60,61
  Zachariah S. 111
Goolsby, Isham D. 41
Gordon, Alexander 135
  A. T. 75,94
  John 98
  Richard 69,75,94
  Thomas 23,54
Green, Caleb 18
  Richard T. 80
Griffin, Nelson 50
  John 63
  Joseph 50
Guerrant, Anderson 21
  Daniel 134
  Peter 134
Guthrey, A. 40
  Bernard 87
  Henry 14
  John 12,55,106
  Sarah 48
  William 12,34,35,61
Guthrie, A. 9

Haistie, Elizabeth 118
  Thomas 118
Hall, John A. 111
  Thomas 138
Hambleton, Ann 73
  Benjamin P. 31
  David 105
  Henry 32
  James 29,61

Hambleton cont.
  John M. 27
  William 54,86
Hamilton, William 41
Hancock, B. 133
Hankley, James 81
Hanley, William W. 50
Hardin, John 120
Harris, Allen H. 126
  Benjamin 28,38,52,95,126,
    130
  Charles 81,123
  Elizabeth 132
  Henry J. 119,130
  James 48,51
  James A. 119
  John 38,63,99,112
  John Jr. 90
  John Skip 38
  Joseph 20,38,130
  Mary 38
  Peter 132
  Rebecca 20
  Rebekah 130
  Samuel, Sr. 63
  Samuel 63
  Sarah 74
  Thomas 95
  William 59,130
Harrison, Benjamin 8,78
  Carter Henry 24
  Cary 18,64,78
  Randolph 19,73,84,10?,
    108
  Randolph, Jr. 64
Haskins, Ch(ristopher) 17,
  64
  Creed 17,82
  Robert 123
  Thomas 17
Hatch, William 28
Hatcher, Ann 75
  Benjamin 30,34,59,109,
    134
  Drury 34,59
  Frederick 22,25,55,60,
    65,68,71,72,125,134
  Henry 106
  Henry, Jr. 65
  John, Sr. 126
  John 55,68,111,126
  John, Jr. 30,51,56,65,
    144
  John H., Sr. 51
  Josiah 65
  Joseph 51
  Milly D. 144
  Samuel 30,31,65,68,75,
    126
  Sarah 60
  Sarah Woodson 25,60,68
Hawkins, Laban 27
Haynes, Curtis 89
Hazlegrove, P. 10
  Pleasant 48,104
  Winston 138
Henderson, Robert 100
Hendrick, Alexander 33
  Adolphus 24,110
  Frances 35
  James 57
  Obadiah 75
  Sutphin 65
  William 36,49
  William Y. 57
Henry, Gov. Patrick 107
Henson, Charles 127
Hill, Jesse 69,109
  John 57
  Joseph R. 67,115
  Thomas 69
  Thomas H. 13
  William C. 106

Hilton, Samuel 137
Hix, John 38
  Josiah 13,38,120
  Mary Ann E. 48
  Samuel 48,66,102
  William 77,138
Hobson, Benjamin 23
  Caleb 36,97
  Catherine 41
  Epa. 33,39,78
  George 81
  James 27,41,90,91,137
  James H. 27
  John, Jr. 117
  Joseph 97,140
  J. S. 81
  Joseph V. 140
  M. L. 55
  Man S. 119
  Maurice L. 40,53,85
  Sally 41
  Samuel 10,33,41,65,86,
    97,141
  Thomas 21,41,45,51,52,
    55,68,71,73,74,76,77,
    94,97,100,123,137,141
  William 33,78,111,121,
    143
  William B. 49,53,84,95,
    101,109
Hodnett, Ayres 108
Hoggard, John 36
Holcombe, J. 146
  Phil. Jr. 146
Holeman, Benjamin 80
  James 87
  John 25,58
  Susan B. 103
Holland, Dick 74
  James 10
  Jesse 36
  John 69
  John S. 22,100
  Mary 10
Holloway, James 131
  John 67,71
Holman, Benjamin 69
  George 14,116,140
  George T. 116
  James 86
  John, Sr. 133
  John 9,64,70,83,116
  John, Jr. 133
  Susan B. 135
  Tandy 25
  William 62
  William T. 116
  Yancey 7
Holt, Jesse S. 92
  John 85
  Joseph 43
  Phillip 38,67,82,85,90,
    94,115
  Polly 85
  Richard 38
Hooton, Samuel C. 47,77,
  101
Hope, John 32
Hopson, Henry 72
Hord, John 32
Horner, Arthur 43
Howard, William 82,130
  Waillium A. 66,102
Howe, Rev. Hiram R. 65
Hubbard, Asa 51
  Benjamin 35
  Bennett 36
  Edward 128
  James W. 136
  Joseph 36
  William 132
Hudgens, Anthony M. 63
Hudgins, Albert 71
  Asa 51

Hudgins cont.
  Holloway 23,83
  Jane 133
  John 15,23,71,72
  John M. 36
  Martha 14
  Mary 43
  Philadelphia B. 27
  Robert 36,44,132,133
  Robert W. 15
  William S. 15
Hudson, Samuel 7,72
  Thomas 7,20
  William 60,94
Huganes, Milly 83
Hughes, Anthony 104
  Billy 72
  Edward 142
  George B. 62
  Isaac 140
  Jane 72
  John 139
  Joseph 36,72,105
  Robert 135,138
  Stephen 44,108
Huse, John 93
Hutchardson, John 11
Hutchinson, James 32

Isbell, Daniel 140
  James 81,133
  Lewis 55,81,133
  Lewis M. 39
  Martha 39
  Polly D. 81
  Thomas H. 77,112
  William 134
Irby, William 123
Irvine, Samuel 110
Irving, Charles 128
  H. P. 83
  Henry P. 40,84
  R. K. 128

James, B. B. 89
  Francis 90
  Frederick 131,136
  Mary 33,90
  Richard 77,90
  Ruby 90
Janney, Isaac P. 77
Jarman, M. B. 56
Jefferson, John 74,123
Jeffries, George R. 129
Jellis, Thomas 78
Jenkins, Allen 79
  Betsey 45
  David 45
  Edward 92
  James 25
  John 75
  John D. 125
  Joseph 45,50,73,75,126
  Joseph Rev. 9,10,11,13,
    21,29,34,35,36,38,55,
    61,77,82,91,92,93,106,
    109,110,114,126,128
  Morman 88
  Stephen 88
  Tarlton 60,74
  William 11,71
Jennings, Gabriel H. 91
Jeter, Burwell 145
  Jesse 145
  Lucy Ann 101
  William 56,80
Johns, James D. 9
  John A. S. 96
  John T. 113
  Thomas 9,96
  Thomas, Jr. 116
Johnson, Anderson 31
  Benjamin B. 66
  Daniel 133

Johnson cont.
  David 108
  Decker 129
  Isaac 129
  Jacob 127
  Job 15
  John 140
  Lucy 76
  Mary 28,46
  Nancy 129
  Obadiah 127
  Peter 46,129
  Polly 30
  Sarah 13
  Thomas 22,45,66,76,96
  William 131
  W. H. 30
Jones, Daniel 11,46,131
  Elijah 77
  Elizabeth 125
  Frederick 30,120
  Hannah 26
  Hanningham 91
  Harrison 78,140
  Joel 77
  John 98,135
  John H. 56,68,71,77
  Joshua 52
  Lewis 12,125
  Mary Ann 78
  Mary Ann S. 140
  Nancy 125
  Rhoda 91
  Robert 39
  Walter 9
  Washington 77
  William 42,57,87,107,125
  William A. 77
  William W. 93
Jordan, Edwin H. 131
  Elizabeth 76
  John 123
  Robert P. 46,83,101
  William B. 77

Keeble, Walter 23
  Walter, Jr. 38,50
Keeling, George 12,139
Kent, William 139
Kerr, Dabney 53,105
  Daniel W. 105
  John 78
  Thomas 29
Kilpatrick, Joseph N. 78
Kinckle, Rev. William H.
  43
King, Henry 123
  Lavinia 103
  Phillip 78
Kinkle, Rev. William H.
  100

Lackland, James 69,131
  Zadock 131
Lacy, Rev. Drury 8,48
Lancaster, John 37,58,145
  Josiah 37,58
  Nat. 56
  William 145
Langhorne, Alexander 70
  Maurice 117
  Maurice, Jr. 93,94
  Maurice M. 52,144
  William B. 11,47,106
Lawson, Michael 97
Layne, Rom. M. 130
Leake, John 92
  John M. 92
Leaker, James 60
Lee, Barrett C. 56
  B. D. 34
  Ch. B. 135
  Charles 13,132
  Charles P. 130

Lee cont.
  Edmund P. 13
  Henry Gov. 14,45,99,115,
    139
  John 13
  Joseph 38,80
  Joseph D. 23,56,129
  Keziah 38
  Patty 144
  Susanna
  Wiley F. Rev. 84
  William 79
Leigh, Rev. Joshua 30,48,
    56,66,73,94
Lennly, John E. 42
LeSueur, Catherine 128
  Charles 12
  David, Sr. 128
  David 114
  David, Jr. 128
  Peter 116
LeVillain, Elizabeth 144
  John 143
Lewis, Charles W. 43
  Gilley 95,103
  Howell 77
  John 24
  Patrick R. 101
  Thomas 24
Ligon, Elijah 84
  Joseph 81,90
  Leonard W. 115
  William, Jr. 125
  William F. 43
Lindsey, James H. 140
Lipford, Amos 107
  Henry 40,96,100,106
  Henry, Jr. 106
  John 100
  Thomas 100
  Thomas W. 96,112
Lipscombe, Henry 104
Lockland, James 37
Lockett, Joel 62
  Royal 85
Logwood, Edmond 95
Lookado, Peter 82
  Peter Anthony 128
Lowry, Rev. F. C. 103,
    126,129,138
  Lewis 119
  S. L. 83
Luck, William 33
Lunsford, John 48
Lyall, Beverly 23
  Elizabeth Ann 70
Lyle, James 79
  Sarah E. 53,62
  William 62
Lyles, John 84
Lynch, Robert 22

McAshan, John T. 31
  William L. 47
  William S. 101
McCann, John 16
McCormack, John, Jr. 21
  Pleasant 25
  Robert 65
  Thomas 114
McKinnie, Charles 127
McLaurine, Archibald 85
  Archer 133
  James 56,70,74,94,95
  James, Jr. 70
  Jane 70
  Joseph 55,65,103,111
  Lewis 126
  Robert Rev. 30
  Robert 122,123,124
McNeal, Charles 40
McTyre, Benjamin P. 31

Macon, John 54

Maddox, Josiah 79,108
  Thomas 108,120
Mann, Ann B. 85,94
  Benjamin H. 85
  Cain 74
  William, Sr. 144
  William 102
  William, Jr. 102
  William F. 133
  William F. Jr. 69,85,92,
    94,102,142
Marshall, Phebe 85
  William 85,138
Martin, Austin, Jr. 118
  Benjamin 86
  Daniel 118
  Henry 99,130,138
  Henry, Jr. 99
  Hezekiah 41
  John 52,86,112,122,132
  Kiah 60
  Obadiah 86
  Stephen, Jr. 86
  Thomas 86
  Valentine 20
Mason, A. 22
  Caty 83
  Joseph 87
Mathis, Sarah 39
Matthews, Elizabeth 119
  G. H. 13
  George H. 103,106
  Gregory 28
  John 9,110
  Mary 39
  Susan 9
Mattox, William G. 27
Maxey, Mary 49,112
  William 41,49,112
Mayes, Jane 58
  Polly 58
Mayo, D. 17,63
  Daniel 17
  James C. 41,120
  Jeffrey 88
  John M. 17,30
  Joseph 88
  Randolph 37
  Robert 88
  Scipio 82,88
  William 82,88,120
  William H. 120
Meador, Albert, Sr. 89
  Drusilla 14
  Henry L. 95
  Hubbard 99
  Isham A. 42
  James 62
  James, Jr. 89
  Jesse 142
  Jonas 17,42,95
  Martha 111
  Robert J. 113
  Swann 120
  Thomas 90
  Thomas L. 42
  Valentine 27
  William 59,71,98
Meddoss, James 12
Melton, John 99,131
  Nathan 50,96,99
  Rhoda 96
Meredith, James 33
  Warren W. 42
  William W. 11
Merritt, Tapley 28
Meriwether, William W. 114
Merryman, Charles A. 95,97
  Edward 31,52,97,109,119,
    132
  Elizabeth H. 72,89
  J. A. 82
  J. D. 97
  Jane 72

Merryman cont.
  Jesse 23,95,125
  John 28,36,69,79,90
  John F. 23
  John T. 21
  Margaret T. 83
  Martha 89
  Mary 90
  Mary J. 90
  Pleasant 133
  R. 90
  Susan Y. 127
  Thomas 28,79,122,127
  Thomas, Jr. 127
Mewburn, W. 44
Michaux, Jesse 60,127,129,
    139
  John 8,57
  Joseph 34,64,66,91,131
  Judith Woodson 34,131
  Paul 36,123
  Richard 108,109
Micou, Laban 54
Miles, John 91
  William 91
Miller, Dabney P. 46
  James 106
  John 40,120
  Lewis T. 71
  Thomas 92
  William 24,92
  William A. 91
Minor, John 32
  John W. 126
Minter, James 23
  Jesse 24
  John 14,27,73,99,125
  John, Jr. 27
  Micajah 99
  William 24,84,120
Mitchell, Cary 113
  John 93
Molloy, David 11,35
Monroe, David W. 44
  James Gov. 8,30,137
Montague, Dudley S. 36
  Henry B. 18
  James M. 71
  Peter 14,31,38,79,135
  R. H. 17,83
  R. M. 93
  Thomas 73,119
  William W. 93,101
Montgomery, William 20,62
Moody, Thomas 36
Morgan, Samuel 99
Morris, Osborne 71
Morrow, Ewing 37
Morton, Charles 110
  Charles A. 83
  Mary A. 83
  S. D. 83
  Thomas A. 68,83,110
Mosby, Alfred D. 95
  Benjamin 49
  Elbert 95
  Jacob 80,90,110,117
  Jacob G. 142
  James 70
  John 72
  Joseph 95
  Littleberry 72
  Micajah 15,18
  Poindexter 138
  Thomas 44
Moseby, Thomas 58
Moseley, Arthur 95,112,
    144
  Major R. 95
  Richard 68,112,123,127
  Robert 17
  Thomas 112
  William 112
Moss, Alexander 34,121

Moss cont.
  Elizabeth 123
  William 99,123
Murray, Alexander 96
  Ann 57
  Anthony 104,136
  George W. 104
  John 72,104,106,111,
    125,126
  Richard 104
  William 136
  William B. 82,96,100

Naish, William 123
Nance, Frederick 109
Napier, Benjamin W. 85
Nash, Abner 39
  John W. 32,108
Nelson, Andrew 55,105,135
  John, Jr. 72
  Matthew 72,135
Netherland, Benjamin 30
  John 33,54
  Wade 30,54,84,144
Newton, Charles 114
  Henry 73
  James 128
  Nancy 128
  Polly 128
Nicholas, Gov. Wilson
  Cary 56,66,118
Noell, Charles 48
Norris, Jesse 97
  Thomas 74,88,97,123
North, John 140
  William 9
Nunnally, John 28,98
  P. H. 29,103,104,142
  Patrick H. 55
  William 28

Oakley, Erasmus 7,75
  John 91
  Shadrack 86
  Shed 89
  Shedrick 140
  Thomas 122
Oglesby, Thomas 86
Old, Phillip 23
Oliver, Hammon 60
  Harmon 61
  Henry B. 138
  John 62
  Maurice 98
Orange, Azariah 41
  Joel 50
  Joshua 67,86
Osborne, James 23
  William 11,136
Oslin, John A. 21
Otey, Benjamin 96
Overton, Thomas 28

Pace, Catharine P. 65
  George W. 69
Page, Henry 73,84
  John Gov. 19,28,61
  John C. 51,68
  Nelson 40,84,100
  Robert B. 51
  Thomas 51,68,73
Palmore, Charles S. 33,
    37,52,58,67,70,80,132
  Fleming 38,72,112
  Jane 27
  John 21
  John P. 48
  John R. 21,68
  Joseph 13
  Joseph B. 52
  Joseph S. 56,104,143
  Lucy Ann 143
  William 12,18,81
  William A. 33

Pankey, Dorothy 70
  John 71
  Thomas 48,70,78,101,114
  Thomas A. 114
Parker, Charles W. 59
  Isham 27,75,102
  Isom 111
  Jane A. 89
  Jesse 27,75,111
  Jesse D. 102,133
  John 27
  John H. 59,75,89,120
Parrack, S. H. 109
Parrish, Valentine 49
Patterson, Charles 102
  Gideon 91
  James P. 63
Payne, George F. M. 95
Paytrim, William 128
Peak, Mary Ann 37
Pearce, Edmund 50
  Jeremiah 10,31,80
  Martha A. 72
  Rachel 80
Peasley, Gabriel 42,114,
    127
  Gabriel B. 116,127
  Gabriel B., Jr. 129
  William D. 107,127
Peek, Polly 91
Penick, Nathaniel 103,131,
    138
Pettit, S. S. 61
Pettus, Overton B. 18
Phaup, William 17,69,77,
    94
Phelps, Samuel 37,104,134
Phillips, James 48
  Peter T. 22,35,48,58,66,
    73,75,110,123
  Randolph 9,82,137
  Richard M. 137
  Thomas 9,53
Pickett, Henry 137
Pillow, Jasper 132
Pittman, James 113
Pitts, Sally 79
Pointer, John 130
Pollard, John 105
  Rev. John 38,93,99
Pollock, John 73
  Susanna 73
Poore, James 107
Porter, Ann 65
  Elizabeth 60
  Thomas 25,65,143,144
  William 65,105
Povall, Holcraft 118
  Richard 33,68,72,81
Powell, Benjamin H. 66
  William 7,47,52,70
Powers, Judith 96
  William 96
Preston, Gov. James Patton
    86
Price, Anne 13
  Benjamin 106
  Charles 99
  Edmund 13,101
  Elizabeth 106
  John 81
  John F. 44
  John L. 42
  John M. 106
  Joseph 13,101,128
  Thomas 99
  William 7,87,126
  William D. 119
  William G. 17,109
  William W. 30
Prince, William H. 113,129
Pringle, Richard 134
Prosser, Thomas 86,87,121
Puckett, John 115

Pulliam, Samuel G. 9
Putney, Richard E. 107
  Samuel 15

Qualls, John 112
Quarles, James 42,107,112
  Nancy 42

Radford, John 49
Raiborne, Polly 137
Raine, George 81
  Hugh 118
  John, Sr. 142
  Richard K. 18
Randolph, Beverly Gov. 9,
    109
  Edmund Gov. 15,43,83,96,
    139
  Henry 119
  Isham 64
  John 137
  Peyton 61
  Richard R. 141
  Thomas Mann Gov. 50,57
  William 61
  William F. 8,17,64,100
Ransone, Ambrose 41
  Ann W. 108
  Henry 8,58,79,144
  John 108
  John F. 108
  Thomas 93,144
  Thomas J. 108
  William 45,65,74,93
Read, Landon C. 68
Redd, John F. 109
Reynolds, Henry 72
  J. J. 113
  J. W. 113
  James W. 27,119,126
  Obadiah J. 77
  S. S. 62
Rice, Alexander 19
Richardson, E. 96
  Elizabeth 27
  James 101
  John 51,98,102
  Mary 74
  Presley D. 49
  Robert 39,120
  Thomas P. 109
Riddle, Joseph W. 58
Ridgway, Samuel 92
Ritchie, John E. 48
Robertson, Alonza 93
  Henry 50
  Jeffrey 125
  John 24,69
  Matthew 93
  Norvell H. 75,114
  Norvell H., Jr. 75
  Phebe 45,93
  Robert 39
  Samuel 21
Robinson, Alonza 9
  Christopher 85
  Edward 111
  Feild 54
  Gross 89,111
  Hatcher 111
  Jesse 89
  John 83,94,99,131,136
  John, Jr. 122
  John B. 102
  Joseph 22
  Levina 112
  Lockey L. 94
  Patsy 142
  Robert 39,125
  Robert S. 15,107,125
  Sally 112
  Samuel 111
  William 21,111
  William A. 39

Rodgers, Martha 20
Rogers, Martha 118
Roper, Charles 144
  James 63
  Randolph 112
Rose, Robert H. 81
Ross, David 44
Routon, William 24
Rowton, William 118
Rowland, Michel 126
Royall, Joseph A. 91
Russell, Anne 38
  James 76
  Tabitha 127
  William 38,76,108
  Yancey 76
Ryall, Vincent C. 73
Rye, John W. 24

Salmon, Jourdon 120
Sandefer, Abraham 118
Sandifur, Abraham 77
Sanders, Bartlett A. 135
  C. G. 61
  James B. 29
  John 19,69
Sanderson, Albert G. 109
  Caroline J. 116
  Elizabeth R. 26
  George G. 113
  George W. 124
  John 11,26,125
  Obadiah R. 144
  Robert 116
  Thomas 132
  Thomas B. 61,113,115
  William 113
Sandidge, B. J. 86,145
  Beverly J. 87,123
  James 86
  John E. 42
  Zachariah 87
  Zachariah A. 61,127,128
Scott, John 57,105,114
  Robert 48,83
  Saymer 29
Scruggs, Benjamin E. 117
  Drury, Sr. 93
  Drury 67
  Drury, Jr. 93
  Edward 8,50,102,107,142
  Edward, Jr. 103
  Edward L. 55
  Elijah 92
  G. P. 29
  Henry 110
  Henry P. 66,70,77
  John 102,115
  Robert 22,29,38,83,90
  Robert R. 43
  Sally 63
  Tabitha 67
  Thomas 114
  Valentine 114,115
Seay, Isham 129,134
  Jacob 71
  James 139
  James A. 115
  John 91,118,142
  Reuben 115
  William 118
  William P. 24
Self, Edmund T. 116
  Ephraim 98
  John E. 15
  William 108
Sharp, Moses 103
Shapard, Mildred 144
Sheperd, William M. 17
Shepherd, James 118
  Nancy 118
  William 121
Shelton, Pheby 84
  Richard 44

Shenault, Patrick 36
Shields, A. 53
  Alfred G. W. 90
  D. 90
  David 90
  Mary C. 90
Shoott, Pat. 116
Shuffield, Collin 43,47
Shurrey, Rev. John 99
Simpson, Leonard 9
  Richard 9,80
  Samuel 141
  Samuel R. 9,80
Sims, Benjamin 63,112
  Benjamin F. 57
  Bernard 30,97,122,125
  Claiborne 73
  Edward 19
  John 54
  Judith 112
  Peyton 63
  Reuben 125
  Reuben T. 63
Skipwith, Henry 110
  Henry, Jr. 20
Skurrey, Rev. John 145
Slaughter, George 28
Smith, A. 42
  Allen 72
  Berry 17
  Bird 43,44
  Byrd 59
  D. C. 29
  Daniel 20,87
  Guy 132
  Harry 28,117
  Henry 112
  James 63,85
  James M. 91,118
  Janie 42
  John 83
  Larkin 9,12,48,117
  Martha 28
  Martin P. 64
  Mary 106
  Pleasant 8
  Poindexter P. Rev. 9,12,
    28,31,43,44,53,71,98,
    107,114,132,138
  Robert 67,98,119
  Thomas 83,93,106
  Thomas J. 34,43
  W. B. 79
  William 34,63,65,87,105,
    119
Smothers, William 74
Snoddy, David 15,30,71,86
  James 15,100
  James C. 71
  Philip 102
  Samuel 120
Southall, Cary 71
  James 86,120
  John 90
  Turner 73,86,90
  William 15
  William A. 65
Spaldin, Thomas 127
Spears, E. W. 88,103,128
  Edward W. 88
  Elizabeth 116
  Leonard D. 53
  Leonard L. 19
  Robert 53,88
  William 53,120
  William, Jr. 120
Speece, Rev. Conrad 125
Spencer, James A. 131
  John 40
  William 34
Spiers, Abraham 117
Stanard, Eliza J. F. 141
Starkey, Robert 14
  William 101

Stegar, Albert G. 73
  Edward 116
  Francis 141
  Francis E. 73
  Francis George 41,49,117
  Francis E. H. 142
  Hanse 85,119
  Isham 122
  John H. 122
  John O. 122
  Rhoda A. 127
  Samuel 121
  Skip H. 118
  Thomas E. 85
  Thomas H. 73,116,141,
    142
  W. C. 124
Stephens, Isaac 30
  Martin 30
Stevenson, John 16,122
Steward, John 26
Stinson, Joseph 135
  Thomas 106
Stokes, Frederick 91,95
Stone, Caleb 123
Stoner, Daniel 96
Stott, Raleigh 32
Stovall, Batt 123
Stratton, David 82
  Frances W. 82
  George 129
  James 138
  Jarman L. 75
  Jerman 122
  John H. 61,104
  Martha 29
  P. 117
  Peter 29,117
  Robert 41
  W. 122
  William 82,124
  William P. 104
Street, Dudley 92,124
  Jesse 46,50
  Jesse S. 72,111
Sutphin, A. B. 69
  James 87
Swann, T. 22,31
  George T. 125
  Thomas Capt. 64
  Thomas T. 39,70
  Thompson 16,63,84,9?,128
  William S. 61

Tabb, Thomas 26,125,133
Talley, Daniel C. 98,110,
  111
  Garland 126
  Jackey 10,105,111
  John P. 111
  Nelson 20,105
  Sally Manning 22
  William 22,126
  William A. 10
  William G. 24
  Zachariah 12,34
Tanner, Emaline 14
  Frances A. 93
  John F. 14,93
  William E. 126
Tatum, Martha L. 71
  Mary 71
Taylor, A. 64
  Admine 76
  Albert G. 92
  Balona 107
  C. 43
  Creed 10,29,57,66,143,
    144
  Daniel 107
  G. 15
  John 50
  Mary P. 21
  Milly 63

Taylor cont.
  Richard 22,39,76
  Samuel 22,39
  Susannah 76
  Thomas 103
  William 34
  Zachariah 77
Terrell, William 82
Thomas, Anne C. 61
  David 82
  Frances 86
  Francis 61
  George T. 116
  James 20,22,61,102
  James A. 28,30,40,42
  Jesse 40,59,110,133,134
  Jesse W. 96
  Joseph 129
  Phill 133
Thompson, Bartlett 73
  Eliza J. 42
  John 42,44,128
  Josiah 135
  Sally 23
  Robert 119,128,134
Thomson, Bartlett 54
Thornton, F. 85
  Robert E. 85
  William M. 30,128
Thurston, John G. 40,103,129
Todd, John 138
Toler, Benjamin 56,76,129
  Bennett 76
  Frances 100
  William L. 133
Tompkins, Rev. Samuel 122
Travis, Joseph 73
Trent, Alexander 13,63,68
  Burleigh 124
  Carter H. 97,98
  Henry 139
  John 64,125,139
  John C. 124
  Stephen W. 34,97,139
  William A. 34,37,125
Tucker, Byrd G. 82
Tuggle, John 122
Turner, Mary J. 15
  William 15,26,27
Turpin, Strabber 75
  Thomas 63,74
  Thomas, Jr. 51,63,74
  Thomas J. 97
  William 74,97,119
Tyler, Gov. John 35,36
Tyree, Benjamin P. 116
  David 129
  David, Jr. 130
  Rhoda 91
  Timothy 61,116

Vaughan, Joseph 37,139
Vawter, Agnes 64
  Edward 131
  John 64
  Samuel 74
Venable, Francis W. 109,110
  Samuel W. 37
  William L. 109

Wade, Claiborne 99
  William 118
Walden, Mary 86
  Richard 43
Walker, Alexander 137
  B. W. 53
  Benjamin 37
  Henry 137
  James 108
  John 91,103
  John S. 59,75,84
  Judith 80

Walker cont.
  S. 135
  Warren 63
  William 19,20,29,56,67,80,84,91,132
  William Rev. 23,50,67,98,107,110
  William B. 20
Wallace, Anthony A. 78
  William 34,37
Wallis, D. M. 32
Walston, Joseph 118
Walthall, Frances 83
  Katherine 83
Walton, Anthony A. 14,141
  Edward 7,106,116,117,121,129,141,142
  Edward, Jr. 7,120
  Edward G. 67
  Elizabeth Ann 115
  George 21
  George C. 29,71,87,90,124,131,133
  Henry 64
  John 15
  Nathaniel 116
  Nathan W. 47
  Robert 26,40,52,73,100,133
  Robert A. 49
  Sarah 14
  Sarah F. 102
  Sherwood 139
  Thomas 21,91,92,95,96,133,134
  Thomas G. 28
  Thomas H. 49,87
  Thomas M. 7
  William 134
  William S. 47,115
Ward, Josiah 26,97,137
  Susanna 81
  Thomas H. 114
Ware, Nicholas 85
Watkins, Abner 82,134
  Abner Rev. 19,20,25,47,53,67,75,80,85,104,105,108,116,133,142,143
  A. R. 40
  Alfred R. 23
  Austin 142
  Charles 36
  Edward 96,134,135
  Harriet S. 82
  Joel 137
  John 96,105
  John T. 40,135,140
  John T. Rev. 8,9,17,18,23,26,40,46,56,62,69,77,80,84,109,116,133,138,140,142
  Maria L. 24
  Peggy 37
  Samuel 135,144
Watson, Abner 97,135
  Drury 97
  Hugh 79
  John, Sr. 97
  Matilda 58
Weatherford, Joseph 17
Weaver, Samuel 31,44
Webber, John 134
  Polly 97
  Richard 43,48
  Samuel 31
  Seth 31
Webster, Archibald M. 46,91
Weymouth, James 106
  James D. 106
Wharton, A. 65
Wheeler, Elizabeth 114
  Henry 14,120

Wheeler cont.
  Nancy 62
  Robert 120
  Samuel 32,35,50,71,99,136
White, John 33
Whitehead, Benjamin 81
Whitlock, D. H. 62
Whitlow, Jackson 99
Whorthy, Thomas 74
Wilbourn, Robert 52
Wilbourne, Jesse 40
Wilkinson, Carter 131
  Francis L. 138
  James T. 138
  Jesse R. 22
  Thomas 39,119,131
  Z. 120,121
Williams, Joseph 56,138
  Matthias 139
  Samuel 19,38,72,103,138,139,145
  William 138
Willmore, Daniel 91
Wilson, Allen 19,105,139
  Benjamin 130,139
  Daniel A. 115
  Elizabeth 130
  J. A. 83
  James 7
  John W. 35,52,106,142
  Matthew 11,130
  Richard 22,106
  W. Col. 25
  W. 68,100,139
  W. W. 106
  William 10,25,35
Winfree, Charles 111
  Elijah 10
  John 15,23,89,140
  Stephen 75
Wingfield, Joseph S. 74
Winn, Edmund C. 77
Womack, Charles 46,52,76,80,91,121
  Charles, Jr. 80
  Charles H. 52,79
  F. 103
  James A. 141
  James W. 140
  Sampson 88
  Thomas F. 44,68
  T. T. 40,100
Wood, Alfred 126
  Henry D. Rev. 86,113
  James Gov. 16
  John F. 46,96,113,130
  Lucy 83
Woodfin, Edmund 141
  Elisha 72
  Samuel Rev. 21,92
  Sarah 141
Woodruff, Clifford 36
Woodson, Alexander 54
  B. B. 21,69,100
  Benjamin 56
  Blake B. 30,58,125,126
  Booker 55,115
  Charles 92
  Charles F. 139
  Christopher 10,40,142
  Drury 59,76,96,103
  Edwin W. 53,114
  Frederick A. 142
  George B. 57
  Henry 8
  Henry H. 92
  Jacob 96,143
  J. B. 97
  James B. 57
  Jesse 15
  John 38,43,54,55,60,65,77,78,83,88,94,100,120,121,131,138,139

Woodson cont.
  John, Jr. 83
  John M. 145
  Joseph 51,92
  Joseph R. 95,106,142
  M. 109,142
  Mary 140
  Mary Miller 65
  Matthew 143,144
  Miller, Capt. 66
  Miller, Sr. 142
  Miller 9,21,27,29,30,
    37,40,43,55,57,64,68,
    87,102,105,108,120,
    125,134,140,143,145
  Miller, Jr. 32,33,39,
    45,55,65,68,80,97,99,
    100,130,135,137,140
  Peter 143

Woodson cont.
  Rebbecca 112
  Sally H. 139
  Susan 129
  Tarlton 40,52,142
  Tarlton H. 40
  Tscharner 11,12,36,55,
    124,134,142
  Wade H. 19
  William 110
  William M. 77
Word, Thomas H. 113
Worley, John 7,58,87
Wright, Archibald 135
  Elizabeth 81
  George T. 102
  John 96
  John R. 19
  John W. 135

Wright cont.
  P. C. 81
  Phineas 61
  Phineas B. G. 27
  Robert 35,104
  Samuel 40
  Saymer 81,134,137,139
  Thomas 30,58,122
  William 8,113,135,139,
    145

Yancey, A. W. 40
  Eliza M. 83
  Robert J. 32
Yarrington, Albert 100
  Alfred 100
  Arana 92
  Mary 121
Young, Matthew H. 144

www.ingramcontent.com/pod-product-compliance
Lightning Source LLC
LaVergne TN
LVHW091551060526
838200LV00036B/786